THE **BIG BOOK** OF FISH & SHELLFISH

THE BIG BOOK OF FISH & SHELLFISH

FRED THOMPSON

MORE THAN 250 TERRIFIC RECIPES

CHRONICLE BOOKS
SAN FRANCISCO

Library of Congress Cataloging-in-Publication Data available.

ISBN-10: 0-8118-4925-2
ISBN-13: 978-0-8118-4925-8

Printed in Canada.

Designed by Leon Yu: LEON YU DESIGN
Food styling by pouké
Prop styling by spork
Typesetting by Leon Yu: LEON YU DESIGN

Distributed in Canada by Raincoast Books
9050 Shaughnessy Street
Vancouver, British Columbia V6P 6E5

10 9 8 7 6 5 4 3 2 1

Chronicle Books LLC
85 Second Street
San Francisco, California 94105

www.chroniclebooks.com

DEDICATION

For Dad, who took the time to take me fishing.

Lil' Bit
And
BB.

ACKNOWLEDGMENTS

Writing a cookbook is never a picnic and takes many hands to complete. The thanks go far and wide.

Bill LeBlond, Amy Treadwell, Doug Ogan, Vanessa Dina, Yolanda Accinelli, and the entire staff at Chronicle Books did yeoman's work on this book, while making it easy on me. They are exceptional people to work with. My agent, Lisa Ekus, who tied up the loose ends, and made sure I had some fun writing this book, is great. She has always believed in my abilities.

What a fun design by Leon Yu and the yummy cover photograph by France Ruffenach. Both will add pleasure to the reader.

I could not have written this book without my neighbors, Barry and Linda Johnson, Robin and Rachel Thomas, and Henry and Nancy Wood, enduring a litany of good and bad seafood dinners. Pableaux Johnson helped keep me on track with his sixth sense as to when I needed a support phone call. His expertise on the Gulf coast also helped immensely. Belinda Ellis, and later her brother Brandon, both burned midnight oil to read my work for errors and just plain stupid stuff. John T. Edge put the seed in my pocket that let this book evolve. Nikki Parrish walked me through my word processing education, allowing my editors to understand and work with my words. The expert knowledge of William Small, Seafood Marketing Specialist, North Carolina Department of Agriculture, was awesome.

A special thanks to Toni Allegra, Don and Joan Fry, and Lynn Swan. They are the soul of the Professional Food Writer's Symposium at the Greenbrier. They have given me a place to gather with others, have a sense of community, and test my skills. The community of folks that have attended the symposium have all had a hand in this book.

Most of all, I want to thank two groups of people: First, the foodies and beginning cooks that have attended my seafood cooking classes at Viking, ICE, and Southern Season. They along with the readers of my newspaper column influenced both the need and the content of this tome. Second, the fishermen and their families, who risk everything each day, yet continue to put seafood on our tables. They are a vanishing breed, who have given me much time and insight, not to mention good food.

TABLE oF CONTENTs

58

THE BIG & STURDY FISH

96

EVERYBODY'S FAVORITE—SHRIMP

"If only I could cook fish like this at home" is a common lament heard in almost every seafood restaurant throughout the country. For the most part, we are a people of fish and shellfish lovers with very little knowledge of what to do with these waterlogged critters in our own kitchens. A few very simple recipes are the extent of our repertoire, unless we are one of the fortunate few that live on and around the coastal areas of America.

A trip to the coastal areas, for many years, included a stop at the local seafood shack, or buying a local product like shrimp or lobsters, and simply preparing them at our vacation house. Other than that, we were trapped by the inland seafood restaurants, which never seemed to be as good. Shipping and packing technology has come a long way over the last twenty years, allowing us to have a different take on seafood. Can you imagine any supermarket chain not having a "fresh" seafood department? And now, a seafood department in North Carolina can feature Dungeness crab from California, Olympic oysters from Oregon, mussels from Prince Edward Island, as well as local grouper, shrimp, and crab. Memphis, Tennessee, can partake of the Copper River salmon season as easily as upstate Washington. Californians are not limited to sand dabs and salmon, but can also enjoy Maine lobsters and Florida's stone crab claws. And New York City can beat everybody to the punch with soft-shell crabs. We now have the ability to get a better selection and fresher seafood to marketplaces all over the United States. As a result, our exposure level to different types and varieties of seafood is growing exponentially. Now our inland restaurants, too, have the opportunity to thrill us with all kinds of different seafood.

But, the lament is still the same—how can I do this at home?

INTRODUCTION

Over the past two decades, seafood consumption has grown at a steady rate. Since 1984, it is the fastest growing food sector, with a growth rate of about 11 percent annually. Seafood consumption per capita in the United States (1999) showed that Americans ate roughly fifteen pounds of edible meat per year, and recent government draft reports show consumption continuing to grow. In 2001, the farmed seafood sector represented 29 percent of all seafood consumed, with annual revenues of 54 billion dollars.

In 1994, nearly 75 percent of all seafood was consumed in a restaurant setting. That figure has dropped steadily to about 50 percent, convincing me that folks will readily accept buying raw seafood and preparing it at home, especially if they have the guides and recipes to help them in their kitchens. But from my experience as a newspaper columnist, cookbook author, and cooking school teacher, these guides and recipes had better be packed with flavor, classic and updated, be easy to understand, be presented in a nonthreatening way, and work. Consumers look to expand their knowledge—with both familiar and new preparations and species.

At the beginning of all my seafood cooking classes, I tell the class that they should leave feeling confident about cooking seafood in their kitchen. That's the goal of this book. No, it is not meant to be "the end all to end all" encyclopedia on fish and shellfish. We will not dissect every possible realm of sea critters, nor explore possibilities that many of us won't have access to buying. I will give you the scoop on cooking some of the more popular seafood items. My hope is that this book will guide you, from the buying process to sitting down to eat. You should feel a bit like I'm in the kitchen with you, or that some of these words will resonate when you step inside the fish market.

The book has been divided into chapters by fish or shellfish types, rather than the standard soups, salads, entrées, etc. This was done after some lengthy discussions with home cooks. Your purchase of fish and shellfish is somewhat different from other food products. If shrimp or salmon, for instance, are on sale, or the tuna seems especially fresh, you seem to want a clear group of recipes in one place representing the possibilities for these products. "Make it easy for me," you seem to say. So, here I will try to do just that. *The Big Book of Fish & Shellfish* is broken into chapters on whole thin fish; thin, delicate fish fillets; the thicker and sturdier fish; and the different shellfish types. There is also a section on squid and octopus, as well as canned seafood, which includes some smoked and salted seafood. I may take you through a few steps in a recipe, but they will be as uncomplicated as possible. Recipes that look long are usually ones giving you some extra tastes surrounding the seafood and you can choose not to do the extras. You will find no recipes for stocks; for home cooks there are acceptable substitutes, in canned and bottled products. The idea is to get you in the kitchen cooking seafood with the least amount of stress and the maximum amount of flavor.

Here's the key to the recipes in this book: The vast majority of the recipes within each of the two fish chapters (pages 24–95) are successful made with any fish in that chapter. When you shop, maybe have a recipe in mind, but don't get caught up in the exact type of seafood you will buy. Buy what is the best all-around value and freshness. Many of the shrimp recipes will also work with scallops and vice versa. Clams and mussels can easily work in each other's territory. But remember that recipes should be a guide. Always prepare a recipe once as suggested, but be creative from that point. Adjust it to your needs and flavor palate.

My love affair with seafood started young—when I was ten years old, with a bowl of blue crab claws and some cocktail sauce. It has grown over the decades as I learned from folks for whom the ocean and lakes, and their bounty, consume their lives. Oyster ranchers on the Potomac, Alaskan crab and salmon boat captains, the watermen of the Chesapeake Bay, lobstermen of Maine, the guys fly-fishing in a mountain stream, fishermen from Noyo Harbor in Northern California, catfish farmers in the Mississippi Delta, marine researchers near Winyah Bay—they and many more have touched my life and thought process about this food group called seafood. These people are fearless, weathered, stubborn, and a breed that's slowly leaving us. Most of them have absolute respect for the water, its power and mercy. "Follow the water" is advice you hear from them all. What they fear is how we gobble up shoreline and with it the birthplace of most wild seafood—the saltwater estuaries. So we must be mindful of our resources and look to new ways to efficiently keep up with the ever-increasing demand for these healthy proteins. Our nation has a growing love affair with these creatures of our waters. Their life depends on that water.

THE BASICS

GETTING STARTED

The first step to cooking seafood at home is finding a good fish market and developing a relationship with the fishmonger. The market doesn't have to be freestanding; the grocery chains are growing in their expertise on what to do with seafood.

When you enter, does the place smell really fishy? Not a good sign. It should smell of the sea; if the place smells like ammonia, there's bad fish lurking. Walk away. If algae are on the lobster or crab tanks, cleanliness may not be a priority here. Are there puddles of blood or water near the fish? Find another vendor.

At a good fish market, there should be copious amounts of ice. Ice is the gold standard in a seafood market. Chilled cases alone don't get it. Whole fish should be buried in ice, a good layer that has to be moved to inspect the fish. However, fillets should never touch the ice. They ideally will be on metal trays sitting on the ice, and covered with plastic wrap. There should be labels on the seafood. Where did the product come from, what country? Was it previously frozen? Is it "wild caught" or farmed? These issues should be answered and displayed as prominently as the seafood. If not, be a bit suspicious. Bivalve shellfish, like oysters that are in their shells, should also be iced and laid flat, even if layered, so none of their precious juices leak out. Bivalves should also be tagged as to point of origin. One of the most telling signs that you are in a good market is the automatic offer to pack your purchases in ice. These folks know what they are doing.

Once you find that great market, be a regular customer. Just as at any business, the best customers get the best treatment, which in the fish business means the freshest catch. Develop a relationship with one or more of the counter people. They want you to be happy. The counter folks can be a wealth of knowledge and will go the extra mile with a little respect from you. There is no request too silly for the fishmongers I use and yours should be that way too.

"FRESH" AND FROZEN

I hate to break this to you, but unless you caught the fish, "fresh" is a bit of an overstatement. The notion that a boat goes out in the morning and comes back to port that night is only in the movies. Get over it. There are "day boats." You see the term on menus for items like scallops. There is some day-boat fishing for certain species of fish, but guess what: The catch from day boats almost always goes to the top restaurants in the country and it is very small in terms of the total pounds landed. Most fishing vessels are out for a week or more. The better restaurants and fish markets buy only what's known as "top of the trip," which are fish caught on the last day or two of fishing before they return to port. The fish could be from two to five days old, even from the "top." So the other fish on board might be five to eight days old, which then in turn get put in the wholesaler market system, which is huge in this country. Another couple of days in the system and, well, you get the picture. This system works OK with big fish like tuna, because properly handled and iced they deteriorate slowly. Because of this market system, a soft-shell crab caught in Pamlico Sound in North Carolina will probably go to New York's Fulton Fish Market before coming back to markets in North Carolina. Crazy, but some-how it works.

Most sashimi and sushi-grade fish has been frozen at sea the day it was caught. This is the fish we eat raw. More ships than ever process their catch at sea, and freezing methods have improved a hundredfold. The notion that "B"-grade fish are the ones headed for the deep freeze just isn't true anymore. Tomi Marsh, a boat owner and sea captain in Alaska, has shared with me the remarkable turn in freezing salmon and halibut that has happened just in the past few years in that state. Most frozen fish today is portioned, blast frozen, and individually vacuum wrapped, allowing you to buy just the prime cuts. When I am in Tokyo, I always go to the tuna auction, which takes place about 5 a.m. Whole tuna, 90 percent of them frozen solid, will sell from $3,000 to $40,000 in the blink of an eye. The Japanese, the largest fish eaters per capita, have discovered the secrets of frozen seafood, and are continually working to make it better. The vast majority of the seafood we eat today has been frozen, and I don't think it is to anyone's detriment. Today, the definition of "fresh" may be how well the product has been handled and the time it's been thawed.

"WILD" OR FARMED

The reality of the fish business today and the worldwide demand just overwhelms the possibility that all our seafood could be "wild caught," making aquaculture a necessary reality. That being said, I will always buy "fresh" wild-caught seafood over farm raised with the exception of catfish, tilapia, crayfish, mussels, oysters, and a few others. Part of that decision is to protect our fishing communities, truly the last of the real hunters and gatherers, still almost frontier folks in a modern world who have survived in our country. Part is flavor. I taste a slightly richer and deeper flavor in wild caught. It could be because I grew up in a coastal state and ate what came from my coastal waters, or because of my profession, or obsession with food. However, when standing at the fish counter, and I can tell the farmed salmon is fresher than the wild-caught King salmon, I'm going home with the farmed. It is all about getting the highest quality "fresh" product in your home. That's what you want to cook.

SPOTTING THE SEAFOOD THAT YOU WANT TO BUY

In the chapter introductions, I will be more specific about what to look for with each species when buying seafood, but here are good general guides for the reality of the market today: To buy the best, you must use your eyes, nose, and touch. And ask questions. Sure, buying a whole fish is the best way to tell its freshness. If it looks alive, with clear eyes, moist and shiny skin, and Christmas red–colored gills, it's fresh. Most of us will be dealing with fillets or steaks. They too should be moist looking and have sharp color for the type of fish, but look a little translucent. Ask to smell the fish. Does it smell like the sea? Ask the fishmonger to touch the fillet and see if the flesh springs back, meaning it is firm, another positive sign. Fish and fillets bruise just like we do, so look for discolored spots on the flesh. Brown and gray spots are signs of age, so pass on these.

Tuna steaks should always be cut off the whole loin to order; if not, look for good color depth. Buy no fillets that have a "rainbow"—little bands of colors that sort of shimmer—because this indicates age. Live shellfish, like lobsters and crabs, should be just that—alive. They should be mobile and feisty. Find out how long the lobsters have been in the tank. Every day out of the ocean, they are losing their meat to shell ratio. Even the docile soft-shell blue crab should move some, especially when picked up. Shrimp should be firm and of consistent color, with no age spots like those on old fish. Oysters, clams, and mussels should have tags showing you the date of harvest. Always buy live shellfish from the most reputable seller. If you have to buy fish in cellophane-wrapped meat trays, make sure there is no liquid in the package. Don't buy the end of the loin piece of tuna or tail pieces of salmon. More likely they are the oldest fillets or steaks.

NOW YOU'RE HOME

There's just one rule for storing fish at home: Keep it cold, just above freezing. That process starts when you buy seafood. Ask for ice, or have a small cooler for your fish purchases, and still ask for ice.

With whole fish, remove the store wrapping and rinse the fish in cold water. Fill a strainer with ice and put the fish on top. Place the strainer in a bowl, pile more ice on the fish, and place it in the refrigerator. Don't let the fish ever sit in water.

Fillets and steaks can stay in their wrappers, but should be placed on ice just like the whole fish. Just as in a good fish market, the fillets should be over ice but not touching it. Shrimp also should be stored this way.

Oysters, clams, and mussels need to be stored in the refrigerator, in a bowl, with a cold damp kitchen towel over them.

Keep live lobsters in the package from the market and in the refrigerator.

Don't plan on keeping seafood more than a day. It really is better to cook the day you buy.

WAYS TO BRING HEAT TO THE SEAFOOD

Here are the basic methods of cooking seafood:

Poaching or Boiling—These are the simplest methods. Poaching is a slower, more delicate way, using a lower temperature. Boiling is faster and just what it implies; bring the liquid to a full boil, and drop in the food. Boiling is good for lobsters and shrimp, although poached shrimp are wonderful. We normally think of poached salmon, but any fish can be poached. While it is a moist cooking method, you still have to take care not to overcook the seafood.

Steaming—Take a large pot with a good lid and a small amount of water and you are ready to steam. Shrimp, lobsters, oysters, clams, and mussels are the usual suspects.

Grilling—Playing with fire. It is a superior way to cook whole fish and many thicker cuts of fish. Shrimp and the rest of the shellfish family also do well with this method.

Panfrying—This is frying with a small amount of oil, usually ½ inch or less. Typically, fish are panfried, and they are usually lightly coated first, usually with a thin coating of flour, cormeal, or even pancake mix that has been seasoned. Some type of moisture is helpful to get the flour to adhere. Milk, buttermilk, and even water are common.

Deep Fat Frying—This is vat frying, using at least three inches of oil. Shrimp, oysters, clams, and fish fingers work well with this method. With deep-frying the coating can run the gamut between a very thin coating of seasoned flour or cornmeal to thick and crusty coatings using breadcrumbs or even a beer batter or tempura-type batter. Deep-frying also incorporates a three-step coating procedure of flour, an egg wash, and finally the batter coating.

Pan Roasting—This is my favorite method with many fish, like sea bass, salmon, and monkfish. Sear the fish in a pan on top of the stove and finish cooking it in the oven. You get a nice crust with lots of flavor, and a bit of help in not overcooking the fish. Restaurants use this method quite frequently.

"Cooking" with acids—Seviche is an example of this method. You use citrus juices, for example, to alter the proteins in seafood so that they are not exactly raw, but not cooked in the traditional sense.

Smoking—Most smoked fish is cold smoked and difficult to do at home. Salmon and tuna take to hot smoking, which is grilling with indirect heat, at low temperatures, with a flavorful wood. The basic "low and slow" method, except that fish smoke fast.

WHAT'S IN MY KITCHEN

Here is an accounting of the products and tools I used in developing these recipes.

Seasonings

I always use unsalted butter. I want to control my seasoning. When it comes to hot sauce, I'm a Texas Pete guy. Frank's and Tabasco are also okay. Chesapeake Bay seasoning refers to any product similar to Old Bay.

Clam juice and clam broth are interchangeable. Bookbinder's clam broth has great flavor. If Basic's Brand Fish Stock is in your area, substitute it for all or part of any recipe calling for clam juice or low-sodium chicken broth.

Sauces

I really like Bennett's Chili Sauce. If you can only find Heinz, add some sweet pickle relish to the recipe. Duke's and JFG are my preferred mayonnaises. Unfortunately, they are Southern products and not available everywhere. They have little or no sugar, letting the natural lemon flavor come out. Check the labels in your area for mayonnaises without sugar. However, when Hellmann's is in a recipe it has a direct effect on the flavor.

Salt and Pepper

Kosher salt to me flavors better, and all the salt used in these recipes was kosher. Freshly ground pepper is imperative. It will add another level to all your food. Some chefs and cookbook authors insist on white pepper with seafood for the visual aspects. If you want to use white pepper, it's fine. I use black in everything. It's your choice.

Breading

For both all-purpose and self-rising flour, I prefer White Lily products, which are not available everywhere. White Lily is quality soft winter wheat flour, milled longer like hard wheat bread flour, giving it a perfect grain. You may have regional millers that have soft wheat flour. I also use White Lily Cornmeal Mix, which has a perfect ratio of cornmeal to flour. For other breading, I like coarse, stone-ground cornmeal. It has more structure, more body. Check your area for local sources.

I use Pioneer Pancake and Baking Mix only. It is less lumpy than the others and coats more evenly.

Equipment

Every household should have a real fish spatula. They are shaped like a fillet, with a slightly diagonal end that is thin and a bit curved upward. Great for turning any fillet of fish. If you start working with chef's tongs, you will be hooked. For deep-frying, I use an electric wok, which I like better than some of the home fryers on the market. The width lets me fry larger pieces of fish or even whole ones easier. I used both a Weber charcoal and gas grill for the grilled items. Most were tested on both, and the cook times were very close. I do use real hardwood charcoal rather than briquettes. The hardwood burns hotter and has a better flavor. All-Clad nonstick sauté pans are my favorite for their good construction and even heating. Plus they are ovenproof. I use a cast-iron skillet for most of the panfrying. A canning pot is a great steamer pot, or when you are boiling lobsters or shrimp for a crowd.

Most of all, bring laughter into your kitchen. Have fun cooking.

Smaller fish can be just as interesting, if not even more versatile, than larger fish. Fish in this chapter include flatfish like flounder, and smaller fish like snapper, sea bass, and a multitude of freshwater farmed fish like catfish and tilapia, mountain trout, and lake fish like crappie. There are even a few that you may not be that familiar with, but are worth your time. Skate is becoming more readily available in larger cities, as are sardines and anchovies. All of these fish take well to a large number of different preparations.

This group likes to be panfried, baked, broiled, poached, cooked in parchment, and some even like to be grilled. These fish nicely swap between recipes in this chapter. There should be no reason for you not to buy the freshest fish for any recipe, whether it is the one called for or not. There are also some "beginner" fish, like tilapia, catfish, and flounder, to get you and your family eating fish if you have not before. Beginner fish are mild and absorb the flavors around them.

FLATFISH & OTHER

Tilapia and catfish are both farmed fish. Many of the freshwater trout varieties are also farmed. There has been a growing movement to farm a hybrid striped bass. Be aware of this at your fish market. Also understand that not all snappers are created equal, or at least not equal to the superior red snapper. Check the skin for color, and any skinless snapper is definitely a different snapper variety. You will have the opportunity to examine more whole fish in this chapter. Remember, it should look almost alive, with clear eyes and vivid red gills. The fish should also be *in* the ice, not on top.

This chapter can be loads of fun, with really interesting recipes to please your palate.

SMALL
FISH

FLOUNDER OR CATFISH
WITH PECAN SAUCE

This is such a simple recipe, yet it explodes with flavor and texture. It's almost too good for a weeknight dinner, but the ease with which it comes together makes it a snap. You are basically oven poaching the fish, which ensures its moisture, but the oven roasting gives the fish another dimension.

SERVES 4 TO 6

1 Preheat the oven to 400 degrees F.

2 Lightly coat with nonstick spray a baking dish large enough to hold the fish in a single layer and arrange the fillets in the pan. Add enough water to come halfway up the fish, then add the lemon juice. Cover the dish with a greased piece of wax paper or parchment. Bake 8 to 10 minutes, or until the fish is firm to the touch. Transfer the fish to a warm platter and tent it with aluminum foil.

3 While the fish is baking, prepare the Pecan Sauce. In a small frying pan, melt the butter over low heat. Add the pecans, lemon juice, parsley, Worcestershire sauce, and zest and cook for 1 to 2 minutes, until the sauce is heated through and the nuts take on a bit of color. Spoon the Pecan Sauce over the hot fillets and serve immediately.

1½ pounds flounder, catfish, or red snapper fillets

1 tablespoon fresh lemon juice (grate the lemon peel before juicing)

PECAN SAUCE

6 tablespoons (¾ stick) unsalted butter

½ cup chopped pecans

3 tablespoons fresh lemon juice

2 heaping tablespoons chopped fresh parsley

1 teaspoon Worcestershire sauce

½ teaspoon grated lemon zest

ALLEGHENY MOUNTAIN TROUT WITH SWEET POTATO HASH

The Greenbrier Resort in White Sulphur Springs, West Virginia, is consistently honored as one of the top five resorts in the country. The food is driven by Master Chef Peter Timmins, an Irish bloke with a great sense of using local foods. Mountain trout is featured on his menu from morning to night. This dish—one of my favorites—couples the fish with that Southern standard, sweet potatoes, for a near perfect balance of flavor.

Eight 10-ounce whole boneless trout

¼ cup extra-virgin olive oil

Kosher salt

Freshly ground black pepper

1 tablespoon chopped fresh thyme or 1 teaspoon dried, divided

SWEET POTATO HASH

4 strips bacon, diced

4 tablespoons (½ stick) unsalted butter

4 cups finely diced sweet potato (1½ pounds)

1½ cups finely chopped onion (1 large)

3 tart apples, peeled, cored, and cut into ¼-inch dice

1 Rinse the fish and pat it dry with paper towels. Brush the fish, inside and out, with the oil and sprinkle with the salt and pepper and two-thirds of the thyme. Cover and marinate them in the refrigerator for 30 minutes.

2 To prepare the hash: In a large sauté pan, cook the bacon until brown and crisp. Remove it with a slotted spoon, leaving the fat in the pan, and drain it on paper towels. Add the butter to the fat, then add the sweet potato and sauté it over medium heat, turning frequently, until the potato is slightly tender and light brown, about 15 minutes. Add the onion and sauté another 5 minutes, then add the apple and cook until all the ingredients are tender and the hash is golden and crispy, another 4 to 5 minutes. Add the remaining thyme, the cooked bacon, and season to taste with salt and pepper. Keep warm.

3 Preheat the broiler. Arrange the marinated fish on a rack or roasting pan and broil it 2 inches from the heat, until just barely opaque in the center, 2 to 3 minutes on each side for a whole fish and 1 to 2 minutes for a fillet. To serve, arrange the hash on a warmed platter or plates and place the broiled trout on top. Serve immediately.

SERVES 8

BAKED FISH FILLETS WITH SPINACH-PINE NUT TOPPING

I'm taking a page from my friend Andy Schloss, one of the country's top cooking school teachers and cookbook authors. Andy has been advocating the use of some convenience products to make our life in the kitchen simpler. Here, I've used a store-bought spinach soufflé as the base for a killer topping for baked fish. With the pine nuts and cheese, you get a bit of a Sicilian flair. This recipe is both fast and fabulous, and works not only with the fish in this chapter, but also with thicker fillets like grouper, Chilean sea bass, and halibut.

SERVES 6

1 Preheat the oven to 400 degrees F. Brush a rimmed baking sheet with butter. Arrange the fish on the prepared baking sheet; sprinkle it with salt and pepper.

2 Combine the spinach soufflé, pine nuts, onions, garlic, and zest in a medium bowl; stir to blend well. Spoon the topping over the fish. Sprinkle with the Parmesan.

3 Bake the fish until they are just opaque in the center, about 15 minutes. Transfer the fish to plates.

Six 6- to 7-ounce sea bass, tilapia, or orange roughy fillets

Kosher salt

Freshly ground black pepper

One 12-ounce package frozen spinach soufflé, thawed

$\frac{1}{2}$ cup pine nuts, toasted

3 green onions, finely chopped

2 garlic cloves, minced

2 teaspoons grated lemon zest

$\frac{1}{2}$ cup grated Parmesan cheese

BEACH HOUSE SEVICHE

Many folks think of seviche as raw seafood. Seviche has been "cooked" with acids like citrus juices or vinegars, and flavored with other bright and fresh-tasting ingredients. This dish is perfect for a hot summer day at the beach. No cooking heats up the place.

1 pound flounder, cut into ½-inch chunks

1½ cups fresh lemon juice (about 10 lemons)

¼ cup olive oil

2 garlic cloves, crushed

½-inch piece fresh ginger, peeled and finely chopped

1 small jalapeño pepper, seeded and finely chopped

½ teaspoon coarse kosher salt

6 to 8 green onions, white parts only, thinly sliced

2 tablespoons chopped fresh dill

¼ cup finely chopped red bell pepper (optional)

1 Place the flounder, juice, oil, garlic, ginger, jalapeño, and salt in a large bowl. Toss to mix and marinate the fish in the refrigerator for at least 6 hours.

2 When ready to serve, stir in the green onions and dill. Taste for seasoning. Garnish with the red pepper, if desired. Serve in chilled bowls.

SERVES 4 TO 6

BRAISED STRIPED BASS
FILLETS IN GREEN CURRY

Striped bass has another name—rockfish. Rockfish is a major sport fish that is fun to catch for its fighting instincts, but it is also fun to eat. Rockfish has a savory, meaty taste that is not very oily, has a good texture, and takes to many cooking methods. This fish was almost depleted in the wild a decade or so ago. Good conservation efforts have brought rockfish back, especially in the Chesapeake Bay. There is a growing movement to farm raise hybrid striped bass in North Carolina, Arkansas, Mississippi, and California with good results. Snapper and catfish are also very good with this treatment.

SERVES 4

1 Preheat the oven to 350 degrees F.

2 Place the fillets in a sauté pan just large enough to hold them in a single layer. Sprinkle them with salt and pepper and pour on the wine and water.

3 Place the pan over high heat and, as soon as the liquid starts to simmer, cover the pan loosely with aluminum foil and slide it into the oven.

4 After about 5 minutes, check for doneness. Cut into one of the fillets to see if it is opaque. Cook longer if it is still translucent.

5 When they are cooked through, transfer the fillets to warmed, shallow bowls. Stir the coconut milk, fish sauce, curry paste, basil, mint, and cilantro into the hot liquid in the pan and bring it to a simmer. Season to taste with salt and pepper, pour it immediately over the fish, and serve.

Four 6- to 8-ounce skinless striped bass fillets, pin bones removed

Kosher salt

Freshly ground black pepper

¼ cup dry white wine

¼ cup water

½ cup unsweetened coconut milk

¼ cup Thai fish sauce

2 tablespoons green curry paste

1 tablespoon finely chopped fresh basil

1 tablespoon chopped fresh mint

1 tablespoon chopped fresh cilantro

BREADED TRIGGERFISH NUGGETS, CAROLINA STYLE

If you see triggerfish fillets in the market, and they pass all the freshness tests, buy them and enjoy. Primarily East Coast creatures, triggerfish are among the best-tasting ocean fish. On the coast of the Carolinas, cutting triggerfish into chunks for "fish nuggets" is a standard treatment. This is also a successful way to bread most any flat or thin-filleted fish.

2 large eggs

3 tablespoons water

1 teaspoon kosher salt

½ teaspoon freshly ground black pepper

2 pounds triggerfish, cut into 1-inch chunks

1 cup self-rising flour

1½ cups fresh breadcrumbs

½ cup peanut oil

8 tablespoons (1 stick) unsalted butter, cut into chunks

Any Region Tartar Sauce (page 322) or your favorite tartar sauce

1   Beat the eggs with the water, salt, and pepper.

2   Dredge the fish thoroughly in the flour. Dip it into the egg mixture and let the excess drain off. Roll it in the breadcrumbs to coat.

3   Preheat the oven to 200 degrees F. Place a rack over a baking sheet to keep the nuggets warm.

4   Heat the oil in large skillet. An electric skillet works perfectly. Add the butter and heat until it registers 375 degrees F on a deep-fat thermometer. Drop a few nuggets in at a time. Cook the fish until it is golden brown on one side, about 5 minutes. Turn and repeat on the other side. Drain on paper towels, then transfer the fish to the rack and slide it into the oven to keep warm while you finish the remaining nuggets. Serve these hot with tartar sauce.

SERVES 6 TO 8

CHESAPEAKE HOUSE FISH STEW

The Chesapeake House in Myrtle Beach, South Carolina, has been open for decades, and any local or regular visitor to the area will tell you that it's on their list of favorites. Still family owned, they have resisted the trend towards huge seafood buffets and continued their traditions of fresh local seafood carefully prepared. The fish stew is very "Low Country," meaning a bit spicy and tomato based. I serve this recipe for Super Bowl parties because it holds well in a Crock-Pot and folks just love the change of pace from wings and chili. Any flat or small fish fillets will work.

SERVES 8 TO 10

1 Fry the bacon until crisp in a medium skillet. Remove it from the pan and drain on paper towels. Add the onions to the bacon drippings and cook until they are lightly brown. Reserve.

2 In a large soup pot, bring the water to a boil. Stir in the onions, drippings, bacon, fish, Worcestershire sauce, celery salt, hot sauce, and pepper to taste. Reduce the heat to a simmer. Cook until the fish begins to fall apart, about 10 minutes.

3 Stir in the ketchup and tomato paste. Simmer the stew for 2 hours, or until thickened. Serve it over rice.

NOTE: For a more souplike result, cut the simmering time to 1 hour.

8 ounces bacon, diced

1 cup chopped onions

5 cups water

3 pounds flounder fillets

2 tablespoons Worcestershire sauce

1 tablespoon celery salt

1 teaspoon hot sauce

Freshly ground black pepper

2 cups ketchup

One 8-ounce can tomato paste

4 to 6 cups cooked rice

CRISPY SEA BASS WITH
CHILES AND CUCUMBER

Nothing is more impressive in an Asian restaurant than a sizzling whole fried fish leaving the kitchen bound for some hungry customer. Wok frying creates a light and crispy coating, letting the fish flavors mingle with the other seasonings, allowing for a delicate balance. Be mindful that the fish may "spit" some oil. You can do this at home, but it's tough to do for a crowd. Save this recipe for a special someone.

One 2-pound whole sea bass, head intact, scaled and gutted

¼ cup peanut oil, plus extra for frying

1 small onion, thinly sliced

1 garlic clove, finely chopped

1 teaspoon grated peeled fresh ginger

2 Thai or jalapeño peppers, seeded and chopped

2 tablespoons brown sugar

2 tablespoons Thai fish sauce

1 tablespoon tamarind puree (available at Asian markets and specialty food shops)

1 lime, zested and juiced

1 large English cucumber, peeled, seeded if needed, and cut into matchsticks

1 tablespoon chopped fresh cilantro leaves

1 Score diagonal cuts on both sides of the fish. Set it aside.

2 Heat the ¼ cup of oil in a wok or large sauté pan over medium heat. When the oil has begun to simmer, add the onion and cook for 2 minutes, stirring, until it begins to soften and color. Add the garlic, ginger, and peppers and cook for another minute, or until lightly golden and crisp. Mix together the sugar, fish sauce, tamarind, and lime juice and add them to the onion mixture. Allow it to simmer for 30 seconds, or until the sauce thickens slightly. Stir in the cucumber and remove the pan from the heat. Transfer the sauce to a small saucepan and set it aside. Clean the wok or pan.

3 Fill the wok or pan 1 inch deep with oil and heat until it registers 350 degrees F on a deep-fat thermometer. An electric skillet also works well. Lower the fish gently into the oil and cook for 4 to 5 minutes, or until golden and crisp, turning once during cooking. Make sure the skin does not stick to the wok by moving the fish around. Spoon the hot oil over the fish as it cooks. Meanwhile, reheat the sauce. Drain the fish on paper towels, then transfer to a platter. Drizzle the sauce over the fish, then sprinkle it with the lime zest and cilantro.

SERVES 2

EDIE BRYAN'S FISH PROVENÇAL

Ms. Bryan was my landlord in Manhattan, who finally got out of the cold and headed to Florida. She developed this dish for tilapia, but catfish, flounder, sea bass, grouper, or just about any white fish works well in this recipe. Her neighbors rave about this dish, as did mine when I first fixed it. This is a great way to have a taste of the Mediterranean at your dinner table.

SERVES 4

1 Preheat the oven to 350 degrees F.

2 Combine the tomatoes, olives, fennel, garlic, and shallot in a 9-by-13-inch glass baking dish.

3 In a small bowl, mix the Creole seasoning and herbes de Provence. Sprinkle them over the fish fillets, coating the fish well.

4 Push the tomato mixture around to make room for the fish. Nestle the fish down into the vegetables.

5 Bake for 20 minutes, until the fish is just cooked through. Remove the fish to a platter and cover them with the tomato mixture. Serve immediately with a green salad and your neighbors will rave.

6 plum tomatoes, quartered and cubed (about 3 cups)

1⅓ cups pitted Kalamata olives (about one 5.8-ounce jar)

1 small fennel bulb, sliced thinly (about ½ cup; this is my addition, Ms. Bryan hates fennel)

4 garlic cloves, finely minced

1 shallot, finely minced

1 teaspoon Creole seasoning

1 teaspoon herbes de Provence

Four 6-ounce fillets tilapia or other white fish

FISH POACHED IN BUTTERMILK

JoJo's restaurant in New York City first brought national attention to the cooking skills of Jean-Georges Vongerichten. He has gone on to create a restaurant empire across the country with his four-star techniques and concepts. His interpretation of fish poached in buttermilk inspired this much simpler, but just as impressive, recipe. Any flatfish (or even halibut or sea bass) adapts well to this cooking method. Even if you hate buttermilk, you will find pleasure here that's hard to resist.

2 tablespoons olive oil, divided

4 tablespoons (½ stick) unsalted butter, divided

1 pound spinach, stemmed and washed

Pinch of sugar

Kosher salt

Freshly ground black pepper

Four 6-ounce fillets flounder, rockfish, snapper, or black sea bass

⅛ teaspoon cayenne pepper

3 cups buttermilk

6 sprigs fresh dill, leaves stripped from stems

Juice of 1 lemon

About ½ cup sautéed mushrooms (optional)

1 Put 1 tablespoon of the oil and 1 tablespoon of the butter in a large sauté pan over medium-high heat. Add the spinach when the butter foams and toss to barely wilt the leaves. Add the sugar and season to taste with salt and pepper. Set the pan aside and keep it warm.

2 Season both sides of the fish with salt and the cayenne pepper. In a sauté pan large enough for the fish to fit in a single layer, combine the fish, buttermilk, and dill. Cover and place the pan over medium heat. When the buttermilk begins to simmer, cook for about 3 minutes. Turn the fish and cook for about another 3 minutes. The fish is done when it is firm to the touch.

3 Remove the fish from the pan and keep warm. In a blender or with an immersion (hand) blender, combine the warm buttermilk with the remaining 3 tablespoons of the butter and remaining 1 tablespoon of the oil. When it is emulsified, season the sauce to taste with salt, pepper, and lemon juice. Fresh lemon juice is key to the final flavor.

4 In 4 shallow bowls, arrange the wilted spinach. Place the fish on top, pour the buttermilk sauce over each, and top it off with a spoonful of mushrooms, if desired. Serve.

SERVES 4

PAN-SEARED TILAPIA IN ORANGE-SAFFRON BUTTER

Tilapia is such an underrated fish. Some call it "beginner fish" for its mild, nonfishy taste, yet firm and meaty texture. Tilapia is a farm-raised, freshwater fish that is available in almost every market across the country. Tilapia is a good place to start if your family frowns a bit on fish, and this recipe has both bold and soothing essences.

SERVES 4

1   In a heavy saucepan, combine the orange juice, wine, onion, carrot, celery, garlic, bay leaf, cinnamon, and saffron. Simmer over medium-high heat for 5 minutes. Reduce the heat to low, cover, and simmer for 1 hour. Remove the pan from the heat; strain the sauce through a fine-mesh strainer. Set aside. This can be made 1 day ahead and stored in the refrigerator.

2   In a shallow dish, combine the breadcrumbs, salt, and pepper. Coat the fillets in buttermilk and dredge them in the breadcrumb mixture.

3   Heat the oil in a large sauté pan over medium heat. Cook the fillets 3 to 5 minutes, or until golden brown. Turn the fillets and reduce the heat to medium-low. Cook 3 to 5 minutes more, or until the fish are cooked through.

4   Warm the strained orange-saffron sauce, stir in the butter, and season to taste with salt and pepper. Spoon approximately 1½ teaspoons of the sauce on each plate and place a piece of tilapia on top.

2 cups orange juice

½ cup dry white wine

½ cup diced yellow onion

1 small carrot, chopped

1 rib celery, chopped

2 garlic cloves, minced

1 bay leaf

1 cinnamon stick

Pinch of saffron

1 cup seasoned breadcrumbs

Kosher salt

Freshly ground black pepper

Four 6-ounce tilapia fillets

½ cup buttermilk

¼ cup safflower oil

1 tablespoon unsalted butter

FLOUNDER EN PAPILLOTE

Fish cooked en papillote, which literally means cooked "in parchment," provides the most dramatic of seafood presentations. To cut open the crackling parchment paper at the table and get that wonderful aroma makes you hungry from the moment you smell it. While the presentation is dramatic, the preparation is simple.

1 tablespoon unsalted butter, plus extra at room temperature for the papillotes

4 green onions, thinly sliced

Freshly ground white pepper

Four 6-ounce fillets flounder, trout, pompano, snapper, or sea bass

8 thin slices lemon

2 medium shallots, thinly sliced

¼ cup chopped mixed fresh herbs, such as basil, dill, parsley

1 Preheat the oven to 475 degrees F.

2 Melt the 1 tablespoon butter in a medium sauté pan over medium-high heat. Add the green onions. Season lightly with white pepper and cook until softened, about 3 minutes.

3 Cut four 16-by-20-inch sheets of parchment paper. Fold each sheet in half and, with scissors starting from the bottom point, cut out half a heart. Each sheet should now resemble a heart when unfolded. Take some of the softened butter and lightly rub it over half of each sheet.

4 Place a fillet over the buttered part of the parchment, 1 fillet on each sheet. Place 2 lemon slices on each fillet. Divide the shallots and onions equally over the 4 fillets. Likewise, divide the herbs equally over the fillets.

5 For each packet, fold the top over the fish so that the edges align. Beginning at the top or bottom, seal the packets by making small overlapping folds each about ½ inch long. Place the packets on a baking sheet. (The packets may be refrigerated for 3 to 4 hours before baking.) Place the baking sheet on the top shelf of the oven and bake for 10 minutes. Transfer the packets to individual plates and, with a knife or scissors, carefully slice through the top of the parchment and first enjoy the aroma, then the taste.

SERVES 4

FRIED CATFISH, MISSISSIPPI STYLE

Most of us might not walk in the door at Taylor's Grocery in Taylor, Mississippi, about ten miles outside of Oxford, Mississippi, home to Faulkner, John Grisham, and Ole Miss University. The place needs paint and the porch looks like it's leaning, but I've found the love of my life, made some of my best friends, and smoked great cigars on that porch. Plus, it was on Taylor's front porch that the great Southern food writer John Egerton and Denver food writer Ellen Sweet sat me down and taught me the proper way to eat catfish. "First it has to be hot, right out of the fryer," stated Egerton. "Then you hit it with some hot sauce and take a bite with raw onion," explained Ms. Sweet. "Wash it down with Jack Daniels, and you've found heaven on earth!" exclaimed John. It's a darn perfect way to eat.

SERVES 4 TO 6

1 Mix the cornmeal, flour, black pepper, lemon pepper, paprika, garlic powder, and salt together in a large bowl.

2 Pour about 4 inches of oil into a large, high-sided pot. Heat to 350 degrees F on a deep-fat thermometer.

3 Mix together the milk and hot pepper sauce in a shallow pan and dip each fillet into the mixture, let the excess run off, and in a separate shallow pan coat each fillet with the flour. Fry the catfish for 6 to 7 minutes or until brown and firm. Drain the fillets on paper towels.

4 Serve the catfish hot with raw onion separated into rings, hot sauce, tarter sauce, and the beverage of your choice.

2 cups yellow cornmeal

½ cup White Lily all-purpose flour

2 tablespoons coarsely ground black papper

1 tablespoon lemon pepper

1 teaspoon paprika

1 teaspoon granulated garlic powder

Kosher salt

Peanut oil for frying

2 cups whole milk

4 dashes hot pepper sauce

8 six-to eight-ounce Mississippi farmed catfish fillets

2 large onions, sliced

A bottle of hot sauce

Any Region Tartar Sauce (page 322)

FRIED FRESH ANCHOVIES OR SARDINES

If your only experience with anchovies and sardines is from a can, then you are ready for a new awakening. Fresh anchovies and sardines are a whole new taste. Both these fish have become more widely available than ever before in their fresh state. However, know what you are buying. Imported sardines are larger fish with a protruding lower jaw. Anchovies are just the opposite. American sardines are actually herring—just as good, but smaller.

This preparation is the way I was served anchovies in Rome. They are lightly fried and delicious. The Europeans have known this for years, and why should they have all the great flavors?

Olive oil for frying (not extra-virgin)

¾ cup all-purpose flour

4 large eggs, lightly beaten

Kosher salt

Freshly ground black pepper

12 ounces fresh medium anchovies or sardines (heads removed), butterflied and filleted

Extra-virgin olive oil for drizzling

Mayonnaise for serving (optional)

1 Pour the oil for frying into a medium pot to a depth of 2 inches and heat over medium heat until it registers 350 degrees F on a deep-fat thermometer. Meanwhile, whisk the flour, eggs, and ¼ teaspoon of salt together in a medium bowl until the batter is smooth.

2 Working in batches, season the fish with salt, dip them into the batter, and deep-fry until they are pale golden and crisp, about 45 seconds per batch. Drain them on a wire rack set over paper towels and season to taste with salt and pepper. Serve hot with extra-virgin olive oil for drizzling, and mayonnaise, if desired.

SERVES 2 TO 4

GRILLED ORANGE
ROUGHY WITH CAPERS

In the 1980s, markets could barely keep enough orange roughy in their cases for the demand. It had become the darling of the fish-eating public with its firm texture, white color, and mild flavor. Of course, it became a victim of its own success. Orange roughy is a slow-growing fish caught off the coasts of New Zealand and Australia. The demand created fishing restrictions that have slowed the amount of orange roughy landed. It has made a comeback in the last two decades, but it now shares its spotlight with catfish and tilapia, and either fish will substitute in this recipe. Buy what is the freshest and best looking.

SERVES 4

1 Combine the wine and fennel seeds in a small heavy-bottomed saucepan. Bring them to a boil over medium-high heat, and cook until reduced by half, about 4 minutes. Add the clam juice and boil until it is reduced by half, about 8 minutes. Stir in the tomatoes, capers, and anchovies. Simmer 2 minutes to blend the flavors. Stir in the parsley. Season to taste with pepper. Cover the sauce and keep it warm.

2 Light a charcoal fire or preheat your gas grill on high. Oil your grill's cooking grate.

3 Brush the fish with oil, and sprinkle it with salt and pepper. Grill the fish until it is opaque in the center, about 3 minutes per side.

4 Transfer 1 fish fillet to each of 4 plates. Spoon warm sauce over it. Drizzle basil oil around the fish on each plate, if desired, and serve immediately.

¼ cup dry white wine

½ teaspoon fennel seeds, cracked

2 cups bottled clam juice

½ cup drained oil-packed sun-dried tomatoes, sliced

2 tablespoons drained capers

1½ tablespoons chopped canned anchovy fillets

1 tablespoon chopped fresh Italian parsley

Freshly ground black pepper

Four 6- to 8-ounce orange roughy fillets

Olive oil for brushing

Kosher salt

2 tablespoons basil oil or extra-virgin olive oil (optional)

CHARCOALED RAINBOW TROUT WITH BACON BUTTER

I took up fly-fishing last year, and I can confess that few foods will taste as good as just-caught rainbow trout cooked over wood or charcoal, sprinkled with crisp cooked bacon. Their flesh just seems to thrive on the gentle nuances of the fire. In place of the bacon butter, just melt some butter and cook a few slices of bacon in the microwave, then drizzle the butter over the grilled trout and sprinkle with crumbled bacon.

2 slices bacon, finely chopped

¾ cup finely minced shallots

½ cup seeded and finely chopped plum tomatoes (about 3)

⅓ cup dry white wine

⅓ cup cider vinegar

¾ teaspoon finely chopped fresh thyme

Kosher salt

Freshly ground black pepper

1 cup (2 sticks) unsalted butter, cut into 4 pieces and at room temperature

¼ cup chopped fresh parsley

Four 10-ounce trout, boned but with heads and tails left on

1 In a medium skillet, cook the bacon until it is crisp. Transfer to paper towels to drain. Add the shallots to the drippings left in the skillet, cover, and cook over medium-low heat, stirring occasionally, for 10 minutes or until softened.

2 Stir in the tomatoes, wine, vinegar, and thyme. Add salt and pepper to taste. Bring the liquid to a boil and cook over medium heat, stirring occasionally, for about 5 minutes, or until thickened. Whisk in the butter slowly, 1 piece at a time, until melted and creamy. Add the reserved bacon and the parsley and remove the skillet from the heat. Keep the sauce warm or pour into a thermos to hold for a couple of hours.

3 Light a charcoal fire or preheat your gas grill on high. Oil your grill's cooking grate.

4 Grill the trout for 4 to 5 minutes on each side. Carefully roll the fish over when turning. They should be opaque in the center and just firm to the touch when done.

5 Place the trout on a warm serving platter, spoon a little of the warm bacon butter over the fish, passing the rest at the table, and serve immediately.

SERVES 4

GRILLED SARDINES

"Grilled" sardines in Europe are actually broiled, but I think they are better when cooked over open flames. This simple recipe is the way my Portuguese friend Joseph Theresa would cook them at the beach, over a driftwood fire, the sardines skewered on a stick. Sounds romantic, but your backyard grill will do the trick.

SERVES 6 AS A
FIRST COURSE
OR 8 TO 10
AS PART OF A
TAPAS BUFFET

1 Layer the sardines and salt in a 9-by-13-by-2-inch baking dish, cover, and let them stand in the refrigerator for 2 to 3 hours. Rinse the salt from the sardines, then brush each liberally with oil.

2 Light a charcoal fire or preheat your gas grill on high. Oil the grill's cooking grate.

3 Place the sardines on the grill and cook for 3 minutes. Gently roll to turn them over and cook for another 3 minutes, until the fish is firm and just thinks about flaking. Transfer them to a warm platter. Serve with very cold white wine and olive oil seasoned with salt and pepper.

2 pounds fresh sardines (about 24), cleaned, dressed, and boned

1 cup kosher or coarse salt

Extra-virgin olive oil for brushing

Freshly ground black pepper

PANFRIED SAND DABS

This is equal time for the West Coast folks. I call sand dabs a "San Francisco treat," since they are almost a cult fish there. Sand dabs, or windowpane fish, are small fish that are cooked whole, usually simply prepared. I use the phrase "pan dressed," which means scaled, gutted, and the head removed. You will see this phrase frequently when buying whole fish, especially trout. This recipe is loosely based on one at the historic Tadich Grill in San Francisco. You can gussy up this recipe and have a crispier crust by substituting Japanese breadcrumbs (panko) for the flour. Any small lake fish like bream, perch, or even freshwater bass are delicious when prepared in this manner.

1 large egg, lightly beaten

2 tablespoons milk or buttermilk

2 cups self-rising flour

1 teaspoon kosher salt

½ teaspoon freshly ground black pepper

3½ to 4 pounds sand dabs, pan dressed

Olive oil for frying

1 lemon, cut into wedges

Any Region Tartar Sauce (page 322) or your favorite tartar sauce

SERVES 4

1   Mix the egg and milk together in a shallow dish.

2   Mix the flour, salt, and pepper together in another dish.

3   Dip the fish in the egg mixture, allowing the excess to run off.

4   Dredge the fish in the seasoned flour to thoroughly coat them.

5   Preheat the oven to 200 degrees F.

6   Pour enough oil into a large nonstick sauté pan to just coat the bottom. Heat over medium heat, add the fillets in a single layer, and cook for 4 minutes on one side or until golden brown. Turn and cook 4 minutes on the second side, or until golden brown. Transfer them to a warm platter and keep them warm in a low oven. Repeat to cook the remaining fillets, adding more oil to the pan as necessary.

7   Transfer the sand dabs to individual plates, garnish with lemon wedges, and serve immediately with tartar sauce.

PAN-ROASTED SKATE
WITH BRUSSELS SPROUTS

Pier fishing as a kid, I seemed to catch more skate than anything, causing me to cut my line and throw them back. I wish I had known then how great tasting skate can be. Only the "wings" of a skate are eaten, and it is best to buy them filleted unless you have great knife skills (they will always be skinned, as the skin is not edible). Only better fish markets will carry them, which is good because they spoil quickly. Buy skate fillets on the day that you are planning to cook them. The flesh is sweet and moist without any oiliness—in short, a wonderful treat.

SERVES 4

1 Prepare the Brussels sprouts: Cook the bacon over medium heat in a large sauté pan with a lid, cooking until the bacon starts to brown. Add the shallot and the garlic and sauté until they are translucent. Add the carrot and the Brussels sprouts and stir to combine.

2 Add ½ cup of water to the pan and cover. Steam the vegetables for 3 to 4 minutes, or until they are tender. Remove the cover and finish the dish with the butter, stirring until it has melted and coated the vegetables. Add salt and pepper to taste, and the parsley, and stir, mixing well. Set aside.

3 Preheat the oven to 450 degrees F.

4 Prepare the skate: Soak the fillets in a shallow dish with the milk for 5 minutes, then drain and lay them on a plate.

BRUSSELS SPROUTS

4 ounces diced bacon

1 shallot, chopped

2 small garlic cloves, finely chopped

1 small carrot, diced

24 Brussels sprouts, quartered

2 tablespoons (¼ stick) unsalted butter

Kosher salt

Freshly ground black pepper

1 teaspoon chopped fresh Italian parsley

SKATE

4 medium skate wings, filleted

1 cup milk

½ cup cracker meal

1 cup self-rising flour

Kosher salt

Freshly ground black pepper

¼ cup canola or peanut oil

8 lemon wedges

5   On a large plate or in a shallow bowl, combine the cracker meal and flour. Season both sides of the fillets with salt and pepper and then dredge them in the flour mixture, coating thoroughly. Pat off any excess.

6   In an ovenproof skillet over high heat, heat the oil until it just begins to shimmer.

7   Place the fillets in the pan, and lower the heat to medium. Cook for 3 to 4 minutes, or until the bottom crust is golden brown, then turn the fillets and put them in the oven for 4 to 5 minutes, until the skate is firm.

8   To serve, divide the Brussels sprouts between 4 plates and place a skate fillet on each. Garnish each plate with 2 lemon wedges.

EAST TENNESSEE FRIED
CRAPPIE WITH ONION SAUCE

Some folks call it crappie. If you're from east Tennessee, it's pronounced like "croppee." Either way, it's one of the best-tasting fish that comes out of a lake. This recipe was given to me by Carole Jones, one of my neighbors in North Carolina. She and her husband, Johnny, moved to the Triangle area from Milan, Tennessee. Carole was quick to tell me that this is her sister Jody Hopper's recipe, but it's been in their family for decades. This method will work on just about any freshwater fish that is typically fried whole. This dish is always served with hot hush puppies and, in Tennessee, an onion sauce.

SERVES 4

1 To prepare the onion sauce: Place the chopped onion in a small bowl and sprinkle the sugar over it. Cover and refrigerate for about 1 hour. Remove from the refrigerator and drain the liquid that has accumulated from the onions. Put the onions back in the bowl and add the mayonnaise, stirring to combine. Put in just a touch of yellow mustard—just enough to give the sauce a bit of color. Cover and refrigerate until ready to serve.

2 To prepare the fish: Whisk the eggs and water together in a small bowl. A pie plate works well for this. Combine the cornmeal mix, flour, and salt and place them on a plate or another pie plate. Dip each fish in the egg mixture, then roll it in the cornmeal-flour mixture.

ONION SAUCE

1 cup chopped onion (about 1 large)

2 teaspoons sugar

2 tablespoons good-quality mayonnaise

A touch of yellow mustard

CRAPPIE

2 large eggs, lightly beaten

¼ cup water

1 cup white self-rising cornmeal mix

2 tablespoons all-purpose flour

2 teaspoons kosher salt

8 to 12 dressed crappie, depending on the size, or other lake fish like bream or perch

Peanut oil for frying

3   In a sauté pan with 3-inch sides or an electric fryer, add enough oil to reach 2 inches deep. Over medium heat, heat the oil until it registers 360 degrees F on a deep-fat thermometer. Carefully add a few fish to the pan. Fry the fish for a total of 7 to 9 minutes, turning so that both sides are golden brown. The fish will be a little flaky when done. Remove and drain them on paper towels. Continue with the remaining fish. Serve them hot with Buttermilk Hush Puppies (page 330) and the onion sauce.

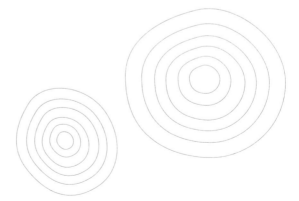

RED SNAPPER WITH SWEET CORN
"SUCCOTASH"

Don't get too caught up with the name snapper. Red snapper, yellow snapper, and even Pacific red rockfish can legally be called Pacific red snapper. All are good, and the freshest variety is what you want. However, you don't want to pay red snapper prices for some other fish. Make sure that you always buy red snapper with the skin on; that way you can see the red tone that starts at the top of the fish and gradually gives way to a pink hue. Plus the skin tastes wonderful.

Succotash is one of those late-summer treats in the South. Usually succotash is corn and butter beans with cream, but I've left out the beans, and added some chiles to give the concept a different twist.

SERVES 4

1   To prepare the succotash: Heat the butter in a heavy-bottomed saucepan over medium heat until hot but not smoking. Add the shallots and the chiles and cook, stirring occasionally, for 6 minutes, or until the chiles are soft.

2   Add the corn, and then run the back of a knife over the cobs to extract all of their milky juices right into the pan. Continue to cook the mixture for another 5 minutes, stirring occasionally. Add the broth and cream, bring the mixture to a simmer, being careful not to let it boil, and cook for another 4 minutes. Stir in the chervil and salt and pepper to taste. Remove the saucepan from the heat and set it aside.

CORN SUCCOTASH

4 tablespoons (½ stick) unsalted butter

½ cup finely minced shallots

1 cup seeded and minced poblano chiles

4 cups fresh yellow corn kernels, cobs reserved

1 cup low-sodium chicken broth or homemade stock

⅓ cup heavy cream

⅓ cup chopped fresh chervil or parsley

Kosher salt

Freshly ground black pepper

SNAPPER

1 cup all-purpose flour

Kosher salt

Freshly ground black pepper

Four 6-ounce red snapper fillets, with skin

1 tablespoon peanut oil

1 tablespoon unsalted butter

3   To prepare the snapper: In a shallow pan mix the flour with 1 teaspoon of salt and $\frac{1}{4}$ teaspoon of pepper. Lightly score the fillets on the skin side with diagonal cuts to keep the skin from shriveling and the fillets from twisting while cooking. Season them with salt and pepper to taste. Dredge the fillets in the seasoned flour, patting them lightly.

4   Heat the oil and butter in a heavy skillet over medium-high heat until hot and the butter has stopped foaming. Place the fillets in the skillet skin side up. Sauté for about 3 minutes on the first side, then sauté for about 2 minutes on the other side. Adjust your temperature so as not to burn the coating. When cooked, the fillets should be opaque in the center and just firm to the touch, with a nice golden brown color.

5   Rewarm the corn mixture. Place 1 fillet on each of 4 plates and divide the corn succotash equally around the fillets. Serve immediately.

WHOLE ROASTED BABY
FLOUNDER WITH SWEET
ONION MARMALADE

If you have never had a whole flounder, then you owe it to yourself to give this a try. My dad used to proclaim, "The nearer the bone, the sweeter the meat!" and it is certainly true when flounder is cooked on the bone. Cooked this way, the flounder is crispy, yet tender, moist, and flavorful. The onion marmalade is a complementing touch that adds a sweet-sour component.

SERVES 4

1   To prepare the marmalade: Bring the onions and broth to a simmer in a heavy-bottomed saucepan over medium-high heat. Reduce the heat to low, cover, and let them gently simmer for 1 hour, stirring occasionally.

2   Uncover the onions, add the salt and pepper, and increase the heat to medium. Cook the onions, stirring occasionally, for about 10 minutes more, or until the liquid gets a bit syrupy. The onions should be very lightly browned. Add the vinegar, stir to combine well, and simmer for 1 to 2 minutes to let the flavors meld. Set the pan aside to keep warm while cooking the fish. (Cooled and then tightly covered, the marmalade will keep in the refrigerator for 2 to 3 days.)

ONION MARMALADE

12 cups finely sliced sweet onions, such as Vidalia or Maui (about 6 large)

1 1/2 cups low-sodium chicken broth

1/4 teaspoon kosher salt

1/4 teaspoon freshly ground black pepper

1/4 cup red wine vinegar

FLOUNDER

Four 12- to 18-ounce dressed baby flounder

1 cup all-purpose flour

1 tablespoon kosher salt

1 tablespoon freshly ground black pepper

¼ cup peanut oil

8 tablespoons (1 stick) unsalted butter

3   Preheat the oven to 400 degrees F.

4   To prepare the flounder: Rinse the fish and pat them dry. In a shallow plate, combine the flour, salt, and pepper. Dredge both sides of the flounder in the seasoned flour, shaking to remove the excess.

5   If you want, cook the flounder in 2 pans, dividing the oil and butter between them. Heat the oil and butter in a large skillet over medium-high heat until the butter begins to sizzle. One at a time, carefully lay the flounder in the skillet, white skin side down. After 2 minutes, check the bottom side to make sure it is browning without burning, but don't be shy—a nice nutty brown color is a good thing. Carefully turn the flounder with a spatula and cook about 2 minutes more, or until browned. Transfer the fish to a baking sheet large enough to hold them all in a single layer.

6   Roast the flounder on the top rack of the oven for 6 to 8 minutes, depending on their size. Look closely: The inside of the fish should be just flaky and opaque. It is important not to overcook them. While the fish are roasting, warm the marmalade to a simmer. Place the fish on warm serving plates, top with the warm marmalade, and serve immediately.

SEA BASS WITH APPLES, CURRANTS, AND WARM SPINACH SALAD

Do you need a trip to the west coast of France? Normandy maybe? Close your eyes and smell this recipe cooking and you will almost be there. Take a bite and enjoy this rustic way with apples, cider, Dijon mustard, and fish. Don't let the length of this recipe put you off; the results are worth a little extra effort, and the recipe does come together fairly quickly. Try it on a weekend so you can savor the plate and a good glass of wine.

SERVES 4

1   To make the vinaigrette: Combine the cider, vinegar, mustard, salt, and pepper in a small bowl. Gradually whisk in the oil and set aside.

2   To make the sauce: Melt 1 tablespoon of the butter in a medium sauté pan over medium-high heat until it foams. Add the apples and sauté, turning frequently, until they are golden brown on both sides. Add the shallots and currants and continue cooking until the shallots are translucent, about 3 minutes. Add the cider and vinegar and simmer to reduce them by half, about 2 minutes.

3   Strain the apple mixture, reserving the liquid. Set the apple mixture aside, and return the cooking liquid to the pan. Simmer over low heat to reduce it by half again. Whisk the remaining 1 tablespoon of the butter into the reduced liquid. Pour the sauce into a thermos to keep it warm.

VINAIGRETTE

3 tablespoons apple cider

1 tablespoon cider vinegar

1 teaspoon Dijon mustard

$1/4$ teaspoon kosher salt

$1/8$ teaspoon freshly ground black pepper

$1/2$ cup extra-virgin olive oil

SAUCE

2 tablespoons (¼ stick) unsalted butter, divided

2 Braeburn, Pink Lady, or Fuji apples, cored and cut into 6 wedges each

2 shallots, thinly sliced

¼ cup dried currants, soaked in hot water for 30 minutes and drained

½ cup apple cider

¼ cup cider vinegar

Four 6-ounce sea bass fillets

Kosher salt

Freshly ground black pepper

2 tablespoons olive oil

2 tablespoons (¼ stick) unsalted butter

10 ounces baby spinach

4 Season the fillets on both sides with salt and pepper. Heat the oil and butter over medium-high heat in a sauté pan large enough to hold the fillets. As the butter foams, add the fillets and cook on one side for 4 minutes, or until golden brown. Turn the fillets over and cook for 3 minutes more, or until golden brown. The fillets should still be a bit springy when pressed gently with your finger. Transfer the fillets to a plate and keep them warm.

5 Return the sauté pan to medium heat, add the spinach, and stir until it begins to wilt. Add the vinaigrette and toss thoroughly.

6 Divide the spinach among 4 plates, place a sea bass fillet on top of each, and equally spoon some of the apple-currant mixture on and around the fish. Pour the sauce around the edge of the greens and serve immediately.

SHAD ROE

Shad roe is one of those distinctly Southern things that has become a connoisseur's delight all over the country. As sure as asparagus signals spring, so does shad roe, and its season is much too short. Chefs like to do a lot of crazy things with shad roe, but the best way to enjoy it is usually the simplest. If cholesterol is not an issue, cook them in bacon fat instead of butter for an absolutely ethereal experience.

SERVES 2 TO 4

1 Heat the butter in a large heavy frying pan until very hot. Season the shad roe with salt and pepper and add it to the pan. Make a few slashes on 1 side of each half with a knife to prevent blistering, reduce the heat to low, and cook for 5 minutes. Turn and cook the other sides until brown, about 5 minutes longer. The roe should still be pink inside.

2 Pour the lemon juice over and serve.

4 tablespoons (¹/₂ stick) unsalted butter

1 double shad roe, separated

Kosher salt

Freshly ground black pepper

Juice of 2 lemons

SOLE MEUNIÈRE

Sole meunière is one of those old classics that fell out of favor with the low-fat craze. However, with a more balanced intake of fats and carbohydrates in our diet today, there is no reason not to serve a fish dish that is simple, has great texture contrasts, and will brighten your week.

½ cup all-purpose flour

Four 6-ounce sole fillets

2 tablespoons clarified unsalted butter or 1 tablespoon olive oil and 1 tablespoon unsalted butter

2 tablespoons (¼ stick) unsalted butter

2 tablespoons chopped fresh Italian parsley

1 tablespoon chopped fresh tarragon

2 tablespoons fresh lemon juice

Kosher salt

Freshly ground black pepper

1 Place the flour on a dinner plate. Take each fillet and press it into the flour, flip the fillet, and press it back in the flour. Shake off any excess.

2 In a sauté pan large enough to hold the fillets (you might need to use 2 pans), add the 2 tablespoons of clarified butter over medium-high heat, and as soon as the butter begins to shimmer, add the fillets. Cook for 4 minutes per side, adjusting the heat as necessary so that the fillets brown but don't burn. Remove the fillets to a plate and tent them with foil.

3 Wipe the pan with a paper towel, removing the fat. Place the pan back over the heat. Add the remaining 2 tablespoons of butter and let it melt. Add the parsley and tarragon. Stir the butter mixture. Add the lemon juice and remove the sauce from the heat. Taste and season with salt and pepper. Plate each fillet and spoon the sauce equally over the sole.

SERVES 4

WHOLE SMOKE-GRILLED MOUNTAIN TROUT

My fish-cooking students rave over this dish. It will transport you to a mountain stream at sunset. The smoky, herbaceous flavors really make the trout jump, but without covering the gentleness of the fish. Anytime you see fresh whole trout at your market, give this a whirl.

SERVES 4

1 Coat the outside of each trout with mayonnaise. In the body cavity of each trout, stuff 2 thyme sprigs, 2 oregano sprigs, 1 rosemary sprig, and 2 lemon slices. Add a little garlic if you like. Refrigerate until ready to grill.

2 Light a charcoal fire or preheat your gas grill on high. Oil your grill's cooking grate. When the coals are almost ready or the gas is close to preheating, add the smoking chips and cover. (For a gas grill, put the chips in a foil pouch and punch lots of holes in it.) Wait until a good head of smoke is obvious, then add the trout. Cover and cook for 5 to 6 minutes on each side, depending on the thickness of the trout. Use the 10-minute-per-inch rule as a guide. Remove the trout from the heat to a platter and let them rest for 5 minutes. Serve with a drizzle of first-rate extra-virgin olive oil.

4 small whole rainbow, golden, or mountain trout, heads removed, scaled and gutted

$\frac{1}{2}$ cup mayonnaise

8 sprigs fresh thyme

8 sprigs fresh oregano

4 sprigs fresh rosemary

8 lemon slices, $\frac{1}{4}$ inch thick

2 teaspoons chopped garlic (optional)

Applewood smoking chips

Extra-virgin olive oil for drizzling

JULIA CHILD'S METHOD FOR BROILING THIN FILLETS

Trying to broil flounder and sole was one of the most frustrating things I've ever tried to do. It seems like they either stuck to the broiling pan or I overcooked them. Then I discovered Julia Child's method, which helps keep the fish moist and gives you a little more "fudge" factor on the cooking time. Quite frankly, it's a simple thing. Pour a little vermouth into a baking dish and you will be amazed at the difference it makes.

Four 6-ounce flounder or other flatfish fillets

Olive oil for greasing

½ cup dry vermouth

2 tablespoons (¼ stick) unsalted butter, at room temperature

Kosher salt

Freshly ground black pepper

4 lemon wedges

1 At least 20 minutes before you plan to cook, preheat the broiler.

2 Lightly oil the bottom of a 9-by-13-inch ovenproof dish. Arrange the fillets in a single layer in the dish. Pour in the vermouth, using only enough to be about ½ inch deep. Put the pan under the broiler and broil the fish as close to the heat as possible for approximately 2 minutes. Remove and quickly spread the softened butter over the fillets. Return the pan to the broiler and cook for about 5 minutes more, until the fish is just cooked through.

3 Remove the fish from the broiler. Salt and pepper each fillet and serve them with the lemon wedges.

SERVES 4

One look at the fish counter in most markets I have visited suggests to me that as a country, we like meaty, firm fish. Tuna and salmon out-display practically every other type of fish. Ask ten people on the street what their favorites are, and invariably tuna, salmon, and Chilean sea bass are named. Monkfish also comes up, but it is only eaten at a restaurant, because when cooked at home, it is tough. We will fix that.

I put wahoo, a great sport fish, in this group. Its meat is similar to tuna—a different color, and milder tasting than tuna, but richer and satisfying. Large Pacific halibut belong in this group, as well as mahi-mahi and grouper. Wild striped bass, or rockfish as they are also called, have the meaty texture to stand with this group. The workhorse of fish, cod, belongs here too.

The recipes in this chapter capture the essence of these fish, both in technique and flavor. Most are bold like the fish themselves. Some quietly show you new ways with this type of fish. But most importantly, they are fish you can buy—maybe not every day—but they are there in your market, whether that market is in Memphis, Tennessee, San Antonio, Texas, or Portland, Oregon. The second beauty to this chapter is how the recipes can accommodate other fish types besides the one called for in that particular recipe. Nothing is more disappointing than having your heart set on a recipe only to find that the tuna you needed is not the best today or didn't come in on the delivery. But perhaps the halibut is perfect. Don't walk away. Buy the halibut, and use the same recipe as for the tuna. I expect you will be happy when dinnertime rolls around.

The big and sturdy fish are sold almost exclusively as fillets, loins, or sides. Rarely will you ever see these fish whole. Remember that it is imperative that fillets not sit directly on ice. They should look moist, with true color, and have a slight translucency about them. No bruised flesh. Ask to smell the fillets—they should smell like the ocean. Don't buy anything that smells of ammonia. Ask the fishmonger to touch the fillet and look for firmness with springiness. See if you can get tuna or wahoo steaks cut straight from the loin. Ask if there is fish that is still

STURDY FISH

frozen, like the possibly prefrozen fillets in their counter. I know a woman who buys a frozen side of salmon when it is on sale at her local grocery, and marches it right down to the meat department to cut into fillets while still frozen. Whatever works.

Tuna, salmon, cod, and halibut can almost always be found frozen, usually cut into perfect-sized portions, and individually vacuum wrapped. These are excellent options.

Salmon usually need pin bones removed from their flesh. You should check for pin bones on every piece of salmon you buy. Sometimes the fishmonger will remove them for you, but it is so easy I try to take care of this myself. Run your fingertips over the flesh of the salmon from the tail to the head. You will feel them if they are there. Tweezers or needle-nose pliers are righteous for the chore. Just press down on the flesh around the bone with your fingers and jerk with the tweezers. You can buy a special tool from a kitchen store, but it doesn't work any better.

Another thought on salmon: Is it wild or farm raised? Most Atlantic salmon is farm raised, and they tend to be smaller than wild Pacific-caught fish. I like wild salmon, especially the different varieties with their own flavor profiles. Special wild salmon runs, such as the Copper River salmon run in late spring, are worth checking out. Copper River salmon are superb in every way. However, no amount of additional flavor can overcome poor quality in a wild salmon. The rule still applies—buy the freshest.

One last comment about this group of fish. There has been much discussion on mercury and PCBs in salmon, swordfish, and tuna. Bigger fish tend to contain more contaminates. If you are pregnant, nursing, have a very young child, or immune system problems, you should avoid fish with known high levels of weird stuff. Check several Web sites, like the USDA site, to get a true picture of the danger. If you don't fall in these categories, the general wisdom holds that the health benefits of eating fish far exceed the potential risks. The best path is to eat many types of seafood, rather than just a couple.

ASIAN SEARED TUNA

Tuna likes to mingle with so many flavors, but the inherent richness plays extremely well with Asian sensibilities. This is a very simple, straightforward preparation. If quickly seared tuna that's still red and cool in the center sounds a little too fast for you, try it once. You can always microwave the tuna to your desired doneness. It's been my experience that once you taste tuna quickly cooked, it will become your preferred method.

Ponzu sauce is a soy sauce–based product with citrus notes that is easily found in major supermarkets, as is wasabi. Don't break your neck trying to find black sesame seeds though—they are more of a visual than a serious effect on the taste of the tuna.

SERVES 4

1   Combine the sesame oil and the ponzu sauce in a shallow baking dish. Add the tuna steaks and cover. Marinate them at room temperature for 20 minutes or in the refrigerator up to 2 hours.

2   Add the mayonnaise and wasabi to a small bowl and combine. Cover and refrigerate until needed. This can be made up to 4 days in advance.

3   When ready to cook, remove the tuna from the marinade, pat dry, and coat each steak with about 1 tablespoon of the wasabi mayonnaise. Spread the sesame seeds out on a plate. Press each tuna steak into the sesame seeds to coat both sides. Heat the oil over medium-high heat in a sauté pan large enough to hold the tuna, until the oil shimmers. Add the tuna and cook on each side for 3 minutes for rare, but not much longer than 5 minutes. Serve with additional wasabi mayonnaise, if desired.

1 tablespoon sesame oil

2 tablespoons ponzu sauce

Four 6- to 8-ounce tuna steaks, cut 1 to 1½ inches thick

¼ cup mayonnaise

½ tablespoon prepared wasabi

¼ cup toasted white sesame seeds

2 tablespoons black sesame seeds, or use all white

2 tablespoons canola oil, or clarified unsalted butter, or 1 tablespoon of oil and 1 tablespoon of butter

BAKED HALIBUT WITH
MOROCCAN SPICES

From the land of Bogart's Rick Blaine comes a simple spice combination that adds a multitude of flavors to fish. The cinnamon works as a nice contrast to the other spices for a very exotic flavor profile. Any white fish will benefit from this treatment—even thinner fillets like sole, flounder, or catfish. I doubt Rick had this on the menu at Rick's Café Americaine, but it would be a mood setter for watching *Casablanca*. Cook it again, Sam.

Eight 6- to 8-ounce halibut fillets (each about 1 inch thick)

2 tablespoons olive oil, plus more for brushing the baking sheet

1 tablespoon ground cumin

1 teaspoon ground coriander

½ teaspoon ground cinnamon

½ teaspoon cayenne pepper

Kosher salt

Freshly ground black pepper

Chopped fresh cilantro for garnish

8 lime wedges

1　Preheat the oven to 400 degrees F. Brush a 17-inch, rimmed baking sheet with oil.

2　Brush both sides of the fish with the 2 tablespoons of oil. Mix the cumin, coriander, cinnamon, and cayenne in a small bowl. Rub the spice mixture all over the fish. Sprinkle the fish with salt and pepper. Place it on the prepared baking sheet.

3　Bake the fish, without turning, until it is just opaque in the center, about 12 minutes. Transfer the fish to a platter. Sprinkle it with chopped cilantro. Serve with the lime wedges.

SERVES 8

BAKED SALMON STUFFED WITH MASCARPONE CHEESE AND SPINACH

There is a blending of flavors here that makes this recipe outstanding. The richness of the salmon against the bitterness present in the spinach and the slight sweet note of the cheese come together for a creamy, pleasing taste experience full of contrasts. You could use this stuffing with halibut or even tuna, but it shines brightest with salmon.

SERVES 8

1   Cook the spinach in a large pot of boiling water just until it is wilted, about 30 seconds. Drain; rinse with cold water. Squeeze the spinach dry, then finely chop it. Place it in a small bowl and mix in the cream cheese, mascarpone, and nutmeg. Season to taste with salt and pepper.

2   Cut one ³/₄-inch-deep, 2 ¹/₂-inch-long slit down the center top side of each salmon fillet, forming a pocket for the spinach mixture. Fill each slit with the mixture, dividing it equally among the salmon fillets. (This can be done up to 4 hours ahead. Cover and chill.)

3   Preheat the oven to 450 degrees F. Brush a rimmed baking sheet with oil.

4   Sprinkle the salmon with salt and pepper. Mix the bread-crumbs, butter, and Parmesan in a medium bowl. Top each of the salmon fillets with some breadcrumb mixture, push-ing it into the slit.

5   Place the salmon fillets, skin side down, on the prepared baking sheet. Bake them until they are just opaque in the center, about 12 minutes (you can cook the salmon a little less if you desire). Transfer the salmon to a platter and serve.

10 ounces fresh spinach

¹/₂ cup cream cheese (about 4 ounces), at room temperature

¹/₂ cup mascarpone cheese, at room temperature

Pinch of freshly ground nutmeg

Kosher salt

Freshly ground black pepper

Eight 6- to 8-ounce salmon fillets, with skin (each about 1 inch thick)

Olive oil for brushing

2²/₃ cups fresh breadcrumbs

8 tablespoons (1 stick) unsalted butter, melted

¹/₂ cup freshly grated Parmesan cheese

BRAISED CURRY FISH

Braising is not commonly thought of as a method for cooking fish, and that's a shame. With so many folks worrying about overcooking fish, and the texture and flavor being bland and dry, braising sets up a natural defense to combat all those negatives. This recipe works as easily for a weeknight dinner as it does for company. Cooked jasmine rice alongside makes for a great meal.

2 tablespoons olive oil

Kosher salt

Freshly ground black pepper

Four 6-ounce fillets any firm white fish such as grouper, monkfish, Chilean sea bass, cod, or tilefish

Instant flour, such as Wondra, for dredging

1 cup chopped onion

1 tablespoon chopped garlic

1 tablespoon chopped peeled fresh ginger

1 cup low-sodium chicken broth

2 tablespoons fresh lime juice

1 tablespoon curry powder

2 teaspoons tamari or light soy sauce

1 jalapeño pepper, seeded and chopped

2 tablespoons chopped fresh cilantro

2 tablespoons chopped fresh chives

1　Heat the oil in a nonstick sauté pan over medium-high heat until it just shimmers. Salt and pepper the fillets. Coat them with the flour. Place the fillets in the hot pan and sear on one side for 3 minutes. Turn the fillets over and cook for 2 minutes. Remove the fillets to a platter.

2　Add the onion, garlic, and ginger to the pan. Sauté them until softened. Add the broth, lime juice, curry powder, tamari, and jalapeño.

3　Bring the liquid to a simmer and add the fish back to the pan. Continue cooking while spooning the liquid over the fish for about 6 minutes, until the fish is just opaque in the center. Remove the fillets and garnish with the cilantro and chives. Serve hot.

SERVES 4

BARBEQUED MONKFISH
WITH CHIPOTLE MAYONNAISE

Monkfish is a joy to eat and overlooked by many home cooks. Monkfish are meaty in texture, without a very strong fish taste. Called *lotte* in France, they are known as "poor man's lobster." I think they resemble lobster in texture only and pleasantly adapt to a number of preparations. Here we treat them with a barbeque spice and serve with a spicy mayonnaise that is also great with grilled chicken. Halibut, Chilean sea bass, and even salmon are good substitutes. With a cold beer, this is a great summertime dish.

In the seafood case, skinned monkfish tails look, well, strange. They tend to have a purplish color to them. The color is a product of a thin membrane that is quite harmless to eat, but when left on makes for one tough piece of fish. Removing the membrane is easy, and essential to a successful monkfish dish.

SERVES 4

1 To make the chipotle mayonnaise: Combine the mayonnaise, chipotle, adobo sauce, lime juice, and garlic. I recommend that you make this at least 2 hours or up to 1 day before serving. Stir in the cilantro, if using, just before serving. Keeps in the refrigerator for about 7 days.

2 Light a charcoal fire or preheat your gas grill on high. Oil your grill's cooking rack.

CHIPOTLE MAYONNAISE

1 cup mayonnaise

1 canned chipotle chile in adobo, finely chopped

1 tablespoon adobo sauce (from the can)

1 tablespoon fresh lime juice

1 garlic clove, pressed

¼ cup chopped fresh cilantro (optional)

MONKFISH

Four 6- to 8-ounce monkfish tail fillets

3 tablespoons of your favorite barbeque rib rub, purchased or homemade

3   To prepare the fish: Remove the purple-gray membrane from the monkfish, by running a knife between the membrane and the meat, pulling the membrane away from the fish with your other hand, the same way you remove silver skin from pork. The membrane comes off easily, but don't worry if you take a bit of the meat with it. It is important to remove all of the membrane. Many people tell me that they like monkfish at restaurants, but can't make it at home. This membrane is the problem.

4   I also like to turn the fish over and remove the clear membrane from the other side using the same method.

5   Sprinkle each fillet with a good coating of the rub, using as much of the rub as needed to cover the fish.

6   When the fire is ready and hot, place the monkfish on the grill. Cook a total of 8 to 10 minutes, turning the monkfish frequently. The fish is done when you press it and it feels similar to pressing the top of your nose between your eyes—firm but with a little give. Serve with a dollop of the Chipotle Mayonnaise on the side.

BRAISED FISH WITH TOMATO-
HORSERADISH VINAIGRETTE

I developed this braised fish recipe for a University of North Carolina Wellness Center cooking class. The flavors are more assertive and bolder than those of other braised fish recipes, contradicting the notion that healthful food has to be boring. The vinaigrette is tasty but not necessary if time is short.

SERVES 4

1 To make the vinaigrette: In a blender, add the tomato paste, vinegar, honey, horseradish, and Worcestershire sauce. Blend until combined. With the motor running, slowly add the oil until emulsified (the oil and other ingredients have blended together). Stir in salt and pepper to taste. (Can be made ahead up to this point.) Just before serving, stir in the thyme.

2 To make the fish: Heat the oil in a nonstick sauté pan over medium-high heat until it just shimmers. Salt and pepper the fillets. Place the fillets in the hot pan and sear on one side for 3 to 4 minutes. Turn the fillets over. Cut the heat down to medium. Add the green onion. Sauté until softened. Add the broth, rosemary, garlic, and Worcestershire sauce. Bring to a simmer and continue cooking while spooning the liquid over the fish for 6 to 8 minutes, until the fish is just opaque in the center. Remove the fillets and keep them warm.

**TOMATO-HORSERADISH
VINAIGRETTE**

2 tablespoons double concentrated tomato paste (located in the tomato paste section in a tube)

2 tablespoons balsamic vinegar

1 tablespoon honey

1 teaspoon prepared horseradish

1 teaspoon Worcestershire sauce

1/3 cup extra-virgin olive oil

Kosher salt

Freshly ground black pepper

1 teaspoon fresh thyme leaves

FISH AND BRAISING SAUCE

1 tablespoon olive oil

Kosher salt

Freshly ground black pepper

Four 6-ounce fillets any firm white fish, such as grouper, Chilean sea bass, cod, or tilefish

1 green onion, thinly sliced

1 cup beef broth

1 tablespoon chopped fresh rosemary leaves

2 garlic cloves, smashed

1 teaspoon Worcestershire sauce

1 tablespoon unsalted butter

2 tablespoons chopped fresh chives

3   Bring the heat to high and reduce the liquid in the pan to about $\frac{1}{3}$ cup. Remove the pan from the heat and swirl in the butter until it is completely blended. Strain the sauce into a bowl.

4   Plate the fish and spoon a little of the vinaigrette over it. Pour a little of the butter sauce around, sprinkle with the chives, and serve immediately.

COLOMBIAN TUNA SEVICHE

This Colombian seviche is adapted from Rafael Palomino, executive chef at the now defunct Sonora, a well-known Latin American restaurant in New York City. This method of "cooking" seafood in citrus juice is perfect for a scorching summer day. Remember that the usual side dish with seviche is popcorn!

SERVES 6 TO 8

1 In a glass bowl, mix the tuna and lime juice, cover, and refrigerate about 2 hours. The tuna should still be pink in the middle.

2 In another bowl, stir together the pineapple, coconut milks, horseradish, ginger, and chile. When the tuna is ready, drain it well, pat dry, and add it to the pineapple mixture. Refrigerate for 2 to 4 hours or up to 8 hours.

3 Serve cold in chilled bowls, and don't forget the popcorn.

1 pound sushi-grade tuna (sometimes frozen is best), diced in 1/4-inch pieces

1/2 cup fresh lime juice

1 cup fresh pineapple chunks

1 cup unsweetened coconut milk

3/4 cup sweetened coconut milk (like Coco Lopez)

2 teaspoons prepared horseradish

2 teaspoons grated peeled fresh ginger

1 teaspoon minced chipotle chiles in adobo sauce

"BRÛLÉED" SALMON WITH FRESH GRILLED FRUIT SALSA

Coating salmon with brown sugar gives it a mildly sweet, moist glaze. Grilled fruit salsa sounded like the perfect thing to go along with it. You'll have leftover salsa, which will be outstanding the next couple of days with chicken, pork, shrimp, or by itself.

Four 6- to 8-ounce center-cut salmon fillets, with skin, pin bones removed

Kosher salt

Freshly ground black pepper

4 tablespoons packed light brown sugar

1 pineapple, peeled and cored

2 nectarines, peeled and sliced into eighths

1 mango, peeled and sliced about ¼ inch thick

2 tablespoons peanut oil

½ cup chopped red onion

3 tablespoons chopped fresh cilantro

1 garlic clove, pressed

1 jalapeño pepper, seeded and finely minced

1 Light a charcoal fire or preheat your gas grill on high. Oil your grill's cooking grate.

2 Take the salmon fillets and sprinkle them liberally with salt and pepper. Take 1 tablespoon of the sugar for each fillet, spread it evenly over the fillet, and pack it down. Reserve.

3 Slice the pineapple into rings, about ¼ inch thick. Toss all the fruit with the oil.

4 When the fire is ready, place the salmon, skin side down, on the grill. Add the fruit to the grill. Cook the fruit 2 to 3 minutes per side, or until it is soft but still firm.

5 While the fruit and salmon are cooking, mix the onion, cilantro, garlic, and jalapeño together in a large bowl. Set aside. When the fruit is done, roughly chop it and add to the onion mixture, stirring to combine.

6 Meanwhile, back to the salmon, cook it for a total of 8 minutes, until it is slightly rare in the center, when checked with a knife. Do not turn it. The skin will probably stick to the grill. That's OK. If that happens, just carefully slide your spatula between the salmon skin and the flesh to remove the salmon fillet and leave the skin on the grill. Serve the salmon with the grilled fruit salsa.

SERVES 4

GRILLED MARINATED
SWORDFISH

This recipe is similar to one I had several years ago at the Grand Central Oyster Bar in New York City. A simple dish with a quick marinade and finished with a seasoned butter, it makes for a fast, sleight-of-hand meal. The marinade works with any thick white fish or tuna. I like doubling the butter and using it atop grilled beef steaks or chicken.

SERVES 4

1   To make the marinade: Whisk together the oil, lemon juice, basil, shallot, salt, and pepper in a medium bowl. Place the swordfish steaks in a shallow baking dish, and pour the marinade over them. Allow the steaks to marinate at room temperature for about 2 hours, turning them over after 1 hour.

2   To make the butter: In a bowl, mash the butter, parsley, and shallot together with a fork. Cover and refrigerate. The butter will keep for about 1 week.

3   Light a charcoal fire or preheat your gas grill on high. Oil your grill's cooking grate.

4   Remove the swordfish steaks from the marinade and let it drain off. You want a little moisture left on the steaks. When the fire is hot, place the steaks on the grill. Cook for 4 minutes on one side, turn, and cook for 3 minutes more, until the swordfish is cooked through and firm to the touch.

5   Remove the fish from the grill, and top each steak with 1 tablespoon or so of the seasoned butter. Serve immediately with the lemon wedges.

MARINADE

1 cup olive oil

Juice of 1 lemon (about 1/4 cup)

2 tablespoons chopped fresh basil

1 shallot, finely chopped (about 1 tablespoon)

1 teaspoon kosher salt

1/2 teaspoon freshly ground black pepper

Four 6- to 8-ounce swordfish steaks, about 1 inch thick

SEASONED BUTTER

4 tablespoons (1/2 stick) unsalted butter, at room temperature

1/4 cup chopped fresh parsley

1 shallot, finely chopped (about 1 tablespoon)

4 lemon wedges

COD DIJON

This is a simple baked fish recipe that really tastes elegant, and is perfect for a busy weeknight supper. Individually frozen and vacuum-sealed cod fillets are perfect for this recipe. The cod processed in Alaska are superior. Most any white fish, even thin fillets like tilapia, take well to this preparation.

Four 6-ounce cod fillets

Kosher salt

Freshly ground black pepper

2 tablespoons (¼ stick) unsalted butter, melted

1 teaspoon fresh lemon juice

1 teaspoon Worcestershire sauce

1 teaspoon Dijon mustard

½ cup cornflake crumbs

4 lemon wedges

1 Preheat the oven to 425 degrees F.

2 Lightly coat a baking dish large enough to hold the fillets with nonstick spray. Lay the cod in the dish, and season it with salt and pepper to taste.

3 Blend the butter, lemon juice, Worcestershire sauce, and mustard together in a small bowl.

4 Spread the sauce over the fillets, covering them completely. Sprinkle the crumbs over the top of the fillets. Bake until they are cooked through, about 10 minutes. Serve with the lemon wedges.

SERVES 4

CORN TORTILLA-CRUSTED GROUPER WITH SPICY SUMMER FRUIT SALSA

Add a taste of the Southwest to your menu with this recipe. I've taken an old method of cooking fish and updated it using crushed tortilla chips rather than breadcrumbs or seasoned flour. Don't expect exploding heat from this dish, but do expect exciting flavor. You might even get a fish hater to come around after a bite of this grouper. Any of the snapper family—tilefish, sea bass, cod, or mahi-mahi—would make grand substitutes for the grouper.

SERVES 4

1 Preheat the oven to 350 degrees F.

2 To make the salsa: Combine the mangoes, papaya, onion, cilantro, oil, jalapeño, garlic, salt, and pepper. Cut the limes into quarters to serve with the salsa. This can be made 1 day in advance and refrigerated.

3 To prepare the grouper: In two shallow pans, first dust the fish with the flour, salt, and pepper, then dredge the dusted fillets in the beaten eggs.

4 Mix the crushed chips, lime juice, cumin, garlic powder, and 1 teaspoon each of salt and pepper and place the mixture in a shallow baking dish. Add the fish, pressing the mixture onto the fillets. Heat the oil in a 12-inch ovenproof sauté pan. When hot, add the fillets and cook for 3 minutes on each side.

SPICY FRUIT SALSA

2 mangoes, peeled and diced

1 papaya, peeled and diced

1 red onion, diced

1 bunch fresh cilantro, chopped

2 tablespoons olive oil

1 jalapeño pepper, seeded and diced

1 garlic clove, pressed

1 teaspoon kosher salt

1 teaspoon freshly ground black pepper

2 limes

GROUPER

Four 8-ounce grouper fillets

2 cups all-purpose flour

Kosher salt

Freshly ground black pepper

3 large eggs, lightly beaten

2 cups crushed tortilla chips (food processor works best)

Juice of 1 lime (about ¼ cup)

2 teaspoons ground cumin

1 teaspoon garlic powder

¼ cup vegetable oil

5   Place the sauté pan in the oven and bake for 7 minutes, until the fish is firm to the touch. Serve with the Spicy Fruit Salsa and lime wedges.

CORNMEAL-CRUSTED
HALIBUT STICKS FOR KIDS

If your kids (big or small) love fish sticks, then you need to try this recipe. If halibut is expensive, or not available, use pollack, cod, or grouper. Once you make these, the supermarket variety may not make it back in your house.

SERVES 6

1   Spray a large rimmed baking sheet with nonstick spray. Place the flour in a shallow dish (pie pans work great). Whisk the salad dressing and eggs together in another shallow dish to blend. Add the breadcrumbs, cornmeal, and parsley to a third shallow dish. Stir to combine.

2   Dip the halibut sticks into flour, then into the egg mixture, then into the crumbs, covering the fish completely. Place them on the prepared baking sheet. They can be coated up to 4 hours ahead; cover and keep refrigerated.

3   Preheat the oven to 400 degrees F.

4   Bake the halibut sticks until they are cooked through, crisp, and firm to the touch, about 15 minutes. Transfer them to a platter and serve warm with tartar sauce, ketchup, or lemon wedges.

All-purpose flour for dredging

1 cup purchased Italian salad dressing

2 large eggs, lightly beaten

3 cups seasoned breadcrumbs

1 cup coarse ground yellow cornmeal

¼ cup finely chopped fresh parsley

1½ pounds halibut fillets, cut into eighteen 4-by-1-by-½-inch strips

EASY POACHED SALMON WITH SAUCE GRIBICHE

This concept, of poaching small pieces of salmon instead of a whole fish or side, gives you the opportunity to enjoy poached fish more often. This fish, served with some dead-ripe tomatoes, is a perfect summer dish. Please don't hesitate to poach other fish, such as sea bass, snapper, and tilefish. For a flatter fish, like fluke or flounder, cut the time off the heat by ten minutes. The sauce gribiche, an old-style sauce based on hard-cooked eggs, improves if made the day before.

SAUCE GRIBICHE

1 cup good-quality mayonnaise

3 large hard-cooked eggs, finely chopped

Juice of ½ lemon

1 tablespoon capers, rinsed and drained

1 tablespoon chopped cornichons

2 teaspoons chopped shallot, rinsed in cold water

2 teaspoons chopped fresh parsley

1½ teaspoons sliced fresh chives

1½ teaspoons chopped fresh dill

1 teaspoon Dijon mustard

SALMON

Four 6-ounce salmon fillets

¼ cup kosher salt

1 tablespoon black peppercorns

1. To make the sauce: Combine the mayonnaise, eggs, lemon juice, capers, cornichons, shallots, parsley, chives, dill, and mustard in a large bowl and stir thoroughly. Refrigerate until ready to serve.

2. To prepare the salmon: Place the fillets in a sauté pan big enough to hold them. Cover the fillets with water, and add the salt and peppercorns.

3. Place the pan over medium-high heat, and bring to a boil. Remove from the heat, cover, and let the fish sit in the water for 25 to 30 minutes.

4. Remove and refrigerate the fish until cold. Serve with the Sauce Gribiche.

SERVES 4

OUTER BANKS FISH MUDDLE

Along the Outer Banks of North Carolina and in the hidden little inlets of the Pamlico River, you will find cauldrons of fish muddle in the making. It really is nothing more than a tasty fish soup, but what differentiates it from so many others is the addition of eggs, which you gently poach in the broth. It reminds me a lot of the Portuguese garlic and tomato soup, where a poached egg has traditionally been the soul of the soup.

SERVES 6

1   Cut the grouper into 1½-inch chunks. In a large frying pan, fry the bacon until crisp; remove it with a slotted spoon, crumble, and set aside. Add the onions to the fat remaining in the pan and cook over medium heat until they are soft, about 5 to 7 minutes. Add the garlic and cook briefly. Add the tomatoes, potatoes, clam juice, vinegar, 1½ tablespoons of the parsley, the thyme, pepper flakes, and 2 cups of water to cover the mixture. Bring to a boil, cover, and reduce to a simmer until the potatoes are nearly soft, about 20 minutes.

2   Add the fish and enough additional water to just cover. Return to a boil, reduce the heat, and simmer for 2 minutes. Season to taste with salt and pepper.

3   Crack the eggs individually into a saucer and slide them, one at a time, onto the top of the soup. Cover and cook, for 1½ minutes, then uncover and baste them with the simmering fish broth. Re-cover and cook approximately 1½ minutes more, until the eggs are lightly poached. Immediately spoon the eggs into 6 soup bowls. Ladle the fish, potatoes, and liquid over the eggs. Mix together the crumbled bacon, green onions, and remaining 1½ tablespoons of the parsley. Garnish the soup with the bacon mixture as you serve.

1½ pounds grouper fillets

8 ounces sliced bacon

4 medium onions, thinly sliced (1½ pounds)

2 garlic cloves, minced

One 28-ounce can Italian plum tomatoes, chopped, with their liquid

4 medium boiling potatoes, peeled and thinly sliced

2 cups bottled clam juice

2 tablespoons cider vinegar

3 tablespoons chopped fresh parsley, divided

1 teaspoon chopped fresh thyme

¾ teaspoon red pepper flakes

Kosher salt

Freshly ground black pepper

6 large eggs

4 green onions or scallions, green and white parts, chopped

FOOLPROOF GRILLED FISH

Grilling fish scares the bejesus out of otherwise confident cooks, and it shouldn't. Grilling fish starts with listening to your mother: "Cleanliness is next to Godliness." Your grill grate has to be impeccably clean. Without a clean grill, you are doomed from the start. Next, a fat has to be involved. Using mayonnaise as that fat keeps the fish lubricated on the grill and also imparts moisture, without adding a flavor. This really is a foolproof way to grill most any thick, lean, white fish.

½ teaspoon ground cumin

½ teaspoon ground coriander

½ teaspoon kosher salt

⅛ teaspoon freshly ground black pepper

Four 6-ounce halibut or sea bass fillets, 1 inch thick

4 tablespoons mayonnaise

1 Light a charcoal fire or preheat your gas grill on high. Oil your grill's cooking grate.

2 Mix the cumin, coriander, salt, and pepper together in a small bowl. Sprinkle evenly over each fillet. With the back of a spoon, spread ½ tablespoon of mayonnaise over both sides of each fillet. It looks messy, but that's OK. Place the fish fillets on a hot grill and cook for 6 minutes. Turn the fillets and cook 4 to 5 minutes longer, until they are opaque in the center. Serve at once.

SERVES 4

GRILLED BARBEQUED SALMON

Probably the easiest fish to grill is salmon. Lately, we have even had a choice in the salmon we can buy. Copper River salmon is a sockeye salmon that is caught as it struggles to get upstream to mate. A lean and rich-flavored fish, Copper River salmon is capable of standing up to the essences of charcoal. But be quick; the season for Copper River is short. Wild King salmon is more and more available, and farm-raised salmon now has much more flavor and is easier to obtain. To grill salmon, thick fillets are best. Ask your fishmonger for 1-inch-thick, center-cut fillets. Stick to your guns here; accept no narrow tail flesh, which does not grill well. You might want to throw a couple of extra fillets on the grill for making salmon croquettes later.

SERVES 4

1   Light a charcoal grill or preheat your gas grill on high. Oil the grill's cooking grate.

2   Lightly spray each fillet with nonstick cooking spray. Sprinkle one side of each fillet with the seasoning mix. Pat the seasoning mix into the fillets.

3   When your grill is ready, place the salmon seasoned side down on the grill. Cook the fillets for about 5 minutes, allowing the seasoning to crust. Turn the fillets and quickly brush each one with barbeque sauce, then cover them. Cook for an additional 4 to 5 minutes, or until your preferred doneness. Please don't overcook. Leaving them a little rare at the middle of the fillet will add to your enjoyment. Serve immediately.

Four 6-ounce center-cut skinless salmon fillets

1 tablespoon seasoning mix or any Cajun or blackened fish seasoning

½ cup of your favorite barbeque sauce

GRILLED TUNA IN THE STYLE OF
THAI STREET FOOD

In northern Thailand, small birds similar to quail are prepared in this manner and sold from street vendors like hot dogs are in this country. The flavors are fabulous, and even better on grilled tuna. Remember to make the Sweet-Hot Garlic Sauce the day before.

SWEET-HOT GARLIC SAUCE

1 cup sugar

½ cup water

½ cup distilled white vinegar

2 tablespoons finely minced garlic

1 teaspoon kosher salt

1 tablespoon chili-garlic sauce (in your supermarket's Asian section)

TUNA

¼ cup coarsely chopped fresh cilantro stems and leaves

¼ cup chopped garlic

2 teaspoons freshly cracked black pepper

3 tablespoons tamari or light soy sauce

Four 6- to 8-ounce tuna steaks, 1 inch thick

Vegetable oil for drizzling

1 To prepare the Sweet-Hot Garlic Sauce: Place a small saucepan over medium heat and add the sugar, water, vinegar, garlic, and salt. Bring to a full boil, stirring to dissolve the sugar and salt. Reduce the heat to low and simmer for about 20 minutes, or until the liquid is a light syrup. Remove it from the heat and stir in the chili-garlic sauce. Cool to room temperature. Pour it into a container and cover with a tight lid and store it at room temperature for 2 to 3 days.

2 To prepare the tuna: Put the cilantro, garlic, and pepper in a food processor. Pulse several times to chop. Add the tamari and run the machine to make a paste. If the paste is thick, add a little water. You want to be able to spread this "pesto" over the tuna.

3 Place the tuna steaks in a baking dish. Add the cilantro pesto and coat the fish evenly. Cover and refrigerate for 1 hour.

4 Light a charcoal fire or preheat your gas grill on high. Oil your grill's cooking grate.

5 Remove the tuna from the marinade, pat dry, and drizzle oil over both sides. Place on a hot grill and cook, about 4 minutes a side for medium, less for medium-rare. Remove the tuna to a platter. Serve with Sweet-Hot Garlic Sauce.

SERVES 4

GRILLED WAHOO WITH CHUNKY TOMATO "BROTH" AND SAFFRON MAYONNAISE

Wahoo is a game fish that's showing up more and more at the fishmonger's. It looks very much like a tuna steak, but is gray in tone. You might pass by on this fish, thinking it to be strong and fishy, as other gray-fleshed fish can be. Not so. Wahoo has a texture like tuna but is milder, creamier tasting, and loves to be grilled. Coupled with the southern French–coast flavors of the broth and the mayonnaise, this recipe is both rustic and surprising. Give it a try.

SERVES 4

1 To make the broth: In a medium sauté pan, heat the oil over medium heat until it shimmers. Add the shallots and sauté until soft. Add the garlic and cook for 1 minute.

2 Add the tomatoes to the pan and cook until they have released their liquid and have become soft. This should take about 20 minutes. Sprinkle in the herbes de Provence and add salt and pepper to taste. Reduce the heat and keep the broth warm, or this can be made a day or 2 in advance, covered and stored in the refrigerator.

3 To prepare the Saffron Mayonnaise: Combine the mayonnaise, sour cream, saffron, and salt and pepper to taste. This sauce improves if made up to a day in advance.

4 Light a charcoal fire or preheat your gas grill on high. Oil your grill's cooking grate.

TOMATO BROTH

1 tablespoon olive oil

2 large shallots, chopped (¼ cup)

2 large garlic cloves, pressed

3 large tomatoes, quartered, then roughly chopped

1 teaspoon herbes de Provence

Kosher salt

Freshly ground black pepper

SAFFRON MAYONNAISE

¼ cup mayonnaise

1 tablespoon sour cream

1 teaspoon saffron

Kosher salt

Freshly ground black pepper

2 tablespoons olive oil

Four 8-ounce wahoo steaks

2 tablespoons herbes de Provence

Kosher salt

Freshly ground black pepper

5   Drizzle the oil over the wahoo steaks. Sprinkle each steak with about 2 teaspoons of the herbes de Provence. Salt and pepper each steak.

6   Place them on a hot grill and cook about 4 minutes per side, but no more than 5 minutes per side, until the steaks are firm but have a little give to the touch.

7   To serve, reheat the broth if necessary and divide it between 4 bowls. Place one steak over the broth in each bowl. Pass the Saffron Mayonnaise at the table.

MAHI-MAHI WITH BLOOD ORANGE SALSA

Mahi-mahi is sometimes referred to as dolphin fish. This is not the mammal (think Flipper), but a regular ocean-dwelling fish. It is also showing up under the name of *dorado*. Mahi-mahi takes well to a wide variety of flavors and really is a very neutral palette.

Blood oranges are now more available across the country. Their flesh is beautiful and their flavor a tad sweeter than regular oranges. If blood oranges are out of season, or just not available, use regular oranges. This recipe is too good to skip for lack of a certain type of orange.

SERVES 4

1 Using a small sharp knife, cut the peel and white pith from the orange. Working over a small bowl, cut between the membranes to release the segments. Add the avocado, onion, jalapeño, and lime juice to the bowl with the oranges. Stir gently to combine. Season to taste with salt.

2 Heat the oil in a heavy, nonstick medium skillet over medium-high heat. Sprinkle the fish with salt and pepper, then add the fish to the skillet and sauté until they are browned and cooked through, about 5 minutes per side.

3 Remove the mahi-mahi to a platter, spoon the salsa atop the fish, and serve.

1 blood orange or regular orange

½ cup ½-inch cubed avocado

⅓ cup chopped red onion

2 teaspoons minced red jalapeño pepper

2 teaspoons fresh lime juice

Kosher salt

1 tablespoon olive oil

Freshly ground black pepper

Four 6-ounce mahi-mahi fillets

GOOD OLD FISH FOR CHIPS

Fish and chips, a dish for the ages, has regained its popularity, as tavern food in general has come back in vogue. I like to think of it as fried fish for the soul. Its thick and comforting batter, sprinkled with malt vinegar, encases the fish like a mother's hug. Some recipes use beer, but I'd rather drink the beer than use it in the batter, plus I like the stability of this batter. Fry your "chips" up first and keep them warm in the oven. You'll want the fish hot!

**3 pounds fresh cod fillets
(choose thick ones)**

Kosher salt

Freshly ground black pepper

**1 cup plus 2 tablespoons
all-purpose flour**

1 tablespoon baking powder

**1 teaspoon freshly grated
lemon zest**

$\frac{1}{4}$ teaspoon cayenne pepper

1 cup water

2 extra-large eggs

Vegetable oil for frying

1 Lay the cod fillets on a cutting board. Sprinkle both sides with salt and pepper. Cut the fillets into $1\frac{1}{2}$-by-3-inch pieces.

2 In a bowl, combine the flour, baking powder, zest, cayenne, $1\frac{1}{2}$ teaspoons salt, and $\frac{3}{4}$ teaspoon pepper. Whisk in the water and then the eggs.

3 Preheat the oven to 200 degrees F.

4 Pour $\frac{1}{2}$ inch of oil into a large (12-inch) frying pan and heat it until it registers 360 degrees F on a deep-fat thermometer. Dip each fillet into the batter, allowing the excess to drip back into the bowl. Place the fillets carefully in the hot oil. Don't crowd the pieces. Adjust the heat as needed to keep the oil between 360 and 400 degrees F. Cook the fish on each side for 2 to 3 minutes, until lightly browned and cooked through. Remove it to a plate lined with a paper towel. Sprinkle with salt and serve hot with the "chips."

NOTE: To keep the fried fish hot for up to 20 minutes, place a rack on a baking sheet, place the fish briefly on the paper towels, then on the rack and into the oven.

SERVES 6

POACHED HALIBUT IN WARM HERB VINAIGRETTE

Why stop with just poached salmon? Most any fish will benefit from this moist treatment. Sometimes folks think of poaching as bland, but I think this presentation will change your mind. The fresh herbs really sing in the vinaigrette, creating a wonderful foil for the creamy, moist fish.

SERVES 4

1 Put the mustard in a medium bowl and slowly whisk in the vinaigrette. Whisk in the shallot. Put the mixture in a small saucepan and set aside.

2 Bring the broth and water to a boil in a 10-inch sauté pan. Season both sides of the halibut with salt and pepper. Add the halibut to the pan and adjust the heat so the liquid just simmers. Poach for 5 to 6 minutes, until a metal skewer inserted into the center of the halibut goes in easily, and the skewer, when left in the fish for 5 seconds, feels barely warm when touched to your lip. The halibut will be rare. Cook for a total of 8 to 10 minutes if you care for a more done fish. Take the steaks out of the liquid as soon as they are done.

3 Meanwhile, add the herbs to the vinaigrette and warm the sauce over low heat. Pull the skin off the halibut and place a steak in the center of each of 4 plates. Spoon the vinaigrette over and around the fish. Serve immediately.

1 tablespoon Dijon mustard

1 cup balsamic vinaigrette, homemade or store bought

1 small shallot, finely diced

2 cups clam broth

1 cup water

Four 8-ounce halibut steaks, with skin

Kosher salt

Freshly ground black pepper

2 tablespoons chopped fresh chives

1$\frac{1}{2}$ teaspoons chopped fresh Italian parsley

2 tablespoons chopped fresh chervil or additional parsley

$\frac{1}{2}$ teaspoon chopped fresh tarragon

ST. AUGUSTINE-STYLE
GROUPER FINGERS

Everywhere I travel around the Jacksonville/St. Augustine area, I find these delectable grouper fingers, always served with what is known as a "shrimp sauce" throughout the north Florida area. I've twisted this just a bit to make them easier to prepare without a deep-fat fryer.

1½ pounds grouper fillets

2 large egg whites, lightly beaten

1 cup self-rising white cornmeal mix

Kosher salt

Freshly ground black pepper

1 cup vegetable shortening or oil, and more as needed

Prepared shrimp sauce, Any Region Tartar Sauce (page 322), or your favorite tartar sauce

1 Cut the grouper into 1-inch fingers. Place the egg whites in a large bowl and add the grouper. Toss to coat.

2 Spread the cornmeal in a plate or Pyrex dish. Take a few pieces of grouper at a time and toss them in the cornmeal mix. Try to keep one hand for the wet mixture of the egg whites and one hand for the dry mixture of the cornmeal. Place the coated grouper pieces on a plate until all are coated.

3 In a high-sided 12-inch sauté pan, add the shortening over medium-high heat. When it begins to shimmer, or it registers 365 degrees F on a deep-fat thermometer, begin to add the grouper fingers. Don't crowd them in the pan or add too many at one time, which will lower the temperature of the shortening. Cook for about 10 minutes, turning frequently so that all sides get crisp. Remove the grouper fingers and drain them on paper towels. Add additional oil if necessary and continue with the remaining grouper fingers. Serve immediately with shrimp or tartar sauce.

SERVES 4

ROAST COD WITH RAGOUT OF SAVOY CABBAGE, CANNELLINI BEANS, AND BLACK TRUFFLES

This recipe is very European in nature and perfect for a cold winter day. The fish gets a simple treatment, but the ragout makes everything jump. If you can't find fresh truffles, just drizzle a little truffle oil over each piece of fish.

SERVES 6

1   In a large saucepan, combine the beans, onion, garlic, and thyme. Add enough water to cover the beans by 2 inches. Bring to a boil, and then reduce the heat to medium-low; simmer the beans for 30 minutes. Add salt and pepper to taste, and continue to simmer until the beans are tender, about 15 minutes more. Set aside 1 cup of the cooking liquid, and drain the beans. Remove and discard the onion, garlic, and thyme. Cover the beans and set aside.

2   Place a large pot of lightly salted water over high heat, and bring it to a boil. Place a bowl of ice water close to the stove. Add the carrot to the pot, and boil for 2 minutes; remove with a slotted spoon, and set aside. Add the cabbage to the pot, and boil until barely tender, for 3 to 4 minutes. Drain, and immediately plunge the cabbage into the ice water. When the cabbage is cool, drain well, and gently squeeze it to remove excess water.

²/₃ cup dried cannellini beans, soaked overnight and drained

1 small onion, quartered

3 garlic cloves, crushed

2 sprigs fresh thyme

Kosher salt

Freshly ground white pepper

1 small carrot, cut into ¹/₄-inch dice

1 small (1 pound) Savoy cabbage, outer leaves discarded, cored and cut into ¹/₂-inch-thick slices

¼ cup heavy cream

4 tablespoons (½ stick) unsalted butter

1 ounce black truffle, sliced as thinly as possible

Six 6- to 7-ounce cod fillets

2 tablespoons canola oil

2 tablespoons finely minced fresh chives

3 In a large saucepan over high heat, bring the reserved bean liquid to a boil. Reduce the heat to medium, add the cream, and bring the mixture to a simmer. Reduce the heat to its lowest setting, and add the butter in 4 or 5 additions, whisking until it has emulsified. Season with salt and pepper to taste, and stir in the beans, carrot, cabbage, and truffle. Keep the pan over very low heat for 5 minutes to warm the ragout and allow the truffle flavor to infuse the mixture.

4 While the ragout is warming, prepare the cod fillets. Place a large nonstick or well-seasoned sauté pan over medium-high heat. Add the oil. Season the fillets on both sides with salt and pepper. Add them to the sauté pan, and cook until golden brown and the centers are opaque, 4 to 5 minutes per side.

5 To serve, use a slotted spoon to transfer some of the ragout to a warm platter or individual serving plates. Arrange the cod fillets on top of the ragout, and spoon over any remaining ragout and sauce. Top with the chives, and serve immediately.

ROASTED CHILEAN SEA BASS WITH CHIVE OIL

Chilean sea bass is the marketing name associated with the Patagonian toothfish. Smart move to rename the fish, don't you think? Chilean sea bass is also one of the most popular fish in this country. Its flesh is snow-white and remains that way after cooking. It has a rich, yet mild flavor, making it a favorite with unsure fish eaters. Since it is a big fish, you have the opportunity to find nice thick fillets, which roast nicely. Most all Chilean sea bass is frozen at sea, so buying well-handled frozen fillets may be your "freshest" choice. Cod and grouper could substitute for the sea bass.

SERVES 4

1 Preheat the oven to 400 degrees F.

2 Place the chives in a food processor. Turn on the processor and add the oil through the feed tube in a thin, steady stream. Season with salt and pepper. Stop to taste, adjust if necessary, adding more oil, chives, salt, or pepper as desired. Strain the oil through a fine-mesh strainer into a bowl and reserve.

3 Place the sea bass in a sauté pan or roasting pan just large enough to fit the fillets. Drizzle them with some of the chive oil and season with salt and pepper. Roast until the fish is just barely cooked in the center. It will continue to cook once it is removed from the oven. For 1-inch-thick fillets, expect it to roast for about 9 minutes.

4 Transfer the sea bass to serving plates and sprinkle it with the chive oil.

¼ cup roughly sliced fresh chives

⅓ cup extra-virgin olive oil

Kosher salt

Freshly ground black pepper

Four 8-ounce Chilean sea bass fillets, around 1 inch thick

SALMON TARTARE WITH RED ONION CREAM

This is an easier take on the salmon "cornets" that greet you soon after you are seated at the French Laundry in Yountville, California. But more important is the number of people that fall in love with these little nibbles and swear they hate raw fish. Talk with a trusted fishmonger when buying the fish. You need sashimi-grade salmon. Many times, buying frozen salmon will result in the freshest possible.

SALMON

6 ounces very fresh, prime skinless salmon, pin bones removed

2 teaspoons minced fresh chives

2 teaspoons minced shallot

1 teaspoon extra-virgin olive oil

1 teaspoon lemon oil

¹/₂ teaspoon kosher salt

Pinch of freshly ground black pepper

RED ONION CREAM

¹/₂ cup sour cream or crème fraîche

1 tablespoon finely minced red onion

¹/₄ teaspoon kosher salt

Two 2.1-ounce boxes frozen phyllo dough cups, baked

Minced fresh chives (optional)

1 Finely chop the salmon. Don't do this with a food processor, as it makes a mush. Mix it with the chives, shallots, oils, salt, and pepper. Cover and chill thoroughly. You can make this 1 day in advance.

2 In a small bowl, combine the sour cream, onion, and salt. Cover and chill. This is better if made 1 day in advance.

3 To serve, spoon the salmon tartare into the phyllo shells. Top each with Red Onion Cream. Garnish with chives, if desired.

MAKES ABOUT 36 HORS D'OEUVERS

SALMON WITH RED WINE SAUCE

This is a rich, elegant, very European dish that was inspired by a recipe I first prepared from a Cordon Bleu cookbook a decade or so ago. It took all day to prepare. I have simplified the recipe for results that still taste like you slaved all day. Make the sauce ahead and your life will be easy. Serve really decadent whipped potatoes for a delightful experience.

SERVES 4

1   Heat 1 tablespoon of the oil in a wide, deep sauté pan set over medium-high heat. Add the shallots, cracked pepper, and thyme, and sauté for 4 minutes. Add the wine and vinegar, then raise the heat to high and bring them to a boil. Let the liquids reduce until about ¼ cup remains. This should take about 10 minutes. Remove the pan from the heat and whisk in the cream. Return the pan to the heat, reduce the heat to medium, and let the cream reduce slightly, about 4 minutes, being careful not to let the cream boil. Remove from the heat and whisk in the butter, one piece at a time. If desired, pour the sauce through a fine-mesh strainer set over a bowl. Discard the solids. Season the sauce with salt and pepper, and set it aside, covered, to keep warm, or pour it into a thermos to hold for up to 4 hours.

2   Warm the remaining 1 tablespoon of the oil in a wide sauté pan set over medium-high heat. Season the salmon on both sides with salt and pepper. Add the salmon to the pan, skinned side up, and cook until it is lightly browned, about 4 minutes. Turn the fillets over, lower the heat to medium, and cook for another 4 minutes, for medium.

3   To serve, place the fillets on a warmed serving platter and drizzle some sauce over each fillet. Pass the remaining sauce alongside in a sauceboat.

2 tablespoons extra-virgin olive oil, divided

2 tablespoons minced shallot (about 1 medium)

½ teaspoon freshly cracked black pepper

1 sprig fresh thyme

2 cups full-bodied, fruity red wine

¼ cup balsamic vinegar

2 tablespoons heavy cream

4 tablespoons (½ stick) unsalted butter, cut into 4 pieces

Kosher salt

Freshly ground black pepper

Four 6- to 8-ounce skinless salmon fillets, pin bones removed

CHILEAN SEA BASS WITH LENTILS AND BACON

Beans and bacon are always the beginnings of a superb meal. Lentils lend an earthiness to most plates and lift the flavors around them. Sauté the fish until it has browned on one side, then flip and finish it in the oven. This gives you some "fudge factor" in the timing and helps generate a nice texture. Grouper or cod are willing substitutes.

4 tablespoons olive oil, divided

4 ounces applewood- or other hardwood-smoked bacon, diced

2 cups chopped onions (about 2 large)

1 large garlic clove, chopped

3½ cups chicken stock or canned low-sodium chicken broth

2 cups lentils (about 13 ounces), rinsed

2 small bay leaves

Kosher salt

Freshly ground black pepper

2 tablespoons (¼ stick) unsalted butter

Six 6-ounce Chilean sea bass fillets

SERVES 6

1   Heat 1 tablespoon of the oil in a large heavy-bottomed saucepan over medium-high heat. Add the bacon and cook until crisp and brown, about 8 minutes. Using a slotted spoon, transfer the bacon to paper towels to drain.

2   Add the onions and garlic to the drippings in the pan. Sauté until they begin to brown, 8 to 10 minutes. Add the stock, lentils, and bay leaves and bring to boil. Reduce the heat to medium-low, cover, and simmer until the lentils are tender and most of the stock is absorbed. Stir occasionally until the lentils are tender, for 40 minutes to 1 hour, depending on the age of the lentils. Season to taste with salt and pepper.

3   Preheat the oven to 400 degrees F.

4   Heat the remaining 3 tablespoons of the oil and the butter in a large, heavy, ovenproof skillet over medium-high heat. Sprinkle the fish with salt and pepper. Add the fish to the skillet and cook until it is browned on the bottom, about 5 minutes. Place the skillet in the oven. Cook for an additional 5 minutes, or until the center of the fish is slightly opaque.

5   Spoon the lentils onto plates and top with the fish. Sprinkle them with the bacon and serve immediately.

SEARED WALLEYE WITH MERLOT SAUCE

Lake Erie without walleye would be a sad state of affairs. It is one of the all-time great American freshwater sport fish, keeping thousands of fishermen (and -women) happy in the north central territories. If you are lucky enough to have some connections for walleye, you are indeed lucky. Salmon, tuna, wahoo, and mahi-mahi are able substitutes for this recipe. I challenge you to prepare this dish. Your efforts will be rewarded with an elegant, rich treat for your palate and soul.

SERVES 6

1 Place the Merlot in a saucepan with the shallots, whole garlic, bay leaf, 1 sprig thyme, the sugar, and peppercorns. Cook over medium heat until only about ¼ cup of liquid remains, about 10 minutes. Set aside in the saucepan.

2 Add the bacon to a cold skillet over medium heat and slowly cook the bacon until it is crisp. Drain the excess fat, remove the bacon, and set aside.

3 Add 2 tablespoons of the butter to the skillet. When the butter begins to foam, add the minced garlic. Return the bacon to the pan and stir in the parsley. Remove the pan from the heat and set aside.

4 Remove the garlic, thyme, and bay leaf from the saucepan that contains the wine and shallots. Place the pan over medium heat. Whisk in 2 tablespoons of the butter bit by bit, until smooth. Remove the sauce from the heat, and season it with salt and pepper to taste. Set aside.

4 cups Merlot

¾ cup finely chopped shallots

5 garlic cloves, 1 whole, 1 minced, 3 crushed

1 bay leaf

3 sprigs fresh thyme

Pinch of sugar

4 black peppercorns, crushed

4 ounces slab bacon, cut into ½-inch dice

6 tablespoons (¾ stick) unsalted butter, divided

1 tablespoon chopped fresh Italian parsley

Kosher salt

Freshly ground black pepper

Six 6- to 8-ounce walleye fillets, with skin

5 Lightly score the skin of the fish with a sharp paring knife. Season with salt and pepper. Heat the remaining 2 tablespoons of the butter in a large cast-iron pan or heavy skillet. Add the crushed garlic and remaining sprigs of thyme. When the butter starts to brown slightly, add the fish, skin side down, and sear until it is crisp, 2 to 3 minutes. Turn it over and sear until it is cooked through, another 5 minutes or so.

6 In the center of 6 plates, place a piece of fish, skin side up. Gently reheat the sauce, add the bacon and parsley, and spoon the sauce around the fish. Serve at once.

SUGAR-SEARED SALMON WITH CREAM SAUCE

Savoy Restaurant in Asheville, North Carolina, is the last place you might think to find a great seafood restaurant, but there it is, specializing in foods with an Italian twist. I had a dish similar to this on the first of many trips I've made to Savoy. It's a fun and a surprising way with salmon.

SERVES 4

1   Mix together the sugar, salt, garlic powder, and pepper in a bowl. Brush the salmon with water to moisten it. Sprinkle it on both sides with all of the sugar mixture.

2   Melt the butter in a large heavy skillet over medium-high heat. Add the salmon and cook until it is crusty on the outside and just opaque in the center, about 4 minutes per side. Transfer each fillet to a plate.

3   Add the clam juice and cream to the skillet. Boil until the sauce thickens enough to coat a spoon, scraping up the browned bits, about 4 minutes. Spoon the sauce over the salmon. Sprinkle it with green onions and serve.

2 tablespoons sugar

1 teaspoon kosher salt

½ teaspoon garlic powder

½ teaspoon freshly ground black pepper

Four 6-ounce skinless salmon fillets, pin bones removed

4 tablespoons (½ stick) unsalted butter

½ cup bottled clam juice

¼ cup heavy cream

Chopped green onions for garnish

WILL'S SMOKY TUNA

Will Johnson has been a fishmonger at Whole Foods in Raleigh, North Carolina, for at least twenty years. This is a recipe he developed and passed on to me years ago, when fresh tuna steaks were just becoming readily available. It is still one of my favorite ways with tuna.

1 cup soy sauce

1 garlic clove, pressed

1 teaspoon grated peeled fresh ginger

8 to 10 dashes liquid smoke

Freshly ground black pepper

4 to 6 tablespoons unsulphured molasses

Four 6-ounce tuna steaks

1   Combine the soy sauce, garlic, ginger, liquid smoke, and pepper to taste in a shallow glass baking dish.

2   Add 2 tablespoons at a time of the molasses until the mixture is just barely sweet to your taste. Add the tuna, cover, and refrigerate for 1 hour, turning after 30 minutes.

3   Light a charcoal fire or preheat your gas grill on high. Oil your grill's cooking grate.

4   Take a disposable foil container about the size of your baking dish, and transfer the tuna steaks into it. Place the foil pan on the grill. Pour in the marinade. Cook the tuna, turning and basting every 3 minutes, for 12 to 14 minutes, or until the tuna is glazed and still rare in the center.

SERVES 4

EVERYBODY'S FAVORITE —

Shrimp is the most popular, or at least the most consumed, seafood in the United States. For that matter, shrimp is a favorite around the world, and with good reason. Shrimp can lead the show all by itself, or it can be a willing playmate with a host of flavors.

For our purposes here, consider shrimp and prawns the same. Some areas of the West Coast seem to call all shrimp "prawns," yet others only refer to the extra-large size as a prawn.

Buying shrimp can also be confusing. Let's start with size. What is medium shrimp? Every fish market that uses terms like "medium," "large," and "jumbo" has a different definition of what those sizes are, and quite frankly, they can change daily at the whim of the manager that day. Of course, these fish dealers may not be the best. Always buy shrimp on a count-per-pound basis. Shrimp are sized in ranges, like 26/30 per pound, and I have always found that the scale leans toward the 30 per-pound size. Each recipe in this chapter has a count per pound rather than a range, as well as a size description. Telling your fishmonger you want a 24-count shrimp will let him know that you know your stuff. I have made them count out the number of shrimp as they put them on the scale, so don't be bashful. It's your money. You may come to agree or disagree with my size assessments, but they will put you on the path to better buying.

Most raw shrimp that you will see are headless. These are called "green headless" in the trade. Some folks, me included, like to grill head-on shrimp, but unless you live in a coastal shrimp-ing region, or have a fishmonger willing to order head-on shrimp, you are unlikely to find them.

Shrimp can be sold raw, unpeeled or peeled, or peeled and deveined (P&Ds), or cooked. I rarely buy cooked, but if you need a shrimp cocktail in a hurry, they can be a lifesaver. My preference is unpeeled or shell on. The shrimp shell has loads of flavor for starters, but also helps protect the natural juices in the shrimp.

The other dilemma with shrimp is whether to buy fresh or frozen. Most all shrimp has been frozen. If I have the time for the shrimp to thaw, and it is fairly quick, I will ask for frozen, unless I know that the market's turnover is rapid. If you are visiting the Southern coast, you

SHRIMP

may get fresh shrimp right off the boat, during the summer months for the most part, when shrimp are in season.

Wild or farm raised is the next question. Virtually all the domestic shrimp is wild caught. That's only about 20 percent of the shrimp eaten here, and at least 85 to 90 percent of imported shrimp is farmed. We eat a lot of farm-raised shrimp. However, I encourage you to buy wild caught whenever they are available, for they are better tasting.

Most shrimp you will find is either pink, white, or brown shrimp. Of the 300 known species of shrimp, Gulf whites are considered by most to be the best, but they usually are expensive. Ecuadorian white is the largest imported shrimp in the United States. Gulf pinks are also of high quality. I prefer the Gulf browns, or "brownies." Some people think they have a stronger iodine taste, but I like their flavor. The Black Tiger shrimp, which is widely farmed in Asia, has caught on in this country. You can easily spot them, with their black or bluish stripes and either red or yellow legs. These can be exceptional for farm raised, and many times are a sale item.

How much to buy depends on who's eating. I routinely purchase 8 ounces per person of unpeeled shrimp for a main course, and 4 ounces for a first course, then I buy a little extra. Folks can be wild about shrimp.

Look for shrimp that have no black spots or bruising. Yellow tints to their shell, or if they don't completely fill their shells, are signs of shrimp you don't want. With frozen, look for shrimp with no gray flesh or an abundance of ice crystals, which means they have been mishandled.

Shrimp can be successfully cooked in most any manner: sautéed, poached, boiled, baked, broiled, or grilled. I would only use 24-count ("large") and larger for grilling. Also, some fish experts believe brining all shrimp is helpful. I do believe that brining shrimp to be grilled is generally necessary, otherwise it's up to you. I tend not to brine for other cooking methods. If you want to try it, a quick brine for 2 pounds of shrimp would be 1 cup salt and ½ cup sugar with 3 cups water. Brine peeled shrimp for 30 minutes, unpeeled for 45 minutes to an hour.

COCONUT-CRUSTED
FRIED SHRIMP

This preparation of shrimp has become a restaurant favorite and it's not very difficult to do at home. Make the Pineapple-Apricot Salsa for a true tropical taste experience.

SERVES 6 AS A
FIRST COURSE
OR 4 AS A MAIN
COURSE

1 To prepare the salsa: Combine the pineapple, onion, preserves, cilantro, lime juice, and jalapeño in a medium bowl. Season with salt and pepper to taste. This can be made 1 day ahead; cover and refrigerate.

2 To prepare the shrimp: Using a small sharp knife and starting at the top of the inward curve, just below the tail, butterfly each shrimp. Cut it more than halfway through toward the outward curve, taking care not to cut the shrimp in two. Open each shrimp and press it slightly to flatten.

3 Mix the cornstarch, salt, and cayenne in a medium bowl. Place the coconut in a pie dish. Beat the egg whites in another medium bowl until frothy. Dredge the shrimp in the cornstarch mixture; shake off the excess. Dip the shrimp into the egg whites, then press them into the coconut; turn the shrimp over and press them into the coconut again to coat both sides.

4 Pour enough oil into a large heavy-bottomed pot or an electric fryer to reach a depth of 2 inches. Heat until it registers 350 degrees F on a deep-fat thermometer. Working in batches, add some shrimp to the hot oil; deep-fry until they are cooked through, about 1 minute. Using a slotted spoon, transfer the shrimp to paper towels to drain. Arrange the shrimp on a platter. Serve them with the salsa for dipping.

PINEAPPLE-APRICOT SALSA

1 cup finely chopped fresh pineapple

1/2 cup finely chopped red onion

1/2 cup apricot preserves

1/2 cup chopped fresh cilantro

2 tablespoons fresh lime juice

1 1/2 tablespoons minced seeded jalapeño pepper

Kosher salt

Freshly ground black pepper

SHRIMP

24 jumbo (16-count) shrimp (about 1 1/2 pounds), peeled, deveined, tails left intact

1/3 cup cornstarch

3/4 teaspoon kosher salt

1/2 teaspoon cayenne pepper

2 cups sweetened shredded coconut

3 large egg whites

Peanut oil for frying

CHESAPEAKE HOUSE
SAUTÉED SHRIMP

This is one of the favorite dishes of the locals who live in the Grand Strand of South Carolina. It's simple, it's quick, and the taste belies how easy it is to fix. It's really best with fresh shrimp in late summer, but frozen farmed work pretty well.

2 pounds medium (40-count) shrimp, peeled and deveined, tails removed

1 teaspoon seasoned salt

8 tablespoons (1 stick) unsalted butter

1 garlic clove, minced

¼ cup white wine

1 Season the shrimp with the salt.

2 In a medium sauté pan, heat the butter over medium heat. When the butter foams, add the shrimp and garlic. Toss the shrimp lightly for even cooking. If the butter begins to burn, reduce the heat.

3 When the shrimp becomes pink and firm, add the wine. (Caution: Wine may flame.) Toss the shrimp in the pan to coat them with sauce. Remove them from the pan and serve immediately.

SERVES 4 TO 6

BARBEQUED SHRIMP ON BISCUITS

Emeril does it, as does just about every other chef and home cook from the Low Country of South Carolina to the Mississippi Delta. Barbequed shrimp on biscuits is one of those Southern things. Biscuits just happen to make it all work and give you something to sop up the juices.

SERVES 4

1 To prepare the sauce: Combine the butter, beer, Worcestershire sauce, ketchup, guava paste, pepper, and salt in a non-reactive saucepan. Simmer over medium heat, whisking continuously, until the butter has melted and the ingredients begin to come together. Continue to simmer for about 10 minutes more, or until thickened. Reserve.

2 Preheat the oven to 425 degrees F.

3 To make the biscuits: Place the flour and chilled butter in a medium bowl. Work the butter into the flour with a pastry cutter, a fork, or your fingertips, until the pieces are a little larger than an English pea.

4 Pour in all of the buttermilk and work the mixture gently until it just holds together. Do not overmix. Handle the dough as little as possible for light biscuits.

5 Turn the dough onto a floured board and knead it quickly, 2 to 3 times, folding like a book. Sprinkle a little flour under the dough so that it won't stick to the board and lightly dust the top of the dough so that it won't stick to the rolling pin. Roll the dough out to about ½ inch thick.

SAUCE

12 tablespoons (1½ sticks) unsalted butter

8 ounces regular beer

2 teaspoons Worcestershire sauce

⅔ cup ketchup

½ cup guava paste or jelly (available at some supermarkets and Hispanic stores)

1 tablespoon freshly ground black pepper

2 teaspoons kosher salt

BUTTERMILK BISCUITS

1½ cups self-rising soft wheat flour, such as White Lily

5 tablespoons unsalted butter, cut into ½-inch pieces and chilled

½ cup plus 2 tablespoons buttermilk

4 tablespoons (½ stick) unsalted butter, at room temperature

SHRIMP

1 pound large (24-count) shrimp, peeled but with the tail left intact

Kosher salt

Freshly ground black pepper

6   Cut the dough into 2-inch rounds, place the disks on an ungreased baking sheet, and bake for about 15 minutes. Remove the baking sheet from the oven and, when they are cool enough to handle, split the biscuits and butter the halves on both sides with the soft butter. You will have extra biscuits.

7   Light a charcoal fire or preheat your gas grill on high. Oil your grill's cooking grate.

8   To prepare the shrimp: Butterfly the shrimp by making a lengthwise slit down the backs. Salt and pepper the shrimp. Grill them for 2 minutes on each side, or until they are pink, turning only once. Remove them to a bowl and cover.

9   Place 4 buttered biscuit halves on each of 4 plates. Spoon 1 tablespoon of the sauce on each biscuit half, and equally divide the shrimp. Spoon more sauce over the shrimp, and serve immediately.

CHILLED SHRIMP AND TOMATO SALAD WITH CLASSIC HERB DRESSING

Make this dish in late summer, when the first of your garden-ripe tomatoes comes off the vine. That's also the time that the shrimp harvest along the East Coast and the Gulf is the greatest. This is a cool, refreshing salad that's perfect for hot and humid days. Pacific prawns will work just as well.

SERVES 6

1   Make the dressing: Combine the shallot, vinegar, herbs, garlic, pepper, salt, and sugar in a small bowl. Whisk in both of the oils slowly, until the dressing comes together. Refrigerate until ready to use. The dressing can be made 1 day ahead.

2   In a large pot, bring the pickling spice bundle and 3 quarts of water to a boil. Boil for 10 minutes to flavor the water, then remove the spice bag and add the shrimp. Stir and cover, then remove the pot from the heat and let the shrimp steep for about 4 minutes. Drain immediately, and place them in a bowl with ice water to stop the cooking.

3   In a sauté pan over medium heat, warm the oil. Add the onion and cook, stirring, until the it is still just crisp, about 3 minutes. Spread on a plate to cool.

HERB DRESSING

2 tablespoons minced shallot

2 tablespoons red wine vinegar

2 tablespoons minced fresh basil

2 tablespoons minced fresh tarragon

2 tablespoons minced fresh mint

1 teaspoon minced garlic

1 teaspoon freshly cracked black pepper

½ teaspoon kosher salt

¼ teaspoon sugar

¼ cup extra-virgin olive oil

2 tablespoons canola oil

SHRIMP

1 teaspoon pickling spices, tied in cheesecloth

1½ pounds large (24-count) shrimp, peeled and deveined

2 tablespoons extra-virgin olive oil

1 cup ½-inch dice Vidalia or sweet Spanish onion

5 fresh tomatoes, peeled, seeded, and cut into ½-inch dice

½ cup julienned fresh basil

2 tablespoons chopped fresh Italian parsley or chives

4 Drain the shrimp and dry them in paper towels. In a large bowl, toss together the shrimp, onion, tomatoes, basil, parsley, and Herb Dressing. Chill for 30 minutes, but allow the salad to sit at room temperature for a few minutes before serving. Serve it in small chilled bowls.

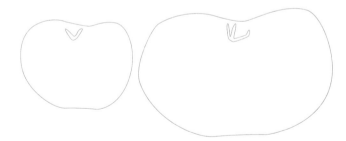

GALATOIRE'S SHRIMP RÉMOULADE

There could not be a more classic New Orleans dish than shrimp rémoulade, and one of its best examples is found at Galatoire's Restaurant, one of the oldest restaurant institutions of New Orleans. You can do most anything with this dish—make it a meal, an appetizer, or a finger food for a party. It's just never in the wrong place. I've been known to make a batch to keep in the refrigerator and not tell anybody, so that I've got a perfect protein fix when needed.

SERVES 6 TO 8 AS A FIRST COURSE

1 Pulse the celery, green onions, onion, and parsley in a food processor until finely chopped. Add the vinegar, ketchup, tomato puree, mustard, horseradish, and Worcestershire sauce, and process until well blended and smooth. Add the mayonnaise and paprika (if using) and process until smooth.

2 In a bowl, toss this mixture with the cooked shrimp to thoroughly coat. Line serving plates with lettuce leaves and divide the mixture among the plates.

4 celery ribs, coarsely chopped

4 green onions, coarsely chopped

1 small onion, chopped (about ½ cup)

¾ cup fresh Italian parsley

½ cup red wine vinegar

½ cup ketchup

½ cup tomato puree

½ cup Creole mustard

1 tablespoon prepared horseradish

1 teaspoon Worcestershire sauce

1 cup good-quality mayonnasie

2 teaspoons paprika (optional)

2 pounds cooked fresh large shrimp, peeled and deveined

Lettuce leaves for serving

PICKLED SHRIMP

Pickled shrimp has a hundred minute variations and they're all good. The novelist Pat Conroy has written how he uses pickled shrimp as "funeral food"—that Southern tradition of taking food to a bereaved family. I think pickled shrimp are much too good to save for such occasions. Keep a jar of pickled shrimp in the refrigerator for a nibble when unexpected company drops by, you need a quick topping for a salad, or for an interesting martini garnish. Get in the habit of pickling shrimp.

1 cup thinly sliced yellow onion (about 1 small)

1 cup white vinegar

½ cup olive oil

1 lemon, thinly sliced

¼ cup fresh lemon juice

One 2-ounce bottle capers, drained and coarsely chopped

4 bay leaves, crushed

1 teaspoon minced garlic

1 teaspoon coarse or kosher salt

1 teaspoon celery seed

1 teaspoon red pepper flakes

2 pounds large (24-count) shrimp, peeled and deveined

1 Mix the onion, vinegar, oil, lemon, juice, capers, bay leaves, garlic, salt, celery seed, and pepper flakes in a large heat-proof glass or ceramic bowl.

2 In a medium stockpot over high heat, bring 4 quarts of water to a boil. Add the shrimp, remove the pot from the heat, and let the shrimp steep for 4 minutes. The shrimp will continue to "cook" in the marinade, so don't worry if they're still a bit raw. Drain and immediately pour the shrimp into the marinade.

3 Place the shrimp and marinade in a glass container with a tight lid. Marinate them overnight in the refrigerator. A few days are better, and they will keep for 2 weeks in the refrigerator. Bring to room temperature to serve.

SERVES 6 TO 8

HERBED SHRIMP IN PARCHMENT

Many of us readily think of cooking in parchment for seafood items like sole or pompano, but rarely do we use the method for shrimp. The moist heat that's generated inside a parchment package is a perfect way to cook shrimp, keeping them tender and flavorful. Use any herb mixture that you desire. You could also easily do this with no herbs and just lemon slices. Give this method a try. I believe it will bring you close to happiness.

SERVES 6 TO 8

1   Preheat the oven to 400 degrees F.

2   Prepare 6 or 8 pieces of 12-by-16-inch parchment. Fold each piece in half and cut out half a heart shape so that, when unfolded, you have a heart. Lightly oil one side of the parchment.

3   Combine the juice, oil, onions, garlic, pepper, salt, cumin, basil, dill, and sugar in a wide, shallow dish. Place the shrimp in the mixture and toss them to coat.

4   Divide the shrimp evenly among the parchment pieces, mounding the shrimp on half of each heart. Fold over the hearts and, beginning at the top or bottom, seal the packets by making small overlapping folds each about $\frac{1}{2}$ inch long. Bake the packets until they are puffy and lightly browned, 10 to 12 minutes. Place them on individual plates. Let your guests cut them open carefully with a knife.

Canola oil for greasing

2 tablespoons fresh lime juice

1 tablespoon olive oil

2 teaspoons minced green onion tops

1 $\frac{1}{2}$ teaspoons pressed garlic

$\frac{3}{4}$ teaspoon freshly ground black pepper

$\frac{1}{2}$ teaspoon kosher salt

$\frac{1}{2}$ teaspoon ground cumin

$\frac{1}{2}$ teaspoon dried basil

$\frac{1}{4}$ teaspoon dried dill

$\frac{1}{4}$ teaspoon sugar

2 pounds medium (40-count) or large (24-count) shrimp, peeled and deveined

JACKY'S DEVILED EGGS
WITH SHRIMP

If there's such a thing as a Renaissance woman, Jacky Robinson would certainly be it. A well-known caterer in Richmond, Virginia, she now puts forth much of her efforts at the Virginia Museum of Fine Arts. Her escape is a place at Virginia Beach, where an invitation to dinner with her is always welcome.

1 cup dry white wine, plus extra to moisten mixture

8 ounces medium (40-count) shrimp, peeled and deveined

12 large hard-cooked eggs, sliced in half lengthwise

2 tablespoons chopped green onion

1 tablespoon sweet pickle relish

Kosher salt

Freshly ground black pepper

½ cup good-quality mayonnaise

Cilantro sprigs for garnish

1 Pour the wine into a 2-quart saucepan over medium-high heat. When the wine begins to simmer, drop in the shrimp, cover, and remove from the heat. Let the shrimp steep for 5 to 6 minutes, or until they are opaque in the center. Remove and allow to cool.

2 Finely chop the shrimp and the yolks of the hard-cooked eggs. You can do this by pulsing the shrimp first in a food processor and then adding the egg yolks. Mix in the onion, relish, and salt and pepper to taste. Fold in the mayonnaise and add additional wine until the consistency is smooth.

3 Stuff the egg whites with the shrimp mixture and top each with a sprig of cilantro. These eggs can be made up to 4 hours in advance; refrigerate until serving time.

SERVES 8 TO 12

JIM VILLAS'S SHRIMP PILAU

Jim Villas is one of America's premiere food writers, and I'm proud to call him a friend and a mentor. This pilau recipe had its beginnings when the Low Country, from Wilmington, North Carolina, to Jacksonville, Florida, was filled with rice plantations. There's some similarity between a pilau and a shrimp Creole. The major difference is that the rice is cooked as part of the dish for the pilau. I think you'll enjoy this modern take on a historic recipe.

SERVES 6

1   In a large heavy-bottomed pot, fry the bacon over medium heat until crisp, drain on paper towels, and set aside. Pour off all but about 3 tablespoons of the fat from the pot, add the onions, and cook, stirring, until the onion is just soft, about 3 minutes.

2   Add the rice and stir till the grains glisten with fat. Add the broth, tomatoes, Worcestershire sauce, nutmeg, bay leaf, cayenne, salt, and pepper and stir. Bring to a low simmer, cover, and cook for 30 minutes.

3   Add the shrimp and reserved bacon and mix well. Return to a simmer, cover, and cook until most of the liquid has been absorbed and the shrimp are pink and curled, about 8 minutes. Fluff the pilau with a fork and serve.

6 slices bacon, cut into small dice

**3 cups chopped onions
(about 3 medium)**

2 cups long-grain rice

3 cups low-sodium chicken broth

**3 cups chopped tomatoes
(about 5 medium)**

2 teaspoons Worcestershire sauce

1 teaspoon ground nutmeg

1 bay leaf

½ teaspoon cayenne pepper

Kosher salt

Freshly ground black pepper

**1½ pounds large (24-count)
shrimp, peeled and deveined**

MEXICAN SHRIMP COCKTAIL

We all love shrimp cocktails. Every now and then I like to get a little off-center and do something special with cold boiled shrimp. Calling this a shrimp cocktail is a bit deceiving. It sets up like one, but the citrus juices, cucumber, avocado, and cilantro make it seem a bit like a seviche, or as one of my friends told me, "This tastes like a shrimp Bloody Mary without the vodka." Whatever it is, it's a very refreshing hot summer day dish.

1^1/$_2$ pounds ripe tomatoes, 1 pound seeded and quartered, and ^{1}/$_2$ pound chopped

Kosher salt

2^1/$_2$ tablespoons fresh orange juice

1 tablespoon fresh lime juice

1 teaspoon Worcestershire sauce

1 teaspoon prepared horseradish

1 pound cooked large (24-count) shrimp, peeled and deveined

1 cucumber, peeled, seeded, and diced

1 large avocado, peeled and diced

2 tablespoons chopped fresh cilantro

Six 3-inch leafy celery stalk tops

6 lime wedges

SERVES 6

1 Place the quartered tomatoes in a glass baking dish and sprinkle them with salt. Let them stand for 1 hour. Place them in a food processor or blender and puree until smooth.

2 Strain the puree into a large bowl, discarding the solids. Pour in the citrus juices, Worcestershire sauce, and horseradish. Season with salt and pepper to taste.

3 Mix the chopped tomatoes, shrimp, cucumber, avocado, and cilantro in a large bowl. Divide the mixture among 6 glasses; pour the tomato puree over them, dividing it equally. Garnish with the celery stalks and lime wedges.

SHRIMP AND GRITS WITH COUNTRY HAM AND "UPSCALE REDEYE GRAVY"

Thanks to Craig Claiborne's reporting in the *New York Times*, shrimp and grits left the secluded foodways of the South. There are hundreds of shrimp and grits recipes along the coastal areas. This one plays to a down-home flavor while "goosing it up a bit." Redeye gravy is a staple pan-made sauce from the browned bits that remain after sautéing country ham. Three solid Southern flavors are here: shrimp, grits, and ham. The gravy can be made a couple of days ahead and the grits can be cooked until almost done and finished with a little more broth when ready to eat. Serve this dish for brunch or dinner. It's especially good at the stroke of midnight on New Year's Eve.

SERVES 4 TO 6

1 To make the gravy: Melt 1 tablespoon of the butter in a 12-inch sauté pan over medium heat. Add the ham and sauté slowly until it is brown. Add the mushrooms and onion and cook, stirring, until they are limp. Pour in the Madeira, then the coffee, scraping the bottom of the pan to get up the browned bits. Simmer for 8 minutes, and then add the cola. Cook an additional 4 minutes. Add the garlic to the pan. Cook 1 minute. Dissolve the cornstarch in the V-8 juice and whisk it into the gravy. Return the sauce to a boil, stirring, add the thyme and chives, and stir to combine. Finish with the lemon juice, remaining 1 tablespoon of butter, and hot pepper sauce to taste, if desired. You can fix this a few days ahead; just hold off on adding the thyme, chives, lemon juice, and hot pepper sauce until you reheat the gravy. Serve immediately or cool and refrigerate until ready to use.

UPSCALE REDEYE GRAVY

2 tablespoons (¼ stick) unsalted butter, divided

8 ounces country ham or bacon, chopped

½ cup sliced shiitake or baby portabello mushroom caps

¼ cup minced onion

½ cup Madeira

½ cup strong freshly brewed coffee

½ cup carbonated cola

1 garlic clove, pressed

1 tablespoon cornstarch

One 6-ounce can spicy V-8 juice

1 tablespoon chopped fresh thyme

1 tablespoon chopped fresh chives

2 tablespoons fresh lemon juice, or as needed

Hot pepper sauce (optional)

CREAMY GRITS

6 cups water or chicken broth

Shrimp shells from your peeled shrimp, if desired and time allows

2½ cups coarse stone-ground grits, yellow or white (no instant stuff)

½ cup cream or half-and-half

Kosher salt

Freshly ground white pepper

SHRIMP

2 tablespoons (¼ stick) unsalted butter

2 pounds large (24-count) shrimp, peeled and deveined

½ cup minced fresh Italian parsley

2   To prepare the grits: Bring the water to a boil in a large saucepan. If flavoring with the shrimp shells, add them now and reduce the heat to a simmer. Cook for 20 minutes. Strain out the shells. Return the broth to a boil. Slowly whisk in the grits. Reduce the heat to low. Continue slowly whisking, for about 5 minutes. This keeps the grits from scorching on the bottom. Cook for about 20 minutes longer, stirring frequently. Add the cream and cook for 5 to 10 minutes more, or until the grits are soft and creamy. Season with salt and pepper to taste. Hold the pot over very low heat or in a double boiler. If the grits get thick, add a little hot water.

3   To cook the shrimp: Melt the butter in a large skillet set over high heat. Add the shrimp and sauté for about 4 minutes, until they are just pink. Stir in the Upscale Redeye Gravy, and remove the pan from the heat just as the sauce warms. Season now with the herbs, lemon juice, remaining 1 tablespoon of butter, and hot pepper sauce (if you have made the gravy ahead). Serve immediately over the Creamy Grits, garnished with the parsley.

MOREHEAD CITY
SHRIMP BURGERS

Morehead City, North Carolina; Georgetown, South Carolina; and Thunderbolt, Georgia, have one delectable food product in common—they are all major centers of the shrimping business, especially brown shrimp, or "brownies." With all due respect to Forrest Gump, Gulf shrimp have nothing on the brown shrimp of the Mid-Atlantic.

SERVES 6

1   In a 3-quart saucepan, bring 1 quart of water to a full boil. Add the shrimp, cover, and remove the pan from the heat. Let the shrimp steep for 4 minutes, then drain. Put the shrimp in a large bowl and cover them with ice to cool. When the shrimp are cool enough to handle, peel and devein them, then roughly chop them.

2   In another bowl, mix the shrimp, celery, green onion, parsley, and lemon zest. Stir in the breadcrumbs, mayonnaise, and egg. Take a wooden spoon and beat the mixture until all the ingredients are well blended. Season with salt, pepper, and hot pepper sauce to taste, and stir once more to incorporate throughout the mixture.

3   From the mixture, make six 3-inch patties. If you wet your hands with water, this process will be a little easier. Heat the oil in a nonstick sauté pan until hot and shimmering. Cook the patties, three at a time, for about 3 minutes per side, or until they are golden. Drain them on paper towels.

1 pound medium (40-count) shrimp

3 tablespoons finely diced celery

2 tablespoons chopped green onion

2 tablespoons chopped fresh Italian parsley

1½ teaspoons lemon zest

1 cup breadcrumbs (cornbread crumbs are out of sight in this recipe)

3 tablespoons good-quality mayonnaise

1 large egg, lightly beaten

Kosher salt

Freshly ground black pepper

A few dashes of hot pepper sauce

1 to 2 tablespoons peanut or canola oil

6 cheap white hamburger buns

Lettuce for serving

Sliced tomatoes for serving

Any Region Tartar Sauce (page 322) or your favorite tartar sauce (optional)

Fred's Basic Cocktail Sauce (page 157) or your favorite cocktail sauce (optional)

4 Serve each patty on a hamburger bun with lettuce, tomato, and tartar or cocktail sauce, if desired.

NOTE: When it comes to cocktail sauce, I'm pretty much a purist. Ketchup, horseradish, and maybe a little lemon juice. I know it is right if my eyes sweat a little.

REALLY GOOD BOILED SHRIMP

The trick to having perfectly boiled shrimp for cocktails, or just to nibble on, is not over-cooking them. Another help is to have a well-seasoned cooking medium. If you will follow this method, you will end up with great tasting, perfectly cooked boiled shrimp to enjoy.

SERVES 4 AS A
MAIN COURSE
OR 8 TO 10
AS AN APPETIZER

1 Place the reserved shrimp shells in a large saucepan. Add the water, vinegar, and pickling spice. Bring the mixture to a boil over high heat, then reduce the heat to low and simmer cook for 20 minutes. Strain the mixture, discarding the solids.

2 Return the shrimp stock to the pan and bring it to a boil. Add the shrimp, cover, and remove the pan from the heat. Let the shrimp steep for about 5 minutes. While the shrimp are steeping, take a large bowl and add the salt and several handfuls of ice. Add enough water to make an ice bath.

3 When the shrimp are cooked through, drain them (you can save and freeze the shrimp stock for cooking shrimp at a later date or to use in fish stews, soups, and sauces). Place the shrimp in the ice bath and leave until they are chilled. Drain and enjoy them with your favorite sauce.

2 pounds large (24-count) or medium (40-count) shrimp, peeled and deveined, shells reserved

6 cups water

2 tablespoons cider vinegar

1 tablespoon pickling spice mixture

2 tablespoons kosher salt

SHRIMP SCAMPI WITH LINGUINE

Shrimp scampi is a classic recipe, and added to pasta it is even better. The sharpness of the garlic against the bright fresh herbs makes for a complete eating sensation.

1 pound linguine

½ cup olive oil

1 pound medium (40-count) shrimp, peeled and deveined

3 garlic cloves, chopped

1 tablespoon chopped fresh basil

1 teaspoon chopped fresh oregano

1 teaspoon chopped fresh parsley

6 tablespoons grated Pecorino Romano cheese (optional)

1   Cook the linguine in boiling salted water. Be careful not to overcook; they should be done but firm (al dente). Drain and toss the pasta with a bit of the oil to keep from sticking. Reserve.

2   In a large skillet, heat the remaining oil over medium-high heat, and cook the shrimp, garlic, basil, oregano, and parsley until the shrimp begin to curl, 4 to 5 minutes.

3   Add the linguine and mix with a fork or tongs. Add the cheese, if desired.

4   Pour the pasta into a large bowl and serve.

SERVES 6 TO 8

SIZZLING SALT AND PEPPER SHRIMP

No trip to Chinatown in any city would be complete without a cold Asian beer and some salt and pepper shrimp. Now don't panic here. You eat the shell and all, and that's part of the fun. The crisp shell of the shrimp, with its tangy salt-and-pepper coating, is such a contrast to the flesh held within. If you want to get really authentic, you would cook the shrimp with the heads on, but that's even a little too fast for me.

SERVES 4

1 Remove the shrimp legs, leaving the shells and tails on. Rinse the shrimp under cold water and set them on several sheets of paper towels. With more paper towels, pat the shrimp dry.

2 In a small bowl, combine the salt, sugar, and pepper.

3 Heat a flat-bottomed wok or large skillet over high heat until a bead of water vaporizes within 1 to 2 seconds of contact. Swirl in 1 tablespoon of the oil, add the jalapeño and garlic, and stir-fry for 30 seconds. Add the shrimp and 1 more tablespoon of the oil and stir-fry for 1 minute, or until the shrimp just begin to turn pink. Swirl in the remaining 1 tablespoon of the oil, add the salt mixture, and stir-fry for 1 to 2 minutes, until the shrimp are just cooked. Stir in the green onions. Serve immediately.

1 pound large (24-count) shrimp

1 teaspoon kosher salt

½ teaspoon sugar

½ teaspoon freshly ground black pepper

3 tablespoons canola oil, divided

2 tablespoons thinly sliced jalapeño peppers

1 tablespoon minced garlic

2 green onions, white and green parts, chopped

SHRIMP DIP

If you ever go to a party anywhere in the state of Georgia, or northern Florida for that matter, part of the buffet will include a shrimp dip. This recipe is quick and easy to make, and is perfect for cocktail parties, receptions, or sharing with your neighbors on the back deck. There are probably a thousand variations on this theme, but this recipe has all the basics. Use any size of cooked shrimp you have on hand.

1 pound cooked shrimp, peeled and deveined

¼ to ½ cup good-quality mayonnaise

2 tablespoons dry sherry

2 tablespoons fresh lemon juice

2 teaspoons finely grated onion

½ teaspoon hot pepper sauce

Kosher salt

Freshly ground black pepper

Assorted crackers for serving

Place the shrimp in the bowl of a food processor and pulse to roughly chop them. Don't make a paste out of this. (You can also chop the shrimp by hand.) Add ¼ cup of mayonnaise, the sherry, lemon juice, onion, and hot pepper sauce. Pulse until well blended. Add the additional mayonnaise if a creamier texture is desired. Season to taste with salt and pepper and serve with crackers.

SERVES 4 TO 6 AND EASILY DOUBLES

SHRIMP LOUIS

Using shrimp in the classic Northern California crab Louis recipe seemed like a no-brainer. On my first attempt, using the exact same type of Louis sauce didn't seem to quite do justice to the shrimp. So I took out a few ingredients and added in the Dijon mustard and found that this blend is as pleasing with shrimp as a regular Louis sauce is with Dungeness crab.

SERVES 4

1   Whisk the mayonnaise, chili sauce, lemon juice, mustard, and zest in a small bowl to blend. Season the dressing with salt and pepper to taste.

2   Divide the greens between 4 chilled salad plates. Top each with 6 of the shrimp.

3   Spoon the dressing over each salad and sprinkle them with green onion. Serve immediately. Any leftover dressing can be refrigerated, covered, for up to 1 week.

½ cup mayonnaise

¼ cup Bennett's chili sauce

2 tablespoons fresh lemon juice

1 tablespoon Dijon mustard

1 teaspoon grated lemon zest

Kosher salt

Freshly ground black pepper

6 cups mixed baby greens

24 cooked, peeled, and deveined jumbo (16-count) shrimp

1 green onion, finely chopped

SPICED-BRINED GRILLED SHRIMP

More people are frustrated when grilling shrimp than with any other seafood. When properly done, grilled shrimp are wonderful. Ten seconds too long, though, and you have rubber. Start with shrimp that are large enough to be grilled. I like to do 24 count per pound and larger. I also have found that brining shrimp gives you a "fudge factor." The cumin and coriander in the brine just enhance the shrimp. I've used this recipe in all of my seafood grilling classes. Invariably people say they will never grill shrimp any other way again.

6 cups water

½ cup kosher salt

2 tablespoons sugar

1 teaspoon ground cumin

1 teaspoon ground coriander

2 pounds large (24-count) shrimp, unpeeled

2 tablespoons peanut or canola oil

1 About 2 hours before you intend to grill the shrimp, mix the water, salt, sugar, cumin, and coriander together to make the brine.

2 With kitchen shears or a paring knife, cut down the center back of each shrimp shell until the last section before the tail. Leave the shell intact and remove any vein. Add the shrimp to the brine. A 2-gallon zipper bag works well.

3 Refrigerate for 90 minutes.

4 Light a charcoal fire or preheat your gas grill on high. Make sure your fire or gas grill is very hot before placing the shrimp on the grill.

5 Remove the shrimp from the brine and pat them dry. In a large bowl, add the oil, then the shrimp, and toss until they are coated.

6 Place the shrimp on a clean grill and cook for 3 minutes. Turn and cook for 3 minutes more, or until the shrimp turns creamy white. This could happen after 2 minutes on the second side, so pay attention. Remove them to a platter, peel, and enjoy with your favorite sauce.

SERVES 6

SPICY BAKED SHRIMP

What a party dish! This recipe can double or triple in the wink of an eye and the shrimp are just as good at room temperature as they are hot out of the oven. But don't save this dish for just company. It's an easy, weeknight celebration of shrimp. Serve this over some rice, add a green salad, and dinner is done.

If you are going to use this recipe for a party and are going to do multiple batches, I suggest you do them one batch at a time so that everyone gets an opportunity for hot shrimp. Also note that just about any spice combination can be used—these happen to be my favorites.

SERVES 2 AS A
MAIN COURSE
OR 4 TO 6 AS
AN APPETIZER

1 Preheat the oven to 400 degrees F.

2 Place the butter in a 9-by-13-inch ovenproof baking dish and put it in the oven while the oven is preheating.

3 Coat the shrimp with the seasoning and place them in the dish with the melted butter. Bake for about 9 minutes, or until the shrimp are barely cooked through and have a gentle C shape. Serve them with your favorite cocktail sauce and a squeeze of lemon juice, if desired.

2 tablespoons (¼ stick) unsalted butter

1 pound medium (40-count) shrimp, peeled and deveined

2 tablespoons Chesapeake Bay–style seasoning or Italian spice blend, or any spice combination you like

Lemon wedges for garnish (optional)

STEAMED SHRIMP

Steamed shrimp is one of those peculiarities of the Mid-Atlantic and is definitely finger-licking good. You are basically coating the shrimp like you would for Maryland-style steamed crabs, so half the fun is peeling the shrimp, getting the seasonings all over your fingers, and just generally creating a mess.

½ cup cider vinegar

½ cup water

2 tablespoons Old Bay or J.O. #2 seafood seasoning

1 pound large (24-count) shrimp, unpeeled

Melted butter for serving

Fred's Basic Cocktail Sauce (page 157)

1 In a saucepan, combine the vinegar, water, and seasoning. Bring the mixture to a boil.

2 Add the shrimp and stir gently. Cover and steam until the shrimp are tender, 3 to 5 minutes. Drain, pour them out onto a newspaper-coated table, then peel and eat. Serve them with melted butter and cocktail sauce.

HOMEMADE CHESAPEAKE-STYLE SEASONING
You can make your own seasoning blend by combining 3 tablespoons paprika, 2 tablespoons kosher salt, 2 tablespoons garlic powder, 1 tablespoon onion powder, 1 tablespoon cayenne pepper, 1 tablespoon dried oregano, 1 tablespoon dried thyme, 1 teaspoon freshly ground black pepper, and 1 teaspoon celery salt. Mix and place the blend in an airtight container. It keeps for several months.

SERVES 2 TO 4 AS A MAIN COURSE OR 4 TO 6 AS AN APPETIZER

STIR-FRIED SHRIMP WITH
CHILI SAUCE

Many of you will find the use of ketchup in a Chinese dish surprising. Ketchup seems to have been derived from the Malaysian word *ketchap,* or fish sauce, and the Chinese word *ke-tsiap.* Now, did our tomato-based sauce really come from Asia? Your guess is as good as mine. I've also been confused when trying to order this dish in local Chinese eateries. Some refer to a close version as "Hunan shrimp." Others call it "Szechuan shrimp." Both versions refer to areas in China known for spicy dishes. I would imagine that this dish was Americanized decades ago, becoming the best effort of new immigrants to hold on to the ways of their country.

SERVES 4

1   To prepare the shrimp: Mix the vermouth, sesame oil, salt, sugar, and pepper in a medium bowl. Combine the shrimp with the marinade. Cover and refrigerate for at least 30 minutes, but no longer than 4 hours.

2   To make the sauce: Mix the ketchup, sugar, vermouth, water, Worcestershire sauce, chili paste, and sesame oil together in a measuring cup or bowl. Have the chopped onion, garlic, and ginger ready to go.

3   Heat a wok or large sauté pan over high heat. Add the canola oil, wait a few seconds, then add the onion and stir-fry for 1 minute or so. Add the garlic and ginger, and cook only for a few seconds. Add the shrimp and cook for 3 minutes, or until they are opaque.

SHRIMP

1 tablespoon vermouth

1 teaspoon dark Asian sesame oil

1/2 teaspoon kosher salt

1/2 teaspoon sugar

1/8 teaspoon freshly ground white pepper

1 pound large (24-count) shrimp, peeled and deveined

SAUCE

3 tablespoons ketchup

1 tablespoon sugar

1 tablespoon vermouth

1 tablespoon water

1 tablespoon Worcestershire sauce

½ tablespoon chili paste with soybeans or garlic

1 teaspoon dark Asian sesame oil

2 cups chopped sweet onion (1 extra large)

2 garlic cloves, finely minced

1 tablespoon minced peeled fresh ginger

2 tablespoons canola oil

4 Pour the sauce into the wok. Cook it, tossing for about 2 minutes, allowing the sauce to thicken and coat the shrimp. Pour the mixture into a heated bowl and serve it at once.

SUCCESSFUL STIR-FRYING

Anytime you are going to whip up a stir-fry dish, there are a few caveats. *Mise en place*, the french term for "everything in its place." or having all your stuff ready to cook. is essential. This type of cooking goes quickly—too quickly for you to be fumbling around grabbing for ingredients. Have everything chopped, diced, and measured. Also have it close at hand. I use little 9-ounce plastic old-fashioned glasses to keep my ingredients separated. Any cup or half-cup container will work, or a plate when you have all dry ingredients. Another critical factor to watch is the shrimp. Please don't overcook them. I guarantee that you will like slightly undercooked shrimp better than the tough texture that an overcooked shrimp takes on. Watch the curl of the shrimp. A nice quarter-moon shape vs. a tight C yields a better-tasting and moister shrimp.

BOURBON-GRILLED SHRIMP SKEWERS

It's amazing how bourbon can bring out the natural sweetness in shrimp, and these skewers will certainly prove that to you. The bacon here works as a basting agent, protecting the shrimp much like the brine does in the other grilled shrimp recipe in this chapter (page 119). Of course, the advantage here is that the bacon fat is also infusing some flavor into the shrimp.

SERVES 8

1 Soak the skewers in water for 30 minutes.

2 Combine the bourbon, sugar, corn syrup, pepper, and shallots in a large sauté pan over medium heat. Be careful: The bourbon might, and probably will, flame. Have a pot lid close by to suffocate the flames if necessary. Simmer the sauce until it is thick enough to coat the back of a spoon, about 10 minutes. Set it aside.

3 Wrap 1 slice of bacon around each shrimp. Pierce it with a skewer. Continue with the remaining bacon and shrimp.

4 Light a charcoal fire or preheat your gas grill on medium. Oil your grill's cooking grate.

5 Grill the shrimp until the bacon is crisp and the shrimp are cooked through, about 10 minutes.

24 wooden skewers

1 cup good Kentucky or Tennessee bourbon

1 cup packed brown sugar

1/2 cup light corn syrup

1 tablespoon freshly cracked black pepper

3/4 cup chopped shallots

24 slices applewood- or hickory-smoked bacon

24 jumbo (16-count) shrimp, peeled and deveined

HUGH LYNN'S
BUTTERFLIED FRIED SHRIMP

Hugh Lynn is probably my best friend, and the one person most responsible for my love of cooking. Hugh is a very accomplished home cook and I've never had anything that he prepared be remotely off. His butterflied fried shrimp are some of the best shrimp you'll ever taste. Shrimp prepared like this are called "in pants," meaning the tail is left on.

2 pounds medium (40-count or less) shrimp, peeled and deveined, tails left intact, wild preferred

3 cups cold water

1 cup evaporated milk

1 large egg, lightly beaten

1 cup all-purpose flour

3 cups plain breadcrumbs

Kosher salt

Freshly ground black pepper

Peanut oil for deep-frying

Any Region Tartar Sauce (page 322) or your favorite tartar sauce

Fred's Basic Cocktail Sauce (page 157) or your favorite cocktail sauce

1 Take each shrimp and slice it down through the middle and two-thirds towards the tail. The shrimp should open a bit like a book, but remain intact.

2 Whisk together the water, milk, and egg in a large bowl. Spread the flour over a plate and the breadcrumbs over another plate.

3 Dip a shrimp in the egg batter, remove, and dip it in the flour, then return it to the egg batter, dip, and then roll it in the breadcrumbs. Repeat this with all the shrimp. Salt and pepper the breaded shrimp.

4 In a Dutch oven or electric frying pan, heat 3 inches of oil until it registers 375 degrees F on a deep-fat thermometer.

5 Preheat the oven to 200 degrees F. Place a rack over a baking sheet.

6 Add the shrimp a few at a time to the hot oil. Cook for 3 to 4 minutes, or until they are golden. Remove and drain them briefly on paper towels. Place them on the rack and put them into the oven to keep warm. Continue until all the shrimp have been fried. Serve them with the tartar and cocktail sauces.

SERVES 4

THE MOST DELICIOUS oF

Crab is always hovering around number 2 or 3 when Americans rate their favorite taste treats. Crab, with its rich, sweet meat, can stand alone or heighten the ingredients around it.

The recipes in this chapter call mainly for crabmeat, not whole crabs. If you live on the coast and have a steady supply of fresh crabs to cook and pick, go to it. To buy live crabs for meat to use in other recipes is work. Only 15 percent of a blue crab's weight is usable meat, and just 25 percent for Dungeness, which means you will pick a lot of crabs. Just remember the best caveat for live crabs is, "If it ain't kicking, it ain't cooking." Blue crabs are the most consistently found live crabs in the market. Some Dungeness or Maine's Jonah crabs are available live, but rarely, and the big Alaskan king crabs are processed before leaving the northland.

Blue crabmeat has different standards. There is jumbo lump, lump (both from the backfin), special, and claw. As you might guess, the lumps are the most expensive, but the claws often have the most flavor. You can substitute any crab variety for the other, including Dungeness, Alaskan king, snow crab, or Maine crabmeat for blue. Again, it's what's available in your area and what's the best buy.

Crabmeat comes "fresh" (although it has been steamed or boiled to get the meat out), pasteurized, vacuum packed, or frozen. All are good choices. I tend to use the "fresh" more during the summer, at the height of blue crab season; otherwise, the others will work just fine in these recipes.

There are a few soft-shell recipes in this chapter. You can get them year-round frozen and they are OK, but a live one in season, which is early spring until fall, is a thing of beauty. Buy only lively ones. Buy "jumbo" or "whales," which are larger graded soft-shells. They must be killed close to the time you cook them. Most fishmongers will do this for you, but it is quite simple. Soft-shell crabs are docile, so pick one up, and with a pair of kitchen shears, cut right behind the eyes. The crab is now dead. Lift the top shell on one side and remove the gills. They are the gray spongy-looking things. They are called "dead man's fingers" and they will make you sick if you eat them. Lift the other side and repeat. You are now ready to go. All crabs have this structure. If you need to clean a cooked blue or Dungeness, simply remove the top shell, pull off the gills, and remove the sand sacks (you'll know). From there, go on a treasure hunt for the meat, which is most abundant where the legs meet the body.

CHINESE BROCCOLI
WITH CRABMEAT

Until a few years ago, Chinese broccoli could be found only at a produce stand in Chinatown. Now, more and more larger supermarkets are handling Asian greens. It's just a different taste than regular, and somewhat exotic. Don't overcook the broccoli; keep it tender-crisp. This makes a wonderful first course or luncheon dish.

SERVES 6 AS A
FIRST COURSE
OR 4 FOR LUNCH

1   Blanch the broccoli in an 8-quart pot of unsalted boiling water for 2 to 3 minutes, or until it is bright green. Drain it in a colander and rinse under cold running water to stop the cooking. Drain the broccoli well.

2   Stir together the broth, 2½ tablespoons of the rice wine, the cornstarch, sesame oil, sugar, salt, and pepper in a bowl until well combined.

3   Heat a wok or large sauté pan over high heat until a bead of water dropped onto the surface evaporates immediately. Add 2¼ teaspoons of the oil, swirling it around to coat the wok. Add the crabmeat and stir-fry 30 seconds. Add the remaining 2 tablespoons of rice wine, then stir-fry for 30 seconds more, and transfer the mixture to a bowl.

4   Add the remaining 2¼ teaspoons of oil to the wok and heat until it begins to smoke. Add the onion and ginger and stir-fry until fragrant, about 10 seconds. Stir to recombine the sauce, then add it to the wok and simmer, stirring occasionally, until it is thickened, 1 to 2 minutes. Add the broccoli and crabmeat, then toss them lightly to combine and transfer everything to a platter. Serve immediately.

1 pound Chinese broccoli (about 1 bunch)

1 cup low-sodium chicken broth

4½ tablespoons Chinese rice wine or dry white wine, divided

2 teaspoons cornstarch

1½ teaspoons dark Asian sesame oil

1 teaspoon sugar

¾ teaspoon kosher salt

⅛ teaspoon freshly ground black pepper

4½ teaspoons canola oil, divided

8 ounces lump crabmeat (any variety), picked over for shell

3 tablespoons minced green onion

2 tablespoons minced peeled fresh ginger

CLASSIC HOT CRAB DIP

Every party, every occasion, and every special event needs a crab dip. This one is wonderfully creamy. The nuttiness of the Gruyère cheese makes this crab dip superior to others.

1 pound cream cheese, at room temperature

8 ounces sour cream

¼ cup mayonnaise

1 tablespoon fresh lemon juice

1 tablespoon Worcestershire sauce

1 teaspoon dry mustard

⅛ teaspoon garlic powder

1 pound fresh backfin crabmeat, blue or Dungeness is OK, picked over for shell

½ cup shredded Gruyère cheese

Assorted crackers for serving

1 Preheat the oven to 325 degrees F.

2 In a large bowl, combine the cream cheese, sour cream, mayonnaise, lemon juice, Worcestershire sauce, mustard, and garlic powder. Gently fold in the crabmeat, being careful to preserved the crab chunks. Place the mixture in an 8-by-8-inch ovenproof dish. Sprinkle the top with the cheese.

3 Bake for 30 minutes, or until it is bubbly. Serve hot or at room temperature, with assorted crackers.

SERVES 10 TO 12 AS PART OF A PARTY BUFFET

CORN AND CRAB CHOWDER

This chowder is standard fare at the Virginia governor's mansion. Originally developed by sous chef Thomas Sears, it survived more than a few administrations. Not heavy, as some chowders can be, it has just the right amount of creaminess to allow the flavor of the crab to blend with the corn.

SERVES 6 TO 8

1   Cut the kernels from the cobs. Be sure to scrape the cobs into a bowl to get all the milky pulp. Reserve both. Cut 3 cobs into 1-inch pieces. In a 3-quart saucepan, simmer the cut cobs with the Spanish onion, carrot, and celery in the water for 30 minutes. Strain and reserve the stock.

2   Simmer the remaining 3 cobs in a 3-quart saucepan with the cream and baking potato over medium heat, until the potato is soft. Be careful not to let the cream boil. Remove the cobs from the cream. Scrape the cobs with the back of a knife and add the scrapings to the cream. Puree the cream mixture in a blender or food processor, strain, and return it to the pot to simmer.

3   Meanwhile, heat the butter in a large sauté pan over medium-high heat. Cook the red onion, peppers, and reserved corn kernels until tender. Add them to the simmering cream with the prosciutto and red potatoes. Simmer until the potatoes are tender but not mushy, 10 to 15 minutes. Add the corn stock to thin it to your desired consistency. Season to taste with salt and pepper.

4   Divide the crab evenly and place in the center of each soup bowl. Top it with a sprinkling of the green onions. Ladle soup over the crab and serve immediately.

6 ears corn on the cob

$\frac{1}{2}$ Spanish onion, diced (about 1 cup)

1 carrot, diced (about $\frac{1}{3}$ cup)

1 rib celery, diced (about $\frac{1}{4}$ cup)

1 quart cold water

1 quart heavy cream

1 medium baking potato, peeled and diced (about 1 $\frac{1}{2}$ cups)

2 teaspoons unsalted butter

$\frac{1}{2}$ red onion, diced (about $\frac{2}{3}$ cup)

$\frac{1}{4}$ green bell pepper, diced (about $\frac{1}{4}$ cup)

$\frac{1}{4}$ red bell pepper, diced (about $\frac{1}{4}$ cup)

4 ounces prosciutto, diced

3 small red potatoes, diced

Sea salt

Freshly ground white pepper

8 ounces jumbo lump blue crabmeat, picked over for shell

3 green onions, thinly sliced on the diagonal

CRAB AND SPINACH LASAGNA

Lasagna is one of my all-time passions. The natural bitterness of spinach plays the foil to the sweetness of the crabmeat. This recipe honors my friend Glen Fischer's memory, for his lifelong support of human rights. Lasagna was his specialty.

9 lasagna noodles

2 tablespoons (¼ stick) unsalted butter

¾ cup finely chopped red bell pepper (about 1)

½ cup finely chopped celery (about 2 ribs)

½ cup finely chopped onion

3 garlic cloves, minced

Three 8-ounce cartons sour cream

¼ cup chopped fresh basil, plus extra leaves for garnish

¼ teaspoon kosher salt

⅛ teaspoon freshly ground white pepper

⅛ teaspoon ground nutmeg

Two 10-ounce packages frozen chopped spinach, thawed and well drained

1 pound fresh lump crabmeat, drained and picked over for shell

2 cups shredded mozzarella cheese (about 8 ounces), divided

2 cups shredded provolone cheese (about 8 ounces), divided

1 Cook the noodles according to the package directions. Drain and set them aside.

2 Melt the butter in a large skillet over medium-high heat. Add the bell pepper, celery, onion, and garlic. Cook for 4 to 5 minutes, or until the vegetables are tender.

3 Preheat the oven to 350 degrees F.

4 Combine the sour cream, chopped basil, salt, pepper, and nutmeg in a large bowl. Stir in the vegetable mixture and spinach. Gently fold in the crabmeat.

5 Arrange 3 lasagna noodles in the bottom of a lightly greased 9-by-13-inch baking dish. Top them with half of the crabmeat mixture. Top with half of the cheeses. Add with 3 more lasagna noodles and the remaining crabmeat mixture (but not the cheese). Top with the remaining 3 lasagna noodles.

6 Cover and bake for 50 minutes, or until thoroughly heated. Uncover and top evenly with the remaining cheeses. Bake, uncovered, 15 minutes more, or until the cheese is melted. Let the lasagna stand for 10 minutes before serving.

SERVES 8

CRAB AND MANGO ROLL
WITH THAI VINAIGRETTE

This is a fun recipe if you've never tried to make maki rolls before. I know it looks simple, yet difficult, when you sit at the sushi bar and watch the master chefs make the rolls. It really is pretty simple to do, though, and these make for a great treat. Crab and mango bounce off each other in rich sweetness. If you can't find mangoes, ripe peaches will work.

SERVES 6

1 To make the vinaigrette: Bring the sake just to a simmer in a small saucepan. Remove it from the heat. Add the sugar; stir until it is dissolved. Transfer the mixture to a small bowl; cool.

2 Whisk the vinegar, fish sauce, garlic, and chili-garlic sauce into the cooled sake. Stir in the cucumber and cilantro. The dressing can be made up to 6 hours ahead. Cover and chill.

3 To make the crab: Bring the water and salt to a boil in a 2-quart saucepan. Add the rice and reduce the heat to low. Cover and cook until the rice is tender and the water is absorbed, about 15 minutes. Stir in the vinegar and cool.

4 Place a slightly damp cloth on your work surface. Place 1 nori sheet atop the cloth. Starting ½ inch from one short end of the sheet, spread a generous ¼ cup rice crosswise in a 2½-inch-wide strip. Top it with ⅓ cup of the greens, then ¼ cup of the crab. Sprinkle with a generous tablespoon of the nuts. Top with 6 mango strips, arranging them parallel to the edge.

THAI VINAIGRETTE

6 tablespoons sake

6 tablespoons sugar

10 tablespoons rice vinegar

2 tablespoons Thai fish sauce (*nam pla*)

2 garlic cloves, minced

1½ teaspoons chili-garlic sauce

½ cup thinly sliced halved, peeled English hothouse cucumber

3 tablespoons chopped fresh cilantro

CRAB AND MANGO

1 cup water

$\frac{1}{2}$ teaspoon kosher salt

$\frac{1}{2}$ cup Italian or sushi rice (short-grain white rice)

2 tablespoons rice vinegar

Five 8-by-7$\frac{1}{2}$-inch dried nori (seaweed) sheets

1 $\frac{2}{3}$ cups packed mixed baby greens

8 ounces fresh crabmeat, picked over for shell

6 tablespoons chopped roasted salted peanuts

2 large mangoes, peeled, pitted, and cut into 2 $\frac{1}{2}$-by-$\frac{1}{2}$-inch strips

5 Using the cloth as an aid, and starting at the end near the filling, roll up the nori sheet gently, but firmly, enclosing the filling. Repeat with the remaining ingredients. Transfer each roll to a plate. Cover and chill them at least 1 hour and up to 4 hours, which is better.

6 Cut each chilled roll diagonally into 4 pieces. On each of 6 plates, stand 3 pieces upright. Serve with the Thai Vinaigrette.

CRAB SALAD NIÇOISE

For you tuna niçoise freaks out there, let me introduce you to an even better version. Based on a recipe from San Francisco's Junior League, this salad is made with Dungeness crabmeat, which really elevates the whole concept. If Dungeness is not available, lump blue crab works just as well. And if you really want a special treat, use half tuna, half crabmeat.

SERVES 6

1 To make the vinaigrette: In a blender or food processor, combine the anchovies, vinegars, lemon juice, capers, tarragon, mustard, parsley, shallot, garlic, salt, and pepper and puree until smooth. With the machine running, gradually add the oil. Taste for seasoning and adjust as needed. Store the vinaigrette in an airtight container in the refrigerator for up to 3 days.

2 To make the salad: Cook the beans in a pot of salted boiling water until they are crisp-tender, 2 to 3 minutes. Using tongs or a slotted spoon, transfer them to a bowl of ice water to stop the cooking. Bring the water in the pot back to a boil and add the asparagus. Cook for 2 to 3 minutes, or until a knife can easily pierce a stalk. Transfer them to the bowl of ice water. Drain the beans and asparagus in a colander.

3 Meanwhile, bring the water to a boil again, and cook the potatoes in it until they are tender, about 15 minutes. Transfer them to a bowl of ice water. Drain them in a colander. Cut them into quarters or halves.

VINAIGRETTE

3 anchovy fillets

3 tablespoons red wine vinegar

1 tablespoon balsamic vinegar

3 tablespoons fresh lemon juice

2 tablespoons capers, rinsed and drained

2 tablespoons minced fresh tarragon

1 tablespoon tarragon mustard or Dijon mustard

1 tablespoon minced fresh Italian parsley

1 shallot, coarsely chopped

2 garlic cloves, chopped

1 teaspoon kosher salt

1 teaspoon freshly ground black pepper

1 cup extra-virgin olive oil

SALAD

8 ounces haricots verts or baby Blue Lake green beans, trimmed

12 asparagus stalks, trimmed

1 pound Yukon Gold or baby red potatoes

4 cups mixed salad greens

2 cups fresh lump Dungeness crabmeat, picked over for shell

6 large hard-cooked eggs, quartered

4 ounces niçoise olives, pitted and halved

2 cups mixed red and yellow cherry tomatoes, stemmed

1 small red onion, thinly sliced

1 Meyer lemon, cut into wedges (optional)

4 On a large serving platter or 6 individual serving plates, place the greens and arrange the beans, asparagus, potatoes, crab, eggs, olives, tomatoes, and onion on top. Drizzle the vinaigrette over the salad and garnish with the lemon wedges, if desired.

EASTERN SHORE CRAB CASSEROLE

Up and down the Eastern Shore, crab casseroles are a tradition on the Wednesday night before Thanksgiving. Easy to put together during a hectic time in the kitchen, it might be a tradition you should adopt.

SERVES 4 TO 6

1   Preheat the oven to 475 degrees F. Butter a 9-by-13-inch baking dish and set it aside.

2   In a large bowl, blend the eggs, mayonnaise, dressing, vinegar, mustard, seasoning, and Worcestershire sauce. Gently fold in the crabmeat until it is well combined. Season with salt and pepper to taste. Pour the mixture into the prepared dish.

3   In another bowl, stir together the cornflakes and parsley. Sprinkle this mixture evenly over the crab mixture. Dot the top with chunks of butter.

4   Bake for 20 to 25 minutes, until the top is golden brown. Remove, let the casserole cool slightly, about 5 minutes, and serve.

2 large eggs, lightly beaten

3 tablespoons good-quality mayonnaise

3 tablespoons salad dressing, such as Miracle Whip

1 tablespoon white vinegar

1 ½ teaspoons prepared mustard

½ teaspoon Chesapeake Bay–style seasoning

Dash of Worcestershire sauce

1 pound crabmeat (any type), picked over for shell

Kosher salt

Freshly ground black pepper

½ cup crushed cornflakes

2 tablespoons chopped fresh parsley

3 tablespoons unsalted butter, cut into small chunks, plus additional for greasing

MARINATED DUNGENESS
CRAB CLAWS

Gene Mattiuzzo has been my educator on all types of Pacific seafood. In the process, he's also become my friend. As far as I'm concerned, Gene runs Noyo Harbor in Northern California. When I asked him to share a recipe with me, this is the one he gave me, and I've also had the pleasure of watching him prepare it. These crab claws are messy to eat but worth the trouble. Gene always says that after the crab has marinated, you should throw out the crab and drink the marinade.

4 Dungeness crabs, cleaned and broken into 8 sections each by the fishmonger

1 cup red wine vinegar

⅓ cup rice vinegar

¼ cup fresh lemon juice

3 cups extra-virgin olive oil

1 small bunch green onions, finely chopped

¼ cup finely chopped fresh parsley

6 garlic cloves, lightly crushed

1 tablespoon dried tarragon

Kosher salt

Freshly ground black pepper

Several fresh rosemary sprigs

Good crusty sourdough bread for serving

1 Run a knife between the sections of the crab legs. Lightly crack the leg sections and set them aside.

2 In a stainless-steel bowl, combine the vinegars and lemon juice. Slowly add the oil while whisking. Add the onions, parsley, garlic, tarragon, and salt and pepper to taste.

3 Gently add the marinade to the crab legs. On top of the crab legs, lay several sprigs of rosemary. With a baster, suck the marinade from the bottom of the container and baste over the top of the crab legs and rosemary. Refrigerate, basting often, for 30 minutes to 2 hours.

4 Discard the rosemary. Remove the legs carefully onto serving plates. Serve them with wine or beer and large amounts of sourdough French bread for dipping into the remaining marinade.

SERVES 4 AS A MAIN COURSE OR 6 TO 8 AS FINGER FOOD

OVEN-ROASTED
DUNGENESS CRAB

Oven roasting a Dungeness crab brings out the unique sweetness of this sea critter. Since you're using crab that has already been cooked, you need to take care not to dry it out. But there's something about oven heat that takes Dungeness to a new level. You could also try this with snow or king crab legs; just break them in half. Even the East Coast, thanks to better transportation, has the ability to get Dungeness on a regular basis. Jonah crab is Maine's version of Dungeness and they're very similar; just a little smaller. So if Jonah is what you come across, you might want to add one more crab to this recipe.

SERVES 4

1   Preheat the oven to 500 degrees F.

2   Melt the butter with the oil in a large heavy ovenproof skillet over medium-high heat. Stir in the garlic, shallot, and pepper flakes. Add the crabs and sprinkle them with salt and pepper. Sprinkle 1 tablespoon of the thyme and 1 tablespoon of the parsley over the crabs. Stir to combine, then place the skillet in the oven and roast the crabs until they are heated through, stirring once, about 12 minutes.

3   Using tongs, transfer the crabs to a platter. Place the skillet on the stovetop, taking care because it will be hot from the oven, and add the orange juice and zest. Boil until the sauce is reduced by about half, about 5 minutes. Spoon the sauce over the crabs. Sprinkle them with the remaining thyme and parsley. Serve.

4 tablespoons (½ stick) unsalted butter

¼ cup olive oil

2 tablespoons minced garlic

1 tablespoon minced shallot

1½ teaspoons red pepper flakes

3 large cooked and cleaned Dungeness crabs, cracked into fourths (about 6 pounds)

Kosher salt

Freshly ground black pepper

2 tablespoons chopped fresh thyme, divided

2 tablespoons chopped fresh parsley, divided

½ cup fresh orange juice

1 teaspoon finely grated orange zest

EXCEPTIONAL CRAB CAKES

I've been on a twenty-five-year quest to make the perfect crab cake. What I found out is there is more than one perfect crab cake. As with all crab cakes, the key is not to over-handle or mash the cakes too much. Also be sure and follow the refrigeration periods, which help to hold the crab cakes together.

2 large eggs, lightly beaten

1 tablespoon fresh lemon juice

1 teaspoon Dijon mustard

1 teaspoon dry mustard

½ teaspoon hot pepper sauce

½ teaspoon Worcestershire sauce

Kosher salt

Freshly ground black pepper

1 pound jumbo lump crabmeat, picked over for shell

½ cup plain breadcrumbs, plus extra for coating

1 tablespoon diced seeded tomato

1 teaspoon chopped fresh chives, plus extra for garnish

2 tablespoons peanut oil

2 tablespoons (¼ stick) unsalted butter

4 lemon wedges

Any Region Tartar Sauce (page 322) or your favorite tartar sauce

1 In a large bowl, use a whisk to combine the eggs, lemon juice, mustards, hot pepper sauce, Worcestershire sauce, and a pinch of salt and pepper.

2 Add the crabmeat, ½ cup of breadcrumbs, tomato, and the teaspoon of chives and toss gently by hand, trying to keep the lumps of the crabmeat together.

3 Form the crab cakes by pressing the mixture into a 2-inch ring mold or a ½-cup measure. Unmold the cakes onto breadcrumbs spread on a sheet pan. Sprinkle the bread-crumbs on the top side of the crab cakes. Cover the whole pan with plastic wrap. Refrigerate the crab cakes on the pan for at least 1 hour—longer is better—and up to 4 hours.

4 Remove the crab cakes from the refrigerator.

5 Preheat the oven to 450 degrees F.

6 In a large ovenproof sauté pan over medium heat, add the oil and butter. When the butter stops foaming, add the crab cakes and cook on one side until they are golden brown. Carefully turn them over and finish cooking them in the oven for 3 to 4 minutes, or until they are golden brown.

7 Transfer the cakes to a platter, and sprinkle with the extra chopped chives. Serve with lemon wedges and tartar sauce.

SERVES 4

"RAVIOLI" WITH CRAB

A little "menu speak" if you please. I had a first course at a bistro in Paris very similar to this. The "ravioli" here are not the normal pasta but thin slices of avocado sandwiching crabmeat that's been sparingly dressed. They're impressive to look at and impressive to eat. Definitely upscale.

SERVES 4 AS A
FIRST COURSE

1   Combine the crab and chives in a bowl. Pour a little of the lime juice on top, and season with salt and pepper. Toss gently to combine. Taste and adjust the seasoning.

2   Just before serving, carefully peel the avocados, taking care not to nick the flesh. Slice 4 to 5 very thin, wide slices from each avocado, dicing the remaining flesh. Arrange one slice on each of 4 small serving plates. Divide the crab mixture in mounds among the slices. Lay a second slice over each mound. Squeeze a little lime juice over each of the "ravioli," and season them lightly with salt and pepper. Drizzle them with almond oil, and divide the remaining diced avocado among the plates. Serve at once.

8 ounces lump crabmeat, picked over for shell

2 to 3 tablespoons chopped fresh chives

1/2 cup fresh lime juice (1 to 1 1/2 limes)

Fleur de sel

Freshly ground black pepper

2 ripe but firm avocados

Almond or walnut oil for drizzling

SALAD OF PEEKYTOE MAINE CRAB

You know the expression "one man's trash is another man's treasure"? It couldn't apply more than to Peekytoe crab. Peekytoe is Maine slang for "picked toe," which is what they call their sand crab. For generations, lobstermen cussed this crab for fouling their gear. Now it's become a gourmet status symbol with all the finest chefs in the country clamoring for this crabmeat. It is truly sweet and tender and is exceptional when left alone as in this salad. Not to worry about all those chefs—more and more Peekytoe is showing up at retail fish counters, allowing you to enjoy this treat at home.

DRESSING

¼ cup extra-virgin olive oil

2 tablespoons fresh lime juice, plus more if needed

2 tablespoons finely chopped fresh cilantro

2 tablespoons finely chopped fresh mint

½ garlic clove, coarsely chopped

Kosher salt

Freshly ground black pepper

SALAD

8 ounces mesclun greens or any assortment of fresh lettuce

One 10.9-ounce can hearts of palm, julienned into 2-by-⅛-inch strips

1 pound Peekytoe Maine crabmeat, chilled and picked over for shell

1 To make the dressing: Combine the oil, lime juice, cilantro, mint, and garlic in the bowl of a food processor or blender, and puree. Season it with salt and pepper, and add more lime juice if necessary to suit your taste. Set the dressing aside.

2 To prepare the salad: Arrange the greens on 6 individual chilled salad plates. In a small nonreactive bowl, toss the hearts of palm with one-fourth of the dressing, and place them over the greens. Then toss the crabmeat with another one-fourth of the dressing and place it on top of the hearts of palm. Spoon the remaining dressing over the salads. Serve immediately.

SERVES 6

SOFT-SHELL CRAB CLUB SANDWICH

A fried soft-shell crab between two pieces of soft white Wonder Bread and slathered with Duke's mayonnaise is really hard to top. But every now and again, you just need to gussy something up. This sandwich brings a few new flavors and textures to a standard "soft" sandwich, as they are called on the Eastern Shore. Use as many or as few as you like. Any way you fix a soft-shell crab sandwich, it is just plain good.

SERVES 4

1 Mix together the flour, cornmeal, and seasoning in a medium bowl, and then pour it into a pie pan.

2 Take another pie pan and add the eggs and water, mixing them well.

3 Dip each dried crab first in the egg, and then in the cornmeal mixture. Use one hand for the wet stuff and one for the dry. Pat the crabs.

4 Pour the oil to a depth of ½ inch in a 12-inch frying pan. Heat the oil until it registers 350 degrees F on a deep-fat thermometer, or until a little of the cornmeal sizzles as soon as it hits the oil.

5 Ease 2 crabs into the pan, and fry until they are golden brown and crispy, 3 to 4 minutes per side. Remove and drain them on brown paper bags or paper towels. Repeat with the 2 remaining crabs.

6 Make sandwiches by spreading 1 tablespoon of the mayonnaise on each roll. Place a crab on each of the bottom halves. Top with bacon, tomato, avocado, and lettuce. Put on the top buns and chow down.

½ cup all-purpose flour

¼ cup cornmeal

1 teaspoon Chesapeake Bay–style seasoning

2 large eggs, lightly beaten

1 tablespoon water

4 soft-shell crabs, cleaned and patted dry

Canola or peanut oil for frying

4 tablespoons mayonnaise

4 crusty rolls

8 slices thick-cut applewood-smoked bacon, cooked until very crisp

4 thick tomato slices

8 slices avocado

Green leaf lettuce, torn

DEVILED CRAB CAKES

If your only experience with deviled crab cakes is the awful plate-filler variety that shows up on many combination platters in seafood restaurants along the coast, then you're in for a happy awakening. These deviled crabs have less filler and more flavor. Originally, deviled crab was always made casserole style, which you could easily do with this by placing it in an ovenproof dish and baking it at 350 degrees F for 10 to 15 minutes.

1 cup best-quality mayonnaise

2 large egg whites, lightly beaten

2¹⁄₂ teaspoons dry mustard

1 teaspoon hot pepper sauce

¹⁄₄ cup minced green onions, white and green parts

3 tablespoons minced shallots

1 pound lump crabmeat, picked over for shell

3 cups fresh breadcrumbs, divided

4 tablespoons (¹⁄₂ stick) unsalted butter, 2 tablespoons melted and slightly cooled

¹⁄₄ cup peanut oil

Rémoulade Sauce (page 328) or your favorite rémoulade sauce

Any Region Tartar Sauce (page 322) or your favorite tartar sauce

1 In a small bowl, whisk the mayonnaise and egg whites together until well blended. Whisk in the mustard and hot peper sauce. Add the green onions and shallots and stir to combine. Carefully fold in the crabmeat, being careful not to break up the lumps. Gently fold in 2 cups of the breadcrumbs.

2 Divide the mixture into 4 to 6 crab cakes, using a 3-inch biscuit cutter as a guide. Mix the melted butter with the remaining 1 cup of breadcrumbs and gently coat each of the cakes.

3 Preheat the oven to 400 degrees F.

4 Heat the oil and the remaining 2 tablespoons of butter in a large skillet over medium-high heat. Add the crab cakes when the butter stops foaming. Cook them for 3 minutes, or until they are golden. Turn them over and place the skillet in the oven. Cook for 4 to 5 minutes longer, until they are golden brown. Serve the crab cakes with spicy rémoulade sauce or tartar sauce.

SERVES 4 TO 6

TABLA CRAB CAKES WITH AVOCADO SALAD

Tabla is one of Manhattan's best restaurants. Some people say it's French-inspired Indian, others say it's Indian-inspired French. No matter, it's a great restaurant whatever you call it. One of the high points has always been their crab cakes. I cornered Chef Floyd Cardoz at the New York City annual barbecue block party of all places and got out of him ingredients for his cakes. After a few tries, I came up with this recipe, which is pretty close. Just a little different from the norm, but not enough to hide the distinct flavor of the crab.

SERVES 4

1 Heat 1 tablespoon of the oil in a small heavy skillet over medium heat. Add ¾ cup of the onion, the ginger, and garlic. Cook for 5 minutes. Add the cumin and turmeric, then ¼ cup of the tomato and cook for another minute. Transfer the mixture to a medium bowl, and cool.

2 When the onion mixture has cooled, add the crab, ½ cup of the panko, 4 tablespoons of the cilantro, 3 teaspoons of the lime juice, the chives, ½ teaspoon of the lime zest, and the cayenne. Season with salt and pepper. Mix in the egg. Form the mixture into four 3- to 3½-inch-diameter patties (a ring mold or 3-inch biscuit cutter are good for this). Spread the remaining 1 cup of panko on a pie plate. Coat the crab cakes with the crumbs, pressing to adhere. Place them on another plate. Cover and chill for at least 1 hour and up to 4 hours. Longer is better.

3 tablespoons corn oil, divided

1 cup finely chopped red onion, divided

1 tablespoon minced peeled fresh ginger

1 garlic clove, minced

½ teaspoon ground cumin

¼ teaspoon ground turmeric

½ cup chopped tomato, divided

8 ounces crabmeat, well drained and picked over for shell

1½ cups Japanese panko breadcrumbs, divided

6 tablespoons chopped fresh cilantro, divided

5 teaspoons fresh lime juice, divided

144

1 tablespoon minced fresh chives

1 teaspoon grated lime zest, divided

¼ teaspoon cayenne pepper

Kosher salt

Freshly ground black pepper

1 large egg, lightly beaten

2 small avocados, peeled, pitted, diced

3 In a medium bowl, mix the remaining ¼ cup onion, ¼ cup tomato, 2 tablespoons cilantro, 2 teaspoons lime juice, and ½ teaspoon lime zest. Add the avocados and toss to coat. Cover; chill up to 2 hours.

4 Preheat the oven to 400 degrees F.

5 Heat the remaining 2 tablespoons of oil in a large heavy nonstick skillet over medium-high heat. Add the crab cakes; cook until they are golden brown, about 3 minutes. Slide the pan into the oven without turning over the cakes and continue cooking for 4 to 5 minutes, or until they are heated through. Serve each cake with some of the avocado salad.

SHE-CRAB SOUP

Nothing says Charleston, South Carolina, and Low Country like she-crab soup. Unless you've got your own crab pots, it might be difficult to come up with enough crab roe to make the real thing. Every now and then, you'll find crab roe in the stores. What I like to do is buy crabmeat that's been processed in either North Carolina or Louisiana. Typically those states seem to have more roe in their picked crabmeat. The roe is also about texture and this recipe has a unique substitute—hard-cooked eggs. They're used in most kitchens throughout this area for she-crab soup. Be sure and pass a little sherry at the table, as that's the signature taste of this soup.

SERVES 8

1   Heat the butter in a heavy-bottomed soup pot over medium heat. Add the onion, leeks, and celery and gently cook, stirring occasionally, for about 15 minutes, or until they are very soft. Add the clam juice, rice, salt, cayenne, thyme, and bay leaf and mix well. Bring the mixture to a simmer, reduce the heat to low, and simmer for 30 minutes, stirring occasionally.

2   Increase the heat to medium-high, add the cream, and bring the mixture to just under a boil. There will be bubbles around the side of the pot. Immediately reduce the heat to medium and simmer for 5 minutes, stirring occasionally.

3   Remove the soup pot from the stove. When the soup has cooled enough to handle, remove the bay leaf and sprig of thyme. Put the soup through a food mill or puree it in a food processor or blender. Return the soup to the pot.

4 tablespoons (½ stick) unsalted butter

1 cup finely chopped yellow onion

1 cup well-cleaned finely chopped leeks, white part only

½ cup finely chopped celery

5 cups bottled clam juice

½ cup converted long-grain white rice

2 teaspoons kosher salt

½ teaspoon cayenne pepper

1 sprig fresh thyme or 1 pinch dried

1 bay leaf

2 cups heavy cream

1 pound lump crabmeat, picked over for shell

6 tablespoons amontillado sherry

½ teaspoon fresh lemon juice

½ cup crab roe, finely chopped, or ½ hard-cooked egg, finely chopped

2 tablespoons finely chopped fresh parsley

2 tablespoons finely chopped fresh tarragon

4 Place the pot over medium heat and add the crabmeat. Bring the soup to a boil, stirring gently to prevent scorching and being careful not to break up the lumps of crab. Stir in the sherry by the tablespoon to your taste and add the lemon juice.

5 In a small bowl, combine the crab roe and herbs. Ladle the soup into warm bowls, add the roe mixture to each bowl, and serve immediately, with some extra sherry to be passed at the table.

SAVORY CRAB CHEESECAKE

Asheville, North Carolina, the eclectic little city nestled in the mountains near Tennessee, may seem like an odd place to find a crab cheesecake. Not that I really want the word to get out, but Asheville is one of the great restaurant cities in this country. It's also filled with superior bed-and-breakfasts. One of my favorites is the Cedar Crest Inn. The husband-and-wife team of Bruce and Rita Wightman do a fantastic job. Bruce is in charge of the kitchen, and this is one of his favorite and best savories for afternoon tea. It will work in just about any party situation and is even great for a light lunch.

**SERVES 8 TO 10
AS AN APPETIZER**

1 Preheat the oven to 350 degrees F.

2 Combine ¼ cup of the Parmesan with the breadcrumbs. Heavily coat the sides and bottom of a 9-inch springform pan with the butter and sprinkle it with the breadcrumb mixture. Set aside.

3 Heat the oil in a large skillet. Add the onion and sauté, stirring, for 4 to 5 minutes, or until it is lightly caramelized. Add salt and pepper to taste. Set aside.

4 Using an electric mixer, beat the cream cheese until smooth. Add the eggs, 1 at a time. Beat in the cream.

5 Stir in the remaining ¾ cup of Parmesan, the Swiss, and crabmeat. Stir in the onion mixture and hot pepper sauce and blend well.

6 Pour the mixture into the prepared pan and bake for 1 hour, or until firm.

7 Allow the cheesecake to cool slightly, approximately 20 minutes, before serving. Make 1 day ahead to allow the flavors to blend.

1 cup freshly grated Parmesan cheese, divided (about 3 ounces)

¼ cup seasoned breadcrumbs

4 tablespoons (½ stick) unsalted butter

1 tablespoon olive oil

1 cup chopped onion (about 1 large)

Kosher salt

Freshly ground white pepper

2 pounds cream cheese, at room temperature

4 large eggs, at room temperature

½ cup heavy cream, at room temperature

1 cup grated Swiss cheese (about 4 ounces)

1 pound crabmeat (approximately 2 cups), picked over for shell

Dash of hot pepper sauce

OPEN-FACE CRAB AND
ARTICHOKE MELT

Crab and artichokes have long been paired, and with good reason. This simple-sounding open-face sandwich is surprising from your first bite. It's a versatile dish that can be used from a bridesmaid's luncheon to a bridge club light supper.

2 cups freshly grated Parmesan cheese (about 6 ounces)

1½ cups mayonnaise

1⅓ cups chopped onion (about 1 medium)

One 13¾-ounce can quartered artichoke hearts in water, drained and chopped

12 ounces fresh crabmeat, drained and picked over for shell

½ cup plus 2 tablespoons chopped fresh parsley

Eight ¾-inch-thick slices sourdough bread

8 plum tomatoes, sliced

8 ounces Monterey Jack cheese, thinly sliced

1   In a large bowl, blend the Parmesan, mayonnaise, onion, artichokes, crabmeat, and ½ cup of the parsley. Transfer the crab mixture to an 8-by-8-by-2-inch glass baking dish. You can do this 6 hours ahead. Cover and refrigerate.

2   Preheat the oven to 400 degrees F.

3   Bake the crab mixture until it is bubbling and heated through, about 25 minutes.

4   Preheat the broiler.

5   Place the bread in a single layer on a large baking sheet. Divide the hot crab mixture among the bread slices, about ½ cup of crab per slice. Top each slice with tomato slices, then cheese slices. Broil the sandwiches until the cheese melts, about 2 minutes, watching carefully to avoid burning. Sprinkle with the remaining 2 tablespoons of parsley and serve.

SERVES 8

GRILLED SOFT-SHELL CRABS

Not that there's anything much better than a panfried soft-shell, but grilling soft-shells results in a unique woodsy flavor. As the fire laps the thinner parts of the shell, giving you a really crunchy treat, the smoke infuses the body, leaving you with hints of driftwood fires on the banks of the Chesapeake.

SERVES 4

1   Light a charcoal fire or preheat your gas grill on high. Oil your grill's cooking grate.

2   Whisk the seasoning into the butter in a shallow pan. When ready to grill, dip each crab into the butter. Shake off the excess. Place the crabs on the grill, top shell down. Grill 2 to 4 minutes per side, until the shells are very deeply red.

3   Remove the crabs from the grill to a warm platter and serve as is, with tartar sauce, or you could even make a sandwich.

2 teaspoons Chesapeake Bay–style seasoning

1 cup (2 sticks) unsalted butter, melted

4 jumbo soft-shell crabs, cleaned (have your fishmonger do this)

CRAB SALAD WITH AVOCADO AND MANGO

Eating a cool crab salad is probably one of the best ways to truly enjoy all the flavors that crab has to offer. This salad will work with just about any kind of crabmeat, but it is especially good with Dungeness. The sweetness of the mango and the soft texture of the avocado balance the ocean goodness of the crabmeat.

¼ cup diced red onion plus ½ cup thinly sliced red onion

¼ cup chopped fresh chives

2 tablespoons finely diced celery

2 teaspoons peeled, seeded, and finely diced cucumber

1 pound lump crabmeat (blue or Dungeness), picked over for shell

¼ cup fresh orange juice

¼ cup fresh lime juice

1 tablespoon olive oil

1 tablespoon chopped fresh cilantro

2 teaspoons Dijon mustard

Kosher salt

Freshly ground black pepper

1 avocado, peeled, pitted, and thinly sliced

1 mango, peeled, pitted, and thinly sliced

1   In a medium bowl, toss the onion, chives, celery, and cucumber together. Gently fold in the crabmeat.

2   In another bowl, whisk together the citrus juices, oil, cilantro, mustard, and salt and pepper to taste. Pour this mixture over the crab mixture and gently fold to blend them.

3   Divide the avocado and mango evenly among 4 chilled plates. Divide the crabmeat mixture evenly, placing it atop the avocado and mango. Serve immediately.

SERVES 4

ONLY

Folks either love 'em or hate 'em. Of course there are those on the fence, who swear by oysters fried but would never touch a raw one. But for the true believer, an oyster in any fashion is a joy to consume.

There are hundreds of oyster types, but they all come from five species that are all found in the United States and Canada: Pacific oysters, which are plump and creamy; Olympias, which have a coppery flavor; Eastern, which are sweet with a briny balance; European flats, which are complex with a mineral-like aftertaste; and Kumamotos, with their deep-cupped bottom shell, are sweet with a touch of brine. The Eastern oyster is the most eaten by three to one over the other varieties. Now, within that group of five comes the real fun. Like wine grapes gathering flavor from their growing location and soil, oysters pick up their special flavors from the waters they grow in. Northern Atlantic oysters are much saltier than the Mid-Atlantic variety. Gulf Apalachicola oysters are saltier than Mid-Atlantic, not to the point of Northern Atlantic, but sweeter than both. I encourage you to try many different regions' oysters, either raw, lightly poached in their own liquor, or steamed, where the flavor differences show the most.

Oysters were once cheap eats, feeding the immigrants that built the great cities on our coasts. "Dime a dozen" was the cry from pushcart oyster vendors of old Manhattan. Oysters are pricey now, even more so with the wealth of raw bars opening across the land. They are now chic, and a bit mystical, probably due to their reputation as an aphrodisiac. You can determine if they work. The point is: We want to buy the best at the market.

FOR

THE

BRAVE—

OYSTERs

Oysters have to be tightly closed. They should always be packed flat. The oyster's liquor is what keeps it alive and adds to the flavor. Oysters not displayed flat may be dry. Ask to see the harvest tag. I was so amused at an oyster festival in lower Maryland, because all the oysters they were steaming were tagged from the Delaware Bay. When you get them home, scrub them clean, lay them out flat, and store them in the refrigerator for up to a week.

What about the R months and the old rule, "Don't eat oysters in a month with an R"? Eating oysters during these months won't hurt you, but the taste will be off, and they will be watery. These are the months that oysters reproduce, and that is what causes the changes in texture and taste. Hey, we need them to reproduce so there's more of them, right?

Opening an oyster can be tricky and usually takes practice. I shuck a lot of oysters, and still need a few to get the hang of it again each time. Many fishmongers will do this for you, and I encourage you to take advantage of the service. Also ask for oyster shell bottoms and wash them in the dishwasher (more on this later). Check the sidebar in this chapter (page 158) on opening an oyster. Steam oysters open much like a clam if you want to use the meat in a recipe.

Hand-dipped shucked oysters, or oysters that have been shucked and vacuum packed, are good as well, and easier to handle. An oyster snob may turn up his nose, but I'll be eating his share. Once you have accumulated some oyster shells, you can use them for half-shell raw oysters, stuffed oysters, or any other recipe calling for a shell. Shucked oysters can be used in most any recipe, especially stews, pan roasts, casseroles, and for fried oysters.

Oysters, like most shellfish, get bad press occasionally. Eat raw oysters and you are taking a risk, though slight. However, pregnant women, older folks, and people with depressed immune systems should never eat raw oysters.

THE OYSTER ROAST

An oyster roast can mean feeding just the two of you or as many as 2,000 along the coastal areas. Many a politician has been elected over his ability to eat oysters. Most large oyster roasts are done by professionals, who can handle huge amounts of folks just like the Brunswick stew masters of Virginia, the Texas barbecue caterers, or the crab feed cooks of the West Coast. But having an oyster roast at home is not difficult. "Roast" is a bit of a misnomer. The oysters are really steam-roasted over an open fire. The old-fashioned way to do this was to dig pits and start oak wood fires, then cover the fires with pieces of sheet metal. When the sheet metal got hot, they poured the oysters along the sheet metal and covered them with wet burlap bags. It's a little simpler now. Your charcoal or gas grill will work just fine. It's a sloppy way to eat, but it's so much fun on a crisp fall day that the butter and juices dripping off your chin don't seem to matter at all.

SERVES 8 AND EASILY DOUBLES OR TRIPLES

1 Light a charcoal fire or preheat your gas grill on high

2 Place as many of the oysters in 1 layer as you can over your grill top. Get your condiments close to the grill on another table and make sure everyone has put on a glove. Have 8 aluminum pie pans available. As the oysters start to open, usually after about 15 minutes, encourage everybody to dig in, start opening their oysters, and use their favorite condiments. Continue cooking the oysters in batches until they're gone. Any oysters that don't open should be discarded. Your pleasure will be enhanced by large amounts of cold beer and a bottle of fine bourbon.

1 bushel oysters in the shell

8 leather garden gloves

8 oyster knives

Fred's Basic Cocktail Sauce (page 157) or your favorite cocktail sauce

Melted butter

Lemon wedges

Corn on the cob (optional)

Cole slaw (optional)

Lots of paper towels

HOME-STEAMED OYSTERS

Steamed oysters are a tradition in just about every coastal area in this country. There is nothing better than the camaraderie of fellow oyster lovers as you pull a stool up to the bar and order a "peck." It's even more fun to do it at home with close friends. Most of us don't have the ability to steam huge quantities of oysters. I've found that using a simple canning pot is the best method for steaming oysters at home, but even then you need to do them in batches, which quite frankly is a plus. Steamed oysters get cold pretty quick. By doing them in batches, you're almost always guaranteed warm oysters. It's a mess to do, but a lot of fun. And don't forget the ice-cold beer.

2 pecks fresh oysters in the shell, scrubbed and rinsed

Melted unsalted butter

Fred's Basic Cocktail Sauce (page 157) or your favorite cocktail sauce

Hog Island–Like Pacific Rim Mignonette (page 157)

Classic French Mignonette (page 158)

You will need 2 large canning pots with racks and lids. Place the racks in the bottom of the pots. Add enough water to just cover the racks. Place each pot over a large burner, cover, and bring the pots to a boil over high heat. Remove the lids. Fill each pot about $2/3$ full with the oysters. Cover and steam them for about 10 minutes. Remove the oysters once they have opened slightly. Place another batch of oysters in each pot and eat the hot oysters with butter and the sauces while the next batch is cooking. Repeat until all the oysters are cooked, discarding any that do not open.

SERVES 6

CHILLED OYSTERS ON THE
HALF SHELL

I praise the brave man who first ate an oyster. He, or maybe she, discovered one of life's simplest and unsurpassed treats. That is, if you like raw oysters, and judging by the number of raw bars and restaurants nowadays, the majority of us must really like raw oysters. They are simple to do at home. The challenge is, of course, opening them, which most fishmongers will do for you in today's market. Just be sure to ask him for the shells. Oysters are like grapes; their flavor develops from their surroundings. If you have access to different types, try to do a mix when you have raw oysters. Each oyster type has its own peculiarities as to sweetness versus brininess. You'll notice that I've listed three sauces: the standard cocktail, and then two types of mignonette. If you've never used a mignonette sauce with oysters before, you might like the way the tart and peppery sharpness accentuates the flavors in an oyster.

SERVES 6
NORMAL FOLKS
OR 3 OR FEWER
OYSTER LOVERS

1 Scrub and rinse the oysters very briskly.

2 Line 6 large plates or pie pans with the crushed ice.

3 Open the oysters, severing the muscle from the shell and leaving each one in the bottom, deeper shell. Equally divide the different types among the plates. Serve with one or more of the sauces on the following pages, lemon wedges, and saltine crackers.

36 oysters in the shells, assorted, if possible, or all one type. (A mix of European flat oysters like Belon; some Atlantic types like Blue Point or Malpeques; Gulf oysters, especially Apalachicola; and some Pacific oysters like Kumamoto)

Lots of crushed ice

One or more of the sauces on pages 157-158

Lemon wedges

Saltine crackers

FRED'S BASIC COCKTAIL SAUCE

I'm pretty much a purist when it comes to cocktail sauce. It's the balance of ketchup and horse-radish that, to me, really makes it work. I would actually use more horseradish than I call for here. I like to see sweat beads right under my eyes when I taste it. Many good oyster bars will serve cock-tail sauce and extra horseradish on the side for you to blend your own. It's not a bad idea.

¹/₂ cup ketchup

1 tablespoon plus 1 teaspoon prepared horseradish, drained, or more if desired

¹/₄ teaspoon Worcestershire sauce

In a small bowl, combine the ketchup, horseradish, and Worcestershire sauce and stir until well combined. Let it sit for 30 minutes before serving. This will keep in the refrigerator, covered, for about 1 week. Let it come to room temperature before using.

MAKES ABOUT
¹/₂ CUP

HOG ISLAND-LIKE PACIFIC RIM MIGNONETTE

There I sat at Hog Island's Oyster Bar at the Ferry Building in San Francisco, shoving their delicious oysters down as fast as I could. What made them really special was this unique take on classic French mignonette. No, they didn't give me the exact recipe, but between my waitress and the sous chef, I did get the ingredients and I've gone from there. I think you will enjoy this interesting twist on a classic.

¹/₂ cup seasoned rice wine vinegar

2 tablespoons finely chopped shallot

1 tablespoon finely chopped fresh cilantro

Copious amounts of freshly ground black pepper, at least 2 teaspoons

1 teaspoon sugar

Kosher salt

In a nonreactive bowl, combine the vinegar, shallot, cilan-tro, pepper, sugar, and salt and mix until well combined. This keeps covered, in the refrigerator for about 1 day.

MAKES ABOUT
¹/₂ CUP

CLASSIC FRENCH MIGNONETTE

This is the sauce of every classic French bistro. The acidity of the vinegar seems to be a match made in heaven with a briny oyster. If you've never tried this classic sauce, I urge you to make a batch. You might discover a whole new joy to eating raw oysters.

MAKES ABOUT
½ CUP

In a nonreactive bowl, combine the vinegar, shallot, pepper, and thyme, if desired. Taste and adjust it to your palate with the lemon juice. This will keep, covered, in the refrigerator for 2 or 3 days.

½ cup red wine vinegar

2 tablespoons finely minced shallot

2 teaspoons freshly cracked black pepper

⅛ teaspoon chopped fresh thyme (optional)

Fresh lemon juice

CRACKING THE OYSTER

To open an oyster, you need a good oyster knife or "church key," a kitchen towel, and a leather garden glove. Place the towel in your gloved hand. Place an oyster in the towel and take your oyster knife and work it into the hinge at the rear of the oyster. Make sure your hand is good and steady and just continue to twist the oyster knife back and forth until the oyster pops open. Slice the oyster muscle away from the top shell and preserve the oyster and as much of its liquor in the rounded, deeper bottom shell. Julia Child liked to open oysters with a "church key," the term for an old-fashioned beer-can opener. The method is basically the same, sticking the pointed end of the beer-can opener into the hinge of the oyster and using leverage to pop the shell open.

If you ever notice oyster shuckers' hands, there are plenty of nicks and cuts. Opening an oyster may not be the safest thing to do, but with some practice, it becomes second nature. Single oysters are always easier to open than clusters. Save the clusters for steaming. And remember, most fishmongers today who sell oysters in the shell will be happy to open them for you.

BAKED OYSTERS BLANCHE

Blanche Brown was the hostess for the Dibble Tobacco Company's entertainment cottage at the north end of Myrtle Beach, South Carolina, for over thirty years. She's passed on and the cottage has been sold to a private family, but the memories of her cooking abound. She, probably more than anyone, influenced my love of all things that come from the sea. This was one of her special recipes, and I'm pleased to share it with you.

BLANCHE'S SAUCE

1 cup good-quality mayonnaise

½ cup chili sauce, Bennett's preferred

2 tablespoons horseradish, or to taste

OYSTERS

24 shucked oysters, liquor and bottom shells reserved

⅓ cup dry white wine

1 tablespoon unsalted butter

½ cup grated Swiss cheese (about 2 ounces)

1 To make the sauce: Combine the mayonnaise, chili sauce, and horseradish in a small bowl and chill, covered, until ready to use. This can be made up to 3 days in advance.

2 Preheat the oven to 400 degrees F.

3 To prepare the oysters: Place the oysters, wine, butter, and the reserved liquor in a sauté pan, then place it over medium heat. Poach the oysters until they just curl at the edges, 3 to 5 minutes. Be sure not to overcook them, because they still get baked. Drain, and put 1 oyster in each reserved shell.

4 Cover each oyster generously with sauce, about 1 tablespoon per oyster. Divide the cheese equally among the oysters. Place the oysters on a rimmed baking sheet and bake them until they are golden brown, 4 to 5 minutes. Serve immediately.

SERVES 4 AS A FIRST COURSE

BAKED OYSTERS WITH
BACON AND LEEKS

Bacon and oysters just seem to go together. Maybe it's a textural thing, but I think it's the smoked flavor against the saltiness of the oyster. Add the gentle flavor and texture of the leeks and you truly have a first course that's pretty impressive. If you don't want to shuck your own oysters, ask your fishmonger for oyster shells and simply put them in the dishwasher before using.

SERVES 6 AS A FIRST COURSE

1 Melt the butter in small skillet over medium heat. Add the flour, and whisk 2 minutes. Add the cream slowly and whisk until the mixture thickens slightly. Remove it from the heat and reserve.

2 Cook the bacon in a large heavy skillet over medium heat until it is crisp, 6 to 8 minutes. Transfer the bacon to paper towels to drain. Discard all but 2 tablespoons of the drippings from the skillet.

3 Add the leeks, celery, bay leaf, and cayenne to the skillet and sauté them over medium heat until the vegetables are soft, about 12 minutes. Add the wine and cook until the liquid has evaporated, about 30 seconds. Add the cream mixture and bring it to a simmer.

4 Stir until the leek mixture thickens slightly, about 3 minutes. Add the bacon and cheese and stir to combine. Season with salt and pepper. (This can be made 1 day ahead. Cool slightly. Cover and refrigerate.)

1 tablespoon unsalted butter

1 tablespoon all-purpose flour

1 cup heavy cream

8 ounces applewood-smoked bacon, chopped

4 cups thinly sliced well-cleaned leeks, white and pale green parts only (about 4)

1 cup finely chopped celery

1 bay leaf

$\frac{1}{8}$ teaspoon cayenne pepper

2 tablespoons dry white wine

2 tablespoons grated Pecorino Romano cheese

Kosher salt

Freshly ground black pepper

18 medium oysters, shucked, bottom shells reserved, or 1 pint shucked oysters with liquor

1 cup fresh breadcrumbs

5 Preheat the oven to 400 degrees F.

6 Place 1 oyster in each shell. Divide the leek mixture equally over each oyster, covering it completely and spreading it to the edge of the shell. Sprinkle the oysters equally with the breadcrumbs. Place the oysters on a rimmed baking sheet. Bake for 5 minutes or so, until the breadcrumbs have browned.

BROWN OYSTER STEW WITH
BENNE SEEDS

Brown oyster stew is one of those quirky, South Carolina, Low Country dishes. "Benne seeds" is the old Low Country name for sesame seeds, which legend has it came over secretly hidden with West Africans headed for slavery. The benne plant is considered to be lucky. How ironic. This sort of stew goes back to the early 1700s and was regularly served at plantations throughout the Low Country. Today it's considered a restaurant menu specialty, with Charleston's Hominy Grill serving some of the best. This recipe incorporates a couple of helpful hints from some Low Country chefs. The depth of the sesame seeds changes the complexion of the oyster stew, giving it a wildlike richness not present in other stews.

SERVES 4

1   Place the benne seeds in a small heavy-bottomed sauté pan over medium heat and dry-roast them for about 9 minutes, or until they become dark and fragrant. Remove them from the heat and pour the seeds onto a cutting board. Crush the benne seeds with a spoon and reserve.

2   Heat the oil in a heavy-bottomed saucepan over low heat. Cook the pancetta for 5 to 8 minutes, or until it is crisp and lightly browned. Remove the pancetta with a slotted spoon and place it on paper towels to drain. Leave the oil and any fat from the pancetta in the saucepan.

3   Add the onion and crushed benne seeds to the saucepan and sauté for about 3 minutes, stirring frequently. When the onion is lightly browned, add the flour, stir well to combine, and cook for 2 minutes.

¼ cup benne (sesame) seeds

2 tablespoons peanut oil

2 tablespoons (about 1 ounce) very finely diced pancetta or other bacon

2 tablespoons finely minced yellow onion

2 tablespoons all-purpose flour

1¼ cups heavy cream

24 fresh oysters, shucked and liquor strained and reserved

1¾ cups bottled clam juice or broth

1 teaspoon chopped fresh thyme

2 tablespoons chopped fresh Italian parsley

1 tablespoon fresh lemon juice

1 teaspoon Asian sesame oil

Kosher salt

Freshly ground black pepper

Oyster crackers for serving

4 In a separate pan, heat the cream to just below a simmer.

5 Add the reserved oyster liquor, clam juice, and thyme to the pan with the onions and simmer, stirring with a whisk, until the mixture is without lumps. Add the warm cream and simmer for 5 minutes. Add the oysters, parsley, lemon juice, and sesame oil. Leave the stew on the heat until the oysters just begin to curl. Remove the saucepan from the heat and salt and pepper the stew to taste.

6 Divide the stew among 4 warm soup bowls. Garnish it with the reserved pancetta and serve immediately, along with oyster crackers.

CAESAR SALAD WITH SPICY FRIED OYSTERS

This is my idea of a hearty salad—warm, crispy, spicy fried oysters atop cool salad greens and a rich Caesar dressing. Which chef came up with this idea is up for debate. Many credit Bob Kinkead, chef-owner of Kinkead's in Washington, D.C., although Louis Osteen at Louis's at Pawley's Island, South Carolina, and Ben Barker of Magnolia Grill in Durham, North Carolina, all lay a little claim to its inception. Not bad. They're all James Beard Award–winning chefs. This salad is a wonderful first course or a great lunch. If you really want to get crazy, throw a handful of cold boiled shrimp on each salad as well.

SERVES 4

1   To prepare the dressing: Put the vinegar, anchovies, garlic, onion, mustard, egg yolk, and lemon juice in a nonreactive bowl, a blender, or a food processor. Whisk or process until well combined.

2   Slowly whisk in the two oils or very slowly pour them into the blender or food processor, teaspoon by teaspoon, with the motor. Add the salt and pepper. Tightly covered, the dressing will keep in the refrigerator for 1 week. If it separates, whisk to bring it back together.

3   To prepare the oysters: Shuck them over a bowl to catch as much of the oyster liquor as possible. Discard the shells, and reserve the oysters and their liquor.

4   On a piece of waxed paper, mix together the flour, cornmeal, paprika, salt, and pepper. Dredge the oysters in the seasoned flour, then shake them well to remove the excess.

CAESAR DRESSING

⅓ cup red wine vinegar

3 anchovy fillets, crushed

2 tablespoons minced garlic

1 tablespoon finely minced onion

1 tablespoon Dijon mustard

1 large egg yolk

1 tablespoon fresh lemon juice

½ cup peanut oil

½ cup extra-virgin olive oil

¼ teaspoon kosher salt

¼ teaspoon freshly ground black pepper

OYSTERS

24 fresh oysters in the shell, scrubbed and rinsed, or one 10-ounce jar fresh shucked oysters, juice strained through a fine-mesh strainer and reserved

$\frac{1}{2}$ cup all-purpose flour

$\frac{1}{2}$ cup cornmeal

1 teaspoon sweet paprika

$\frac{1}{4}$ teaspoon kosher salt

$\frac{1}{4}$ teaspoon freshly ground white or black pepper

Peanut oil for frying

SALAD

1 head romaine lettuce, rinsed, drained, spun dry, and separated into individual leaves

1 head red leaf lettuce, rinsed, drained, spun dry, and separated into individual leaves

5 In a deep pot or electric fryer, heat 2 inches of oil until it registers 350 degrees F on a deep-fat thermometer. Working in batches, fry the oysters in the oil for 2 minutes, or until they are golden, transferring them as they are fried to paper towels to drain.

6 To prepare the salad: Place several whole lettuce leaves on individual plates. Position 6 oysters around the perimeter of each plate, and a ramekin of Caesar Dressing on the side for dunking the oysters and lettuce leaves.

CHRISTMAS EVE PAN ROAST OF OYSTERS

This oyster concoction is the mainstay of my Christmas Eve feast, which really is an oyster overload that includes raw, roasted, and grilled oysters. Inspired by a pan roast I enjoyed at the Trellis restaurant in Williamsburg, Virginia, this recipe is highlighted by the use of shiitake mushrooms and finished with a chiffonade of fresh spinach. The mushrooms deepen the broth and add an earthiness to the dish, while the spinach adds another texture and a correcting bitterness. I've served this dish to friends and family at Christmas for over twenty years. If I didn't, I'd be afraid of the consequences.

SERVES 6 AS A MAIN COURSE OR 10 TO 12 AS A FIRST COURSE

1   No more than 4 hours before serving, add the cream and thyme to a 3-quart saucepan. Bring the cream to a slight simmer over medium heat. Cook until the cream has reduced by half. DO NOT let the cream come to a full boil, and use a ladle in the cream as a safety device to stir it if it gets too hot and begins to foam. The reduction process will take 30 to 45 minutes. Salt and pepper the cream to taste. Strain it into a warm thermos or double boiler and hold it until ready to serve.

2   As the cream reduces, blanch the leeks in boiling water for 30 seconds, strain, and put them in an ice bath. If you are doing this while the cream is reducing, then stir the cream. After a minute or two, drain the leeks, and refrigerate until needed.

2 cups heavy cream

1 sprig fresh thyme

Kosher salt

Freshly ground black pepper

2 leeks, white parts only, well cleaned and thinly sliced

2 tablespoons (¼ stick) unsalted butter

2 tablespoons dry white wine, such as vermouth

8 ounces shiitake mushrooms, stemmed and sliced

3 pints shucked oysters, with liquor

20 light green, flat-leaf spinach leaves, cleaned, dried, and cut into chiffonade (see sidebar)

3   Heat the butter and wine in a large nonstick sauté pan. When a full boil has been reached, add the mushrooms and sauté for 2 minutes. If doing this ahead, remove the mushrooms and any liquid from the pan. Reserve.

4   When it's show time, rewarm the mushrooms in that large sauté pan. Add the leeks and the oysters. Cook over medium heat until the oysters are just beginning to curl, usually 4 to 6 minutes. Stir in the reduced cream, and just barely rewarm it, for no more than 2 minutes. Adjust the seasoning, if needed, with additional salt and pepper. Serve in warmed shallow soup bowls. Equally divide the spinach over the servings. Serve immediately.

GETTING FANCY: HOW TO CHIFFONADE

To chiffonade spinach, or any other green leafy item like basil, stack up 5 to 10 leaves, then roll them up into a cigar shape. Take a sharp knife and slice the roll crosswise as thin as you like. Toss the pile to separate the strands and use them for a garnish.

EASY OYSTER STEW

Some people consider easy oyster stew to be hot milk with oysters and pepper. Okay. That's easy but not as delicious as this recipe. The key to really good oyster stew is taking time for the soup-base flavors to develop. The chicken broth may seem odd here, but it helps intensify the flavor of the cream. Please don't overcook the oysters. As soon as they begin to curl, serve the stew.

SERVES 4 TO 6

1 In a medium saucepan, bring the broth to a boil over high heat. Boil until it is reduced by about one-third, about 5 minutes.

2 Lower the heat, and add the cream and pepper. Simmer very slowly 30 to 45 minutes to mellow the flavor. Do not boil.

3 When ready to serve, add the oysters and as much of their strained liquor as desired and heat just until the edges of the oysters curl, 4 to 6 minutes. Season to taste with salt. Serve immediately, garnished with the parsley, and a bowl of saltine crackers to pass at the table.

1 cup low-sodium chicken broth or homemade stock

2 cups heavy cream

1 tablespoon freshly ground black pepper

36 shucked oysters, liquor strained and reserved

Kosher salt

Finely chopped fresh Italian parsley for garnish

Saltine crackers for serving

HANGTOWN FRY

A hangtown fry is distinctly San Franciscan. Developed at Tadich Grill during the Gold Rush days for a miner who had just struck it rich, the fry is really an open-faced omelet (frittata) and has been on the menu for decades. I'll never forget my first one, sitting at the dark-stained bar at Tadich and marveling how well eggs and oysters go together. This recipe is for one, but quite frankly one hangtown fry might feed two people. If you need more than one, I suggest using two pans and doubling the ingredients.

2 slices bacon

½ cup fine breadcrumbs, seasoned and toasted, or flour seasoned with salt and pepper

6 oysters, shucked

1 tablespoon unsalted butter

3 large eggs, lightly beaten

3 or 4 shakes hot pepper sauce

Kosher salt

Freshly ground black pepper

1 Fry the bacon in a nonstick sauté pan over medium heat until crisp. Transfer it to paper towels to drain.

2 Meanwhile, put the breadcrumbs in a small bowl, add the oysters, and toss until each oyster is evenly coated. Remove the oysters from the bowl and shake each one to remove any excess coating.

3 Pour off the bacon fat. Add the butter to the pan and melt it over medium heat. Add the oysters and sauté for about 1½ minutes on each side, or until they just plump up.

4 Crumble the bacon into pieces and toss it with the oysters. Pour the eggs into the pan. Season with the hot pepper sauce, salt, and pepper, and cook until the eggs are almost set, lifting the edges of the cooked eggs to let the uncooked eggs run under them.

5 Carefully flip the frittata over and cook for about 2 minutes, or until it is cooked on the bottom. Transfer it to a plate and serve immediately.

SERVES 1

FRIED OYSTERS WITH HORSERADISH CREAM SAUCE

Fried oysters are serious business in New Orleans. This recipe blends the best of Creole seasoning and the tart, slightly bitter acidity of horseradish for a wonderful taste temptation. The Creole seafood seasoning makes more than you need for the oysters. It's great sprinkled over most any fish or any flour mixture for frying other seafood. Poached eggs are uplifted by a little sprinkle of the seasoning, and adding some to hollandaise sauce gives it a distinct New Orleans flair.

SERVES 4 AS A
FIRST COURSE

1   To make the seasoning: In a bowl, stir together the salt, garlic powder, pepper, paprika, onion powder, thyme, and cayenne. The Creole Seafood Seasoning keeps in an airtight con-tainer for 6 months. Makes about $2/3$ cup.

2   To make the oysters: In a heavy saucepan, simmer the cream with the horseradish and pepper for 15 to 20 minutes, or until the sauce is reduced to about $1\frac{1}{2}$ cups. Season the sauce with salt, and keep it warm.

3   In a deep pot or electric fryer, heat 2 inches of oil until it registers 350 degrees F on a deep-fat thermometer.

CREOLE SEAFOOD SEASONING

2 tablespoons plus $\frac{1}{2}$ teaspoon kosher salt

2 tablespoons garlic powder

2 tablespoons freshly ground black pepper

2 tablespoons plus $\frac{1}{2}$ teaspoon paprika

$1\frac{1}{2}$ tablespoons onion powder

1 tablespoon dried thyme

1 tablespoon cayenne pepper

OYSTERS AND SAUCE

2 cups heavy cream

**4 ounces finely grated peeled
fresh horseradish, or one 4-ounce
jar, drained and squeezed dry**

**½ teaspoon freshly ground black
pepper**

Kosher salt

Peanut oil for deep-frying

**3 tablespoons Creole Seafood
Seasoning**

1 cup all-purpose flour

24 oysters, shucked and drained

4 While the oil is heating, combine the Creole Seafood Seasoning and flour. Working in batches, coat the oysters with the flour mixture, shaking off the excess. Don't let the oysters sit in the flour for very long or the end result will be soggy oysters. Fry them in the oil for 2 minutes, or until they are golden. Transfer the fried oysters to paper towels to drain.

5 Divide the sauce among 4 plates and arrange the oysters on it.

OYSTER PO'BOYS
There's no reason why the folks in New Orleans should have all the fun. Oyster po'boys are simple to make. Choose your favorite fried oyster recipe. Plan on 4 to 6 oysters per sandwich. Buy the very best French or Italian loaf bread that you can. Split it in half, slather it with tartar sauce, top with oysters, sliced tomatoes, and shredded lettuce, and you, my friend, are in business.

SWAN OYSTER DEPOT'S
OLYMPIA OYSTER COCKTAIL

On every trip that I make to San Francisco, my first stop is at Swan Oyster Depot. To grab one of the sixteen or so stools in this Polk Street institution is to be fed and entertained by the boisterous countermen. The first time I ordered one of their oyster cocktails, I was a little taken aback. I mean, it was in a school cafeteria Jell-O cup and they had poured the cocktail sauce right over the oysters and oyster liquor. I got over it. Letting the cocktail sauce thin out with the oyster liquor gave a new dimension to what an oyster cocktail should be. If you ever make a trip to the restaurant, watch out for their horseradish. It's made in-house, and it's got plenty of kick.

SERVES 4

1   In a small bowl, mix together the ketchup, 2 tablespoons of horseradish, the lemon juice, and hot pepper sauce.

2   Divide the oysters and their liquor evenly among 4 chilled cocktail glasses or small bowls. Spoon the cocktail sauce on top, garnish with lemon wedges, and serve immediately with hot pepper sauce and extra horseradish on the side.

²/₃ cup ketchup

2 tablespoons prepared horseradish, plus additional for serving

2 tablespoons fresh lemon juice

Dash of hot pepper sauce, plus additional for serving

80 to 100 Olympia oysters, freshly shucked, liquor reserved, and chilled

1 lemon, cut into wedges

OYSTER PAN ROAST IN THE STYLE OF GRAND CENTRAL TERMINAL'S OYSTER BAR

One of New York City's most impressive structures is Grand Central Terminal. On the lower level is one of the grand restaurants in Manhattan, Grand Central Oyster Bar. The Oyster Bar, has fed millions as they've traveled through that building. The best place to sit is at the oyster bar itself, watching experts shuck your oysters and make your pan roast. What distinguishes this pan roast from many others is the inclusion of a chili sauce, which spices the cream just a bit. And don't snicker over that piece of toast—it's a critical part of the whole. For a true New York experience, give this recipe a try.

16 freshly shucked oysters, liquor reserved

4 tablespoons (½ stick) unsalted butter, divided

2 tablespoons chili sauce

2 tablespoons Worcestershire sauce

1 teaspoon paprika, plus additional for serving

Dash of celery salt

1 cup heavy cream

2 slices dry toast

SERVES 2

1   Put the oysters, ½ cup of oyster liquor, 2 tablespoons of the butter, the chili sauce, Worcestershire sauce, paprika, and celery salt together in the top part of a double boiler over boiling water. Make sure that the bottom of the top pot doesn't touch the water below.

2   Whisk constantly for about 1 minute, or until the oysters are just beginning to curl. Add the cream and continue whisking. Do not boil.

3   Place 1 slice of dry toast in each of 2 soup plates. Divide the pan roast equally between the 2 bowls. Top each with 1 tablespoon of the remaining butter and sprinkle with additional paprika. Serve immediately.

NOTE: The Oyster Bar also serves pan roast of shrimp, scallops, lobster, clams, and a combination, so don't hesitate to use other shellfish in this preparation.

SIMPLE GRILLED OYSTERS IN THEIR SHELLS

Did you know that folks who farm oysters are called ranchers? I didn't until I took in the St. Mary's County, Maryland, annual oyster cook-off and national shucking contest. If you don't like oysters, you really don't need to go. I talked this recipe out of the guys from the Circle C Oyster Ranch as they were grilling oysters and selling them as fast as they could get them off the grill. It truly is a great way with an oyster. The Circle C Ranch is trying to bring back the Chesapeake Bay oyster, which has virtually disappeared from the bay. While smaller than the Chesapeakes I remember as a kid, they have that hearty flavor and heaviness of the old bay oysters.

SERVES 6 TO 8 AS A FIRST COURSE OR 2 AS A MAIN COURSE

1 Light a charcoal fire or preheat your gas grill on high. Oil the grill's cooking grate.

2 In a shallow baking pan, combine the butter and garlic, and place the pan at the edge of the fire to melt the butter. When it has melted, add the Worcestershire sauce, lemon juice, hot pepper sauce, and salt and pepper to taste, and stir to combine.

3 Place the oysters on the grill directly over the fire and cook for 2 to 3 minutes. At this point you can pull them off and open them with an oyster knife, or you can leave them on the fire for another 2 to 3 minutes until they open completely.

4 Remove the oysters from the fire, pull off the top shells, and sever the bottom muscles. Sprinkle the oysters with the parsley, douse them with the butter sauce, and then serve them in their shells with lemon quarters.

8 tablespoons (1 stick) unsalted butter

1 tablespoon minced garlic

¼ cup Worcestershire sauce

2 tablespoons fresh lemon juice

2 to 3 teaspoons hot pepper sauce

Kosher salt

Freshly ground black pepper

24 oysters of your choice in the shell, scrubbed and rinsed

3 tablespoons roughly chopped fresh parsley

2 lemons, quartered

OYSTERS WITH SPICY
JICAMA SALAD

This is a fresh and interesting way with raw oysters. The jicama, an underused vegetable, creates a wonderful crunch against the succulent inherent creaminess of a raw oyster. Throw in the mint and cilantro and you cross a few cultures. If you are skittish about raw oysters, warm them gently with 1 tablespoon of unsalted butter in a saucepan until the edges just begin to curl. It won't be quite the same, but it will still be good.

¹/₂ cup bottled chili sauce

5 tablespoons rice vinegar, divided

Kosher salt

Freshly ground black pepper

One 10- to 12-ounce jicama, peeled, cut into matchstick-size strips (about 2 ¹/₂ cups)

¹/₄ cup chopped fresh mint

¹/₄ cup chopped fresh cilantro

2 tablespoons sugar

1 tablespoon minced peeled fresh ginger

1 teaspoon minced seeded serrano or jalapeño pepper

24 oysters, shucked

1 Mix the chili sauce and 3 tablespoons of the vinegar in a small bowl. Season the sauce to taste with salt and pepper.

2 Mix the jicama, mint, cilantro, sugar, ginger, serrano pepper, and remaining 2 tablespoons of the vinegar in a medium bowl. Season the salad to taste with salt and pepper. (The sauce and salad can be prepared 8 hours ahead. Cover separately and refrigerate.)

3 Divide the chili-vinegar sauce between 2 small bowls; place 1 bowl in the center of each of 2 plates. Spoon 6 mounds of jicama salad around each sauce bowl. Top each mound of salad with 2 oysters, and serve.

SERVES 2 AS A
FIRST COURSE

NEW ENGLAND OYSTER ROLL

Once you hit Massachusetts and start heading toward Maine, shellfish on a roll is going to be something you want to try at every little shack you see. Sure, you've heard of the lobster roll and even the clam roll, but if you're an oyster lover, this is a great way to eat oysters. The key to any roll is taking the time to griddle the bread in butter. Feel free to use your favorite fried oyster recipe, whether lightly cracker meal coated or crispy cornmeal fried, they're both good. Try to find the top-load hot dog buns, but if you can't, regular buns work almost as well.

SERVES 4

1   In a large sauté pan over low to medium heat, melt the butter. Place the hot dog buns on their sides in the butter. Grill the buns in the butter, flipping them a couple of times so that both sides are coated with butter and brown evenly. Remove the buns from the pan and place them on a large plate.

2   Spread tartar sauce in the bottom of each bun. Place 6 fried oysters on top and serve with shoestring fries and coleslaw, if desired.

4 tablespoons (¹⁄₂ stick) unsalted butter

4 Pepperidge Farm top-loading hot dog buns

Any Region Tartar Sauce (page 322) or your favorite tartar sauce

24 fried oysters from your favorite recipe (or facing page)

Shoestring fries (optional)

Mother's Coleslaw for Fish (page 336; optional)

CRACKER MEAL-FRIED OYSTERS

This is probably my favorite way to fry oysters. The coating is light, crisp, and lets the oysters really shine. It's not exactly, but very similar to, the way the restaurants in Calabash, North Carolina, the self-proclaimed seafood capital of the world, fry oysters.

32 medium oysters, shucked and liquor reserved

Peanut oil for frying

1¹/₂ cups cracker meal

¹/₃ cup all-purpose flour

Kosher salt

1   Place the oysters in a bowl in their liquor and refrigerate them until ready to fry. In a deep saucepan or pot, heat the oil until it registers 350 degrees F on a deep-fat thermometer.

2   Mix the cracker meal and flour in a large shallow dish. A baking dish works well.

3   Drain the oysters, and drop them into the coating one by one, keeping them separated. Coat each oyster well, shaking off the excess cracker meal and flour mixture. Drop each oyster gently into the hot oil and fry until it is golden brown, 3 to 4 minutes. It is important not to overfry them. Drain them on paper towels and sprinkle with kosher salt.

SERVES 4

ROMAN GRILLED OYSTERS

While Rome may not immediately come to mind as an oyster-eating city, Romans seem to consume quite a few during their antipasti courses. Most that I saw were cooked in a method similar to this recipe below. Here again, if shucking the oyster is not your thing, have your fishmonger do it for you. Just tell him you want the shells. I keep two to three dozen oyster shells for times when I can't get oysters in the shells and have to rely on shucked oysters. It's not a sin to put an oyster in a shell that it didn't come out of.

SERVES 4 TO 6

1 Shuck the oysters, removing the flat, top shells.

2 Light a charcoal fire or preheat your gas grill on high. Oil your grill's cooking grate.

3 In a medium bowl, mix the breadcrumbs, parsley, garlic, and pepper to taste. Put a teaspoon or more of this mixture on top of each oyster. Sprinkle a few drops of lemon juice on each oyster and drizzle it with oil and salt to taste.

4 Place the oysters in the half shell on the grill, covered, and cook until the breadcrumbs are golden and have a little charring, about 15 minutes. If your grill doesn't have a lid, cover the oysters with disposable aluminum roasting pans or steam table–size pans. Serve with lemon wedges.

24 oysters in the shell, scrubbed and rinsed

1 ½ cups breadcrumbs

6 tablespoons finely chopped fresh parsley

2 garlic cloves, minced

Freshly ground black pepper

Juice of 1 lemon

Olive oil for drizzling

Kosher salt

Lemon wedges for garnish

ABSOLUTE BEST THANKSGIVING OYSTER CASSEROLE

OK, I'm biased. This oyster casserole is a standard with my family at Thanksgiving. As a matter of fact, there has been a discussion of forgetting the turkey altogether. This is an "it depends" recipe. By that I mean the amount of butter that you use depends on the amount of oyster liquor that you get. You're looking for about 1½ cups of total liquid. You want the top of the casserole heavily peppered. If you'll notice, it's the only spice there is. If there's a bunch of oyster lovers around, keep your eye on them; they might get into the raw oysters before you assemble the dish. I always buy an extra pint to keep them happy.

1 quart plus 1 pint shucked oysters with liquor

1-pound box regular Ritz crackers

About 1 cup (2 sticks) unsalted butter, melted

At least 1 tablespoon freshly ground black pepper

1 Preheat the oven to 350 degrees F.

2 Place the oysters in a colander with a bowl underneath to drain the liquor. Reserve the liquor.

3 Roughly crush the crackers. Make sure you have some large pieces. In a 9-by-13-inch glass baking dish, sprinkle one-third of the crushed crackers on the bottom in an even layer.

4 Layer about half the oysters over the crackers. Cover the oysters with another layer of crackers, layer the remaining oysters over the crackers, and take the remaining crackers and layer them over the top.

5 Mix the butter together with the reserved oyster liquor to get 1½ cups. Pour the mixture evenly over the casserole. Sprinkle the casserole with copious amounts of black pepper. You want to be able to see the black pepper.

6 Bake for 15 to 20 minutes, until the casserole is a little brown but still moist. Serve hot.

SERVES 12

sCAllops.

For my taste, scallops are the best tasting of the sea dwellers. They are by far the most popular bivalves in this country. Didn't know they were in the same class with clams and mussels? That's because most of us will never see a scallop in its shell. Unlike their cousins, scallops never totally close their shells. This causes the scallop to spoil rapidly once out of water, so most scallops are cleaned and processed at sea. Lucky us—no shell to deal with.

We are basically going to find three types of scallops in the market: sea, bay, and calico. Most will be wild-caught off the Atlantic coast, but some farming is being done on the Pacific coast. Sea scallops are the larger scallops that most of us will encounter. They can be sold like shrimp, so many per pound, but unless you are grilling the scallops, you really don't need the huge or superhuge sea scallops.

Sea scallops take nicely to most all cooking methods, but my favorite is a quick pan sear. Undercook them slightly, leaving the center a bit translucent, and you will get more pleasure from them. Quick frozen at sea may even be better than fresh, since scallop boats stay out for several days.

Bay scallops are smaller, about 1 inch by ½ inch. They are harvested from October 'til March, between Massachusetts and Long Island, and may be referred to as "Nantucket" bay scallops. They are the sweetest and most prized of the American scallops. They are also very expensive, fresh costing $28 a pound or more, and if you are not paying that for fresh bay, you are probably buying large calicos. Once a year they are worth the price. I like bays quickly seared with a rich creamy sauce. To overcook any scallop is a sin, but doubly so with bays. Calico scallops are small, most the size of a pencil eraser. Because they are so small, they get steamed to open them and of course partially cooked in the process. That makes them easy to spot at the market, because they will be white and opaque, rather than multitoned and translucent like other scallops. They are never great, but work OK quickly cooked in butter, or as the base for a scallop cake.

The most important question you have to ask at the fish counter is, "Are these wet or dry pack?" Many scallops are treated with tripolyphosphates to preserve their shelf life and weight. Avoid these. When heat is applied, the fluid runs right out, and if you are trying to pan sear a scallop it is hopeless—they will steam in the liquid. Good fishmongers will be up-front about this, but protect yourself by being able to spot the difference. Wet, which are preservative-soaked scallops, are almost perfectly white and slide together in a mass, even looking a bit slimy. Nontreated will be white and ivory and pinkish in color. They will also look separate and seem sticky.

Buy 3 to 4 ounces of any scallop per person for a first course, and about 6 ounces for a main course. Always remove the little "foot," or side muscle, before cooking. It will pull right off.

Are there fake scallops out there? Maybe. The skate wing plug legend would make such fakes more expensive than scallops, and they look nothing like scallops; and for the shark plugs, you could tell when you look closely, since the shark has more muscle separations. The little side muscle is the best way to know for sure if you have the real thing.

Please don't overcook scallops unless you like tough, chewy matter. Make sure they are slightly firm but springy to the touch.

FROM SEA TO

BAY

SEARED SEA SCALLOP
SAGANAKI WITH FETA

This is my best interpretation of a dish I had at the fine Greek restaurant Molyvos in New York City. It's amazing to me how well the salty, bitter earthiness of feta cheese marries with the sweet succulence of sea scallops.

SERVES 4 AS A
FIRST COURSE

1 In a large skillet over high heat, heat 2 tablespoons of the oil. Season the scallops with pepper, place them in the skillet, and cook, turning once, until they are well browned and slightly firm to the touch, about 2 minutes per side. Transfer them to a plate and cover them with aluminum foil. Discard the oil, wipe out the skillet, and return it to the heat.

2 Heat the remaining 1 tablespoon of the oil, and add the garlic. Cook until fragrant, about 30 seconds. Add the wine and cook until it is reduced by half, 3 to 4 minutes. Add the broth, bring it to a boil, and cook until it is reduced to $^3/_4$ cup, about 5 minutes. Remove it from the heat and stir in the lemon juice, green onions, chopped parsley, dill, and mustard.

3 Place 3 scallops in each of 4 bowls. Add 3 sun-dried tomatoes to each bowl. Spoon some of the sauce over the top, and sprinkle the bowls with feta. Garnish with the parsley sprigs, and serve.

3 tablespoons olive oil, divided

12 large dry-pack sea scallops, side muscles removed

Freshly ground black pepper

2 large garlic cloves, thinly sliced

1 cup white wine

2 cups low-sodium canned chicken broth

Juice of 1 lemon ($^1/_4$ cup)

2 green onions, green ends only, thinly sliced on the diagonal

2 tablespoons coarsely chopped fresh parsley, plus sprigs for garnish

2 tablespoons coarsely chopped fresh dill

1 teaspoon Dijon mustard

12 oil-packed sun-dried tomatoes with a little of the oil

5 ounces feta cheese, crumbled

BACON-WRAPPED GINGER-SOY SCALLOPS

A lighter, more interesting take on the classic hors d'oeuvre angels on horseback, the ginger and soy here let the scallop flavor penetrate more thoroughly than when they are brushed with teriyaki sauce. With or without the bacon, these are really good little bites.

¼ cup soy sauce

1 tablespoon dark brown sugar

1½ teaspoons minced peeled fresh ginger

6 very large dry-pack sea scallops (about 12 ounces total), side muscles removed

One 8-ounce can sliced water chestnuts, drained

12 slices bacon, cut in half crosswise

1   Set a rack in the upper third of the oven. Line the bottom of a broiler pan with aluminum foil, then place the slotted top part on the pan. Place the whole pan on the oven rack while the oven preheats.

2   Preheat the oven to 450 degrees F.

3   In a medium bowl, combine the soy sauce, sugar, and ginger. Cut each scallop into quarters. Marinate the scallop pieces in the soy mixture for 15 minutes. Reserve the marinade.

4   When ready to cook, stack 2 slices of the water chestnuts in the center of a piece of bacon. Put a piece of scallop on top of the water chestnuts. Wrap each end of the bacon over the scallop and secure with a toothpick. Repeat with the remaining bacon, water chestnuts, and scallops. (If you have some leftovers, it's OK.)

5   Remove the broiler pan from the oven and quickly arrange the bacon-wrapped scallops on the hot pan so that an exposed side of each scallop faces up. Drizzle the scallops with the reserved marinade. Bake, turning the scallops over once after 10 minutes, until the bacon is browned around the edges and the scallops are cooked through, about 15 minutes total.

MAKES 24 HORS D'OEUVRES

BASIC GRILLED SCALLOPS

Grilling sea scallops adds an extra dimension of flavor to this already rich and sweet treat. The cumin and coriander help to bring out the natural flavors in the scallops without adding any sort of distinctive flavor. The key here is to get as thick a scallop as you possibly can. Touch the scallops frequently during cooking—an overcooked scallop, especially a sea scallop, is nothing more than a hockey puck. This recipe also works well in a stove-top grill pan—it's all about caramelizing the natural sugars in the scallop.

SERVES 4

1 Lay the scallops out on a platter. Sprinkle them with pepper.

2 In a small bowl, combine the cumin and coriander. Sprinkle this mixture over both sides of the scallops, lightly tapping on the seasoning. Drizzle them with oil and let them sit at room temperature while you prepare your grill.

3 Light a charcoal fire or preheat your gas grill on high. Oil your grill's cooking grate.

4 Over a very hot fire, place the scallops on the grill. Cook for about 5 minutes on one side. Turn and cook an additional 3 minutes, or until they are slightly firm to the touch but with some give.

5 Remove the scallops to a platter. Sprinkle them with sea salt and serve.

1 pound large dry-pack sea scallops, at least $3/4$ inch thick, side muscles removed

Freshly ground black pepper

1 teaspoon ground cumin

1 teaspoon ground coriander

Olive oil for drizzling

Coarse sea salt

SCALLOP CHOWDER WITH
PERNOD AND THYME

This chowder reminds me of the south of France. The dash of Pernod and the hint of thyme raise this chowder's level from the norm. They replace the standard salt pork or bacon as the main flavoring ingredient. This chowder does justice to the scallops.

1 tablespoon unsalted butter

1 large sweet onion, such as Vidalia, finely chopped (about 1¹/₂ cups)

2 large white potatoes, peeled and cut into ¹/₂-inch dice (about 1 cup)

1 pound dry-pack sea scallops, side muscles removed

1 quart heavy cream

¹/₄ cup Pernod

1 teaspoon chopped fresh thyme

Kosher salt

Freshly ground black pepper

Milk for thinning, if needed

Chopped fresh chives for garnish

1 In a large saucepan over low heat, melt the butter. Add the onion and cook until soft, 5 to 8 minutes.

2 Stir in the potatoes and cook for 2 minutes. Add the scallops and cook for 2 additional minutes, stirring frequently. Add the cream and simmer for 30 minutes. Add the Pernod, thyme, and season with salt and pepper to taste. Continue cooking for another 10 minutes, or until the potatoes are tender.

3 Thin the chowder with a little milk if it is too thick. Ladle the chowder into bowls and sprinkle it with the chives.

SERVES 4

GRILLED SCALLOPS WITH
HOISIN-ORANGE SAUCE

The interesting twang of Chinese hoisin sauce blended with orange juice and other ingredients creates a backdrop to let the enhanced sweetness of grilled scallops come to the forefront. Grilling scallops is a bit easier than shrimp but care must be taken not to overcook. Scallops actually are much better when still cool in the middle. Test them with your finger. If they still give a little, they're done.

SERVES 4 AS A
FIRST COURSE
OR 2 AS A MAIN
COURSE

1   To make the sauce: Mix the hoisin sauce, juice, vinegar, zest, garlic, and ginger in a bowl. This can be made 1 week ahead. Cover and chill in the refrigerator. Bring it to room temperature before using.

2   To prepare the vegetables: Mix the juice, oil, chili-garlic sauce, and fish sauce in a large bowl. Add the watercress, cucumber, carrot, cilantro, and onion and toss to blend. Season with salt and pepper to taste. Let the mixture stand for 30 minutes or chill up to 1 hour, tossing occasionally.

3   To prepare the scallops: Combine the oil, ginger, and coriander in a medium bowl, then add the scallops. Let them stand at least 30 minutes or chill up to 1 hour.

4   Light a charcoal fire or preheat your gas grill on high. Oil your grill's cooking grate.

SAUCE

One 8½-ounce jar hoisin sauce

⅓ cup fresh orange juice

1½ tablespoons rice vinegar

1 tablespoon freshly grated orange zest

2 garlic cloves, minced

2 teaspoons minced peeled fresh ginger

VEGETABLES

3 tablespoons fresh lime juice

2 tablespoons Asian sesame oil

1 teaspoon chili-garlic sauce

1 teaspoon Thai fish sauce (*nam pla*)

1 bunch watercress, trimmed

1 medium cucumber, peeled, seeded, and cut into matchstick-size strips

1 medium carrot, peeled and cut into matchstick-size strips

¾ cup fresh cilantro leaves (from a large bunch)

½ red onion, very thinly sliced

Kosher salt

Freshly ground black pepper

SCALLOPS

1 tablespoon Asian sesame oil

1 tablespoon minced peeled fresh ginger

1 teaspoon ground coriander

12 large dry-pack sea scallops, side muscles removed

4 wooden skewers (soaked in water for 30 minutes)

5 Thread 3 scallops onto each of 4 soaked wooden skewers. Grill the scallops until they are just opaque in the center, about 3 minutes per side. Divide the vegetables among 4 plates. Top each with 3 scallops and serve, passing the Hoisin-Orange Sauce separately.

PAN-SEARED SCALLOPS ON RED ONION MARMALADE

This is another classic dish from the famous Greenbrier Hotel and Spa in White Sulphur Springs, West Virginia. It actually is part of their spa, or "light," cuisine, of which they have a nightly offering. In some ways, eating this dish is almost like having dessert, with the inherent charm of scallops and the red onions cooked until their sugar is exposed and caramelized.

SERVES 8

1 Rinse the scallops. In a bowl large enough to accommodate all the scallops, mix together the water, juice, sugar, Worcestershire sauce, ginger, salt, and pepper. Add the scallops and toss to coat thoroughly. Marinate them in the refrigerator about 30 minutes.

2 To make the Red Onion Marmalade: In a large heavy-bottomed saucepan heat the oil over medium heat and add the onions. Cook until they begin to soften, about 10 minutes, then add the sugar and stir to coat. Season with salt and pepper. Continue cooking over medium heat, stirring frequently, until the onions are golden brown, another 10 to 15 minutes. Add the vinegar and cook until it has completely evaporated, then add the wine and repeat the process, stirring the onions frequently to prevent sticking and burning. When the wine has evaporated, taste and correct the seasoning. Remove the marmalade from the heat and keep it warm. The marmalade may be made up to 2 days ahead.

2½ pounds dry-pack sea scallops, side muscles removed

1 cup water

¼ cup fresh lemon juice

2 tablespoons packed brown sugar

1 tablespoon Worcestershire sauce

1½ teaspoons ground ginger

½ teaspoon kosher salt

¼ teaspoon freshly ground white pepper

RED ONION MARMALADE

3 tablespoons extra-virgin olive oil

4 pounds red onions, thinly sliced (10 cups)

1 tablespoon brown sugar

Kosher salt

Freshly ground white pepper

¾ cup red wine vinegar

1¼ cups red wine

Vegetable oil (such a canola, soy, or safflower), for cooking

2 tablespoons chopped fresh chives

3   Drain the scallops and pat them dry with paper towels. Heat a nonstick frying pan until very hot. With a paper towel, rub a thin film of oil on the pan, then add the scallops in a single layer. Sear them over high heat until they are just barely opaque in the center, 3 to 4 minutes on each side for large scallops. Cook them in batches if necessary to avoid crowding the pan so that the scallops will caramelize nicely, not boil.

4   To serve, arrange the warm onion marmalade on a warmed platter or plates. Arrange the hot scallops on top, sprinkle with the chives, and serve immediately.

PAN-SEARED SEA SCALLOPS AND
BEURRE BLANC SAUCE

For my taste, scallops have the most complex, enjoyable flavor and texture, with the exception of a cold briny oyster, of any of the mollusk family. And while scallops are the most popular of all the bivalves we consume, there are all grades of weird tales about them. Yeah, I guess you can plug a skate wing or shark meat into a scallopy-looking thing, and there are times when I distrust the breaded and frozen variety; but it's hard to fake that little knot of tissue on the side of all scallops, whether sea, bay, or calico.

The sauce is a basic butter sauce, which really sets off the scallop flavor. If you think it's too much trouble, then skip it. When shopping for scallops, look for dry-pack scallops.

SERVES 4

1   To make the sauce: Combine the vinegar, wine, and shallots in a small saucepan. Place them over medium heat and cook until almost all the liquid is gone.

2   Add the cream and reduce by half, 3 to 5 minutes.

3   Remove the pan from the heat and whisk in the butter, several small pieces at a time. Season to taste with salt and pepper. Pour the sauce into a thermos to keep warm.

4   To prepare the scallops: Combine the salt, sugar, basil, thyme, garlic powder, and onion powder in a small bowl. Sprinkle the scallops lightly with the seasoning mixture.

SAUCE

¼ cup white wine vinegar

¼ cup white wine

¼ cup chopped shallots

½ cup heavy cream

8 tablespoons (1 stick) unsalted butter, cut into small pieces

Kosher salt

Freshly ground black pepper

SCALLOPS

$^1/_2$ teaspoon kosher salt

$^1/_2$ teaspoon sugar

$^1/_2$ teaspoon dried basil

$^1/_2$ teaspoon dried thyme

$^1/_4$ teaspoon garlic powder

$^1/_4$ teaspoon onion powder

$1^1/_2$ pounds dry-pack sea scallops (must be dry pack, and don't try this recipe with bay or calico scallops), side muscles removed

2 tablespoons canola oil

2 tablespoons ($^1/_4$ stick) unsalted butter

Chopped fresh chives

5   Heat the oil and butter in a heavy sauté pan (cast iron is great). Add the scallops in a single layer so that they don't touch each other. Cook 3 to 4 minutes, or until the bottoms are browned. Turn and cook an additional 2 to 4 minutes, depending on size, until the other sides are also browned.

6   Spoon 1 to 2 tablespoons of the butter sauce on a plate, add a few scallops, and sprinkle them with the fresh chives.

SCALLOP CAKES WITH CILANTRO-LIME MAYONNAISE

I have a close friend who challenged me to make a scallop cake as delicious as my crab cakes. I think this result fills the bill. The texture is completely different from a crab cake—meatier, more substantial. But the wonderful sea-filled flavor of the scallop does not disappear in this mixture.

SERVES 4

1   To make the mayonnaise: Blend the cilantro, lime juice, garlic, mustard, and hot pepper sauce in a food processor until the cilantro is finely chopped. Add the mayonnaise and process just to blend. Transfer the mixture to a small bowl. Season with salt and pepper to taste. This can be made 1 day ahead. Cover and refrigerate. Makes about 1 cup.

2   To make the cakes: Heat the olive oil in a medium nonstick skillet over medium heat. Add the onion and cook until it is tender, about 8 minutes. Remove the pan from the heat and cool.

3   Place the scallops in a food processor and use the pulse feature to coarsely chop them, or chop them by hand. Transfer the scallops to a large bowl. Stir in the onion, chives, egg, parsley, flour, ginger, lime juice, salt, zest, and pepper.

4   Mold the scallop mixture into eight ½-inch-thick patties, each 3 to 3 ½ inches in diameter. Place the scallop cakes on a baking sheet. Cover and chill them for 1 hour. They can be prepared 6 hours ahead. Keep in the refrigerator.

CILANTRO-LIME MAYONNAISE

1 cup packed fresh cilantro

3 tablespoons fresh lime juice

1 garlic clove, peeled

1 teaspoon Dijon mustard

¼ teaspoon hot pepper sauce

¾ cup mayonnaise

Kosher salt

Freshly ground black pepper

SCALLOP CAKES

1 tablespoon olive oil

1 cup finely chopped onion

2 pounds dry-pack sea scallops, side muscles removed

$\frac{1}{2}$ cup chopped fresh chives

1 large egg, lightly beaten

2 tablespoons chopped fresh parsley

2 tablespoons all-purpose flour

1 tablespoon minced peeled fresh ginger

1 tablespoon fresh lime juice

2 teaspoons kosher salt

1 teaspoon grated lime zest

$\frac{3}{4}$ teaspoon freshly ground black pepper

2 tablespoons peanut oil

Fresh cilantro sprigs for garnish

5   Preheat the oven to 450 degrees F.

6   Heat the peanut oil in a large nonstick skillet over medium-high heat. Working in batches, add the scallop cakes to the skillet and cook until they are browned, about 2 minutes per side. Transfer the cakes back to the baking sheet. Bake until they are cooked through, about 7 minutes.

7   Place 2 scallop cakes on each of 4 plates. Top with Cilantro-Lime Mayonnaise. Garnish with cilantro sprigs.

SCALLOPS IN **BLACK** BEAN SAUCE

The quick cooking necessary for scallops makes them a perfect candidate for any kind of stir-fry recipe. As with any stir-fry dish, this one goes quickly and it's imperative that all of your ingredients be assembled before you start. I think you'll enjoy the brininess of the fermented black beans and the way they couple with the sea-like flavors of the scallops.

SERVES 4

1　Heat 1 tablespoon of the canola oil in a wok or heavy skillet, and when the oil shimmers, add the scallops. Cook for 2 minutes, or until they are just firm. Remove them to a plate.

2　Mix together the rice wine, soy sauce, and sugar in a cup with 1 tablespoon of water and set aside.

3　Add the remaining 1 tablespoon of canola oil to the wok and heat until it is beginning to smoke. Add the onion, garlic, and ginger. Cook for 30 seconds. Add the beans and the soy sauce mixture and bring it to a boil. Return the scallops to the sauce, add the sesame oil, and simmer for about 30 seconds. Serve immediately with rice and steamed vegetables.

2 tablespoons canola oil, divided

24 dry-pack sea scallops, side muscles removed

2 tablespoons Chinese rice wine

1 tablespoon soy sauce

1 teaspoon sugar

1 green onion, finely chopped

1 garlic clove, finely chopped

½ teaspoon finely grated peeled fresh ginger

1 tablespoon salted fermented black beans, rinsed and drained

1 teaspoon roasted sesame oil

Cooked rice for serving

Steamed vegetables for serving

BAY SCALLOP EGG SCRAMBLE

Supper, that late-night meal after the theater, can be so fashionable. And it really needs to be tasty. Scrambled eggs and bay scallops fill that bill perfectly. It's quick to prepare and soothing. It also surpasses expectations for brunch. Just add a mimosa or Bloody Mary.

4 slices lean bacon

6 large eggs, lightly beaten

4 tablespoons (½ stick) unsalted butter, divided

Kosher salt

Freshly ground black pepper

2 tablespoons heavy cream, half-and-half, or milk, according to your conscience

1 tablespoon chopped fresh Italian parsley

1 teaspoon chopped fresh tarragon or chives

8 ounces very fresh bay scallops, side muscles removed

4 slices toast or 4 biscuits

1   Broil or fry the bacon over medium heat. Drain them on paper towels and set aside in a warm oven.

2   Break the eggs into a colander over the top of a double boiler or heat-safe bowl and beat them gently, using a whisk or a wooden spoon to push the eggs through. Once they're strained, add 1 tablespoon of the butter and the salt and pepper to taste.

3   Cook the eggs over medium heat in the double boiler or place the bowl over a pan of simmering water, whisking constantly, scraping the sides of the pot where the eggs first coagulate. When the eggs begin to thicken, add the cream.

4   Remove the eggs from the heat when they have formed small, bright yellow curds. Add the parsley and tarragon to the eggs.

5   Meanwhile, pat the scallops dry with a paper towel and melt the remaining 3 tablespoons of butter over medium-high heat in a 10-inch nonstick pan. When the butter bubbles, but before it darkens and begins to smoke, add the scallops in 1 layer. Cook until they turn brown, about 3 minutes. Turn and cook until they are browned on the other side, about 2 more minutes. Remove the scallops with a slotted spoon and drain them on paper towels. Stir them into the eggs, and add the bacon, crumbled.

6   To serve, pour the scramble onto a platter, surrounded by the toast.

SERVES 2

SEA SCALLOPS IN THYME-LEEK SAUCE

Thyme and leek join together here to make a quick pan sauce that gently surrounds the sea scallops. This method of making a sauce yields a tongue-satisfying concoction in a short amount of time. This recipe could work just as well with tarragon, chervil, or even parsley. If leeks are difficult to find, shallots or a sweet onion could be substituted. However, one of the main taste elements of this recipe comes from the sear on your scallops, which makes it imperative that you only try this recipe with dry-pack scallops. Wet scallops will not generate the caramelization necessary for a pleasing and outstanding dish.

SERVES 6

1 Cook the bacon in a medium saucepan until it is crisp. Remove the bacon and place it on a paper towel. Reserve 1 tablespoon of the dripping in the pan and discard the rest. Crumble the bacon and reserve.

2 Place the saucepan back over the heat. Add the leeks and cook until they are soft, about 2 minutes. Pour in the wine, and simmer until almost evaporated, about 3 minutes. Add the cream and thyme; bring it to a simmer and cook until it is slightly thickened, about 3 minutes. Season with the salt and pepper; keep this sauce warm.

3 Heat a nonstick skillet over high heat until very hot. Working in batches, sear the scallops until they are nicely golden brown, about 2 minutes per side. Spoon a portion of sauce onto each plate and top each with 4 scallops. Sprinkle them with the bacon and serve.

6 ounces bacon (about 8 slices, depending on the bacon)

1 medium leek, white part only, well cleaned and julienned

1/3 cup dry white wine

1 1/2 cups heavy cream

1 teaspoon minced fresh thyme

1/2 teaspoon kosher salt

1/4 teaspoon freshly ground white pepper

1 1/2 pounds dry-pack sea scallops, side muscles removed

CAPE COD SCALLOPS WITH
CITRUS BEURRE BLANC SAUCE

This is my version of a recipe that I had at a restaurant called the Impudent Oyster in Chatham, Massachusetts. It was also the first time I ever had true Nantucket bay scallops. They are a heavenly treat. But alas, the season for Nantucket bays is short and they can be extremely pricey. So don't hesitate to try this recipe with other bay scallops or even sea scallops that have been cut into quarters. I was actually pleasantly shocked recently at the high quality of some frozen bay scallops I had purchased. So don't overlook these at your seafood market.

BEURRE BLANC SAUCE

½ cup fresh orange juice

¼ cup dry vermouth

3 tablespoons minced shallot (about 1 large)

8 tablespoons (½ stick) unsalted butter, cut into chunks

2 teaspoons grated orange zest

Kosher salt

SCALLOPS

1 tablespoon canola oil

1 pound bay scallops, side muscles removed

1 tablespoon grated orange zest

1 To make the Beurre Blanc Sauce: Combine the juice, vermouth, and shallots in a 1-quart saucepan. Bring them to a boil over high heat and cook until the liquid has almost evaporated, about 5 minutes.

2 Reduce the heat to low. Remove the pan from the heat. Whisk in 1 tablespoon of the butter. Return the pan to the heat and whisk in the remaining butter, 1 tablespoon at a time. Whisk in the zest, and salt the sauce to taste. Serve immediately or hold it in a thermos for 3 hours.

3 To prepare the scallops: Heat the oil in a sauté pan large enough to hold the scallops without crowding. Toss the scallops with the zest. When the oil is hot, add the scallops and cook them no more than about 2 minutes per side. Remove the scallops using a slotted spoon. Divide them between 4 plates and pour equal amounts of the Citrus Beurre Blanc Sauce over each serving. Serve immediately.

SERVES 4

DOWN EAST FRIED SCALLOPS

Cracker meal, I think, makes one of the greatest coatings for any fried seafood. It has just the right amount of crunch without being heavy or covering the flavor of the food that it encases. To me, this is the best way to fry a scallop, but you could easily substitute peeled and deveined shrimp, oysters, or clams in this recipe with outstanding results. You could use milk in place of the buttermilk, but you would miss the slight lemony note that buttermilk imparts.

SERVES 4

1 Place the scallops in a large bowl and add the buttermilk and salt and pepper to taste. Toss to coat. Let them sit for 30 minutes. Drain.

2 Place the cracker meal in a large bowl. Add the drained scallops and toss to coat. Let them sit while the oil heats.

3 Preheat the oven to 250 degrees F. Place a rack over a baking sheet. Heat the oil in a deep pot until it registers 350 degrees F on a deep-fat thermometer.

4 Add a few scallops at a time to the oil and fry until they are golden brown, about 3 minutes. Remove and drain them on paper towels. Place them on the rack and put it in the oven. Repeat with the remaining scallops. Serve them hot with tartar sauce.

1 pound bay scallops, side muscles removed

1 cup buttermilk

Kosher salt

Freshly ground black pepper

2 cups cracker meal

Peanut oil for frying

Any Region Tartar Sauce (page 322) or your favorite tartar sauce

SCALLOP YAKITORI

If you travel to Japan, you will find yakitori bars on just about every corner. Yakitori means "grilled fowl," and it is almost always served on a stick. Typically you sit at a bar and get to watch all the action; scallops take nicely to this method. The Japanese seven-spice mixture will be available at all Japanese markets and markets that stock predominantly Asian goods. Or you can sprinkle the scallops with a little salt, pepper, and cayenne pepper for a similar taste experience.

YAKITORI SAUCE

6 tablespoons Japanese dark soy sauce

¹⁄₄ cup sake

2 tablespoons mirin

1 tablespoon sugar

12 wooden skewers (soaked in water for 30 minutes)

15 medium dry-pack sea scallops, side muscles removed

Japanese seven-spice mixture

1   To make the Yakitori Sauce: Combine the soy sauce, sake, mirin, and sugar in a small saucepan and bring it to a simmer. Simmer gently for 1 minute. Remove from the heat and let the sauce cool. Yakitori Sauce will keep in the refrigerator, covered, for several weeks. Makes ³⁄₄ cup.

2   Cut the scallops in half crosswise so you end up with 30 disks. Marinate the scallops in the Yakitori Sauce for 15 minutes.

3   Slide 5 scallops onto 2 skewers (like a ladder) to make the scallops easy to turn on the grill. Make sure the scallops are close together so no wood remains exposed. Pour the Yakitori Sauce onto a plate.

4   Light a charcoal fire or preheat your gas grill on high. Oil your grill's cooking grate.

5   Grill the scallops for about 1 minute on each side and then dip them in the Yakitori Sauce. Grill the scallops again for 1 minute on each side and dip them once more in the sauce. Grill them for 30 seconds more on each side, or until they slightly give when touched, and serve immediately, along with the seven-spice mixture to sprinkle on at the table.

SERVES 6 AS A FIRST COURSE OR FINGER FOOD

SCALLOP SEVICHE

It's the middle of the summer, hot and humid. The last thing you want to do is cook. That's when you pull out this seviche recipe. The sea scallops are actually "cooked" in the acid of the citrus juices. Blending them with the other ingredients in this recipe, you get a very fresh, refreshing, and cooling sensation. Seviche can be great as a whole meal or as an appetizer any time of the year. Don't think of this dish as raw—think of it as delicious.

SERVES 4 AS A
FIRST COURSE
OR 2 AS A MAIN
COURSE

1 Slice the scallops into disks about ½ inch thick.

2 Combine the scallops with the juices, onions, cilantro, peppers, salt, and pepper in a nonreactive bowl, and refrigerate for 20 minutes. Serve the seviche in small chilled bowls, or in wide glasses such as a martini glass.

1 pound dry-pack sea scallops, side muscles removed

¼ cup fresh lime juice (about 2 limes)

⅓ cup fresh orange juice (about 1 small)

4 green onions, green and white parts, finely chopped

3 tablespoons chopped fresh cilantro

2 jalapeño peppers, seeded and finely chopped

Kosher salt

Freshly ground black pepper

SCALLOPS WITH CAVA AND
SAFFRON SAUCE

A little Spanish twist on scallops: Cava is Spanish sparkling wine, i.e., Champagne, if we could legally call it that. An American or French sparkling wine will work just as well, although I think there is some extra effervescence to Cava that adds a bit to this plate. The unique bitterness of saffron plays an interesting taste game in your mouth with the scallops. Be sure to slightly undercook the scallops in the first step so they won't over-cook when you return them to the sauce to reheat.

2 tablespoons (¼ stick) unsalted butter

20 large dry-pack sea scallops, side muscles removed

1 ½ cups dry Cava or other sparkling wine

Pinch of saffron threads, crushed

1 cup heavy cream

Fresh lemon juice for seasoning

Kosher salt

Freshly ground black pepper

Minced fresh parsley for garnish

1 Melt the butter in a large heavy skillet over medium-high heat. Add the scallops and sauté until they are not quite cooked through, turning occasionally, about 2 minutes. Transfer them to a plate.

2 Add the Cava and saffron to the skillet and boil until the liquid is reduced by half, about 7 minutes. Add the cream and boil until it is reduced to a sauce consistency, about 10 minutes. Season the sauce to taste with lemon juice, salt, and pepper. Return the scallops to the sauce and stir just until they are heated through.

3 Divide the scallops and saffron sauce among 4 plates. Sprinkle them with the parsley and serve.

SERVES 4

OVEN-FRIED SCALLOPS

This is a pretty good method of keeping your food out of fat—deep fat, that is. Oven frying works well here for scallops, and the same recipe could be used with shrimp. There are a couple of advantages to oven frying. One, you don't get the fast-food smell of hot vats of oil throughout your house. You also don't have to worry about cooking these scallops in batches as you would when you deep-fry them. These oven-fried scallops are great by themselves but also make a wonderful topping for salads. I used to frequent a restaurant called Caroline's, and one of their best dishes was what they called a "hot and cold salad." It was a plate of salad greens piled high, and over half they put cold boiled shrimp. The other half had either fried oysters or fried scallops. The contrast was amazing and delicious.

SERVES 4

1 Preheat the oven to 450 degrees F.

2 Place the scallops in a small bowl. Combine the oil and juice and pour them over the scallops. Marinate them in the refrigerator for 30 minutes, turning occasionally.

3 Remove the scallops from the marinade, discarding it. In a bowl, combine the egg and water and stir well. Combine the breadcrumbs, salt, pepper, and paprika in a pie plate. Dip each scallop in the egg mixture, then dredge it in the breadcrumbs.

4 Place the scallops in an ungreased 8-inch square pan. Drizzle the butter over them. Bake, uncovered, for 15 to 20 minutes, or until the scallops are golden. If desired, serve them with lemon wedges and tartar sauce.

12 dry-pack sea scallops (about 1 pound), side muscles removed

2 tablespoons vegetable oil

2 tablespoons fresh lemon juice

1 large egg, lightly beaten

2 tablespoons water

½ cup dry breadcrumbs

½ teaspoon kosher salt

Dash of freshly ground black pepper

Dash of paprika

4 tablespoons (½ stick) unsalted butter, melted

Lemon wedges for garnish (optional)

Any Region Tartar Sauce (page 322) or your favorite tartar sauce (optional)

SCALLOP PIE

Seafood casseroles seem to like to go by the name of pie, and this one has an Irish pie heritage. Whatever we call it, this is an excellent dish. Mushrooms, potatoes, and scallops—it can only be so bad, right? If you have leftover mashed potatoes, you're a step ahead. And if you're in a real hurry, just skip to Step 2 and you'll have a nice sauté of scallops and mushrooms.

1 pound boiling potatoes, peeled and cut into chunks

3 garlic cloves, divided

5 tablespoons unsalted butter, divided

1 pound small white mushrooms, cleaned and trimmed

$\frac{1}{2}$ cup minced green onion

2 tablespoons all-purpose flour

1 cup light cream or half-and-half

$\frac{1}{4}$ cup sweet sherry

2 pounds bay scallops, side muscles removed

About 3 tablespoons milk (optional)

2 tablespoons chopped fresh parsley

1 Put the potatoes in a pot, cover them with cold water, and bring them to a boil over high heat. Reduce the heat to a simmer and cook until they are tender, about 30 minutes.

2 Meanwhile, mince $2\frac{1}{2}$ of the garlic cloves. In a heavy-bottomed nonreactive saucepan, melt 3 tablespoons of the butter. Add the minced garlic and sauté for 2 minutes. Add the mushrooms and onions and sauté to soften them, 3 minutes. Sprinkle the flour over the mixture and stir well. Slowly add the cream, stirring constantly, and bring it to a boil. Add the sherry and scallops and immediately remove the pan from the heat.

3 Preheat the oven to 350 degrees F.

4 Remove the potatoes from the heat and drain. Add 1 tablespoon of the remaining butter. Mince the remaining $\frac{1}{2}$ garlic clove and add it to the potatoes. Mash the potatoes until they are fluffy, adding the final 1 tablespoon of butter and a few tablespoons of milk if the potatoes are too dry.

5 Pour the scallop mixture into an 8-inch deep-dish pie plate. Spoon the potatoes on top of the scallops and spread it evenly with a fork. Use the tines of the fork to draw furrows into the top. Bake until the tips of the furrows are golden brown, 20 minutes. Garnish with the parsley and serve.

SERVES 6 TO 8

BAY SCALLOPS WITH
GINGER AND JALAPEÑO

I could just as easily name this recipe "Editors' Scallops," because it seems to have made the circles of book editors around the country. Book editors tend to be busy folks and when they cook, it needs to be fast and furious, but they're also demanding. So a recipe has to be full of flavor. This one fits those priorities. It can be a weeknight meal or part of a brunch on the weekend. Either way, the assertive flavors in this recipe will please you.

SERVES 4

1 Warm the oil in a nonstick skillet over medium heat. Add the garlic and jalapeño and cook to soften them, 30 seconds. Add the onions, ginger, and salt and pepper to taste.

2 Add the scallops, increase the heat to high, and cook, stirring constantly, until the scallops are just cooked through, 2 to 3 minutes. Remove them to a warmed platter and garnish with the parsley.

3 tablespoons peanut oil

3 garlic cloves, minced

1½ teaspoons minced jalapeño pepper

4 green onions, trimmed to 3 inches, split

3 thin slices fresh peeled ginger

Kosher salt

Freshly ground black pepper

1½ pounds bay scallops, side muscles removed

2 tablespoons chopped fresh Italian parsley

BROILED STUFFED SCALLOPS

If you want to impress somebody, this is a good dish to do it with. The flavors are unbelievable. The basil, mint, and garlic all infuse the scallops from the inside. It also looks impressive, with that horizontal band of the stuffing. Now the real plus side: This dish could not be easier to prepare. If you're feeling extremely flush and have access to black truffles, you could also slide a slice of truffle in the middle, but that's almost overkill.

¼ cup fresh basil leaves

¼ cup fresh mint leaves

1 garlic clove

½ teaspoon kosher salt

¼ teaspoon freshly ground black pepper

3 tablespoons olive oil, divided

20 extra large dry-pack sea scallops (1½ to 2 pounds), side muscles removed

1   Finely mince the basil, mint, and garlic together. Add the salt and pepper and, using the back of your knife, press down on the mixture and scrape it back and forth over your cutting board to make a paste. Place it in a bowl and add 1 tablespoon of the oil, stirring to combine.

2   Preheat your broiler. Set an oven rack as close as possible to the heat source. Line the bottom of a broiling pan with aluminum foil. Replace the slotted top and place it in the preheating oven.

3   Into each scallop, make a deep horizontal cut, taking care not to cut completely through the scallop. Stuff each scallop with about ½ teaspoon of the herb mixture.

4   Take the remaining 2 tablespoons of oil and baste both sides of the scallops. Place them on the hot broiling rack and broil for 2 to 4 minutes per side, until they are golden and slightly firm to the touch. Take care not to overcook them. Remove, and divide the scallops among 4 plates. Serve immediately.

SERVES 4

LOBSTER

Can you imagine a time when lobsters were thought of as poor man's food? A century and a half ago, that was a lobster's place in the world. What a change from today's culinary standards!

For me, a boiled lobster is a thing of beauty. It's simple, and needs little other than melted butter. However, lobster can be prepared in many other ways that you might love. Either whole lobster or tails are wonderful grilled. They can be baked or broiled, steamed, or the meat sautéed. It's all in the taste of the beholder.

For this book, whole American lobsters, the ones in the tanks, spiny lobster tails, and cooked lobster meat are our heroes. Many of the recipes call for cooked lobster meat, and you can get there a couple of ways. Obviously, cook the lobster yourself and pick the meat. I will sometimes cook spiny lobster tails and pick the meat. There are more and better sources now for frozen cooked lobster meat than ever before. I use the cooked meat frequently, especially if the price is fair. Most 1½- to 2-pound lobsters will yield about 3¾ to 4 ounces of meat. Check the price of the whole lobster against the price of the meat, plus your time and trouble factors, to make the correct decision. Since many markets will steam lobsters for you, that becomes a factor as well.

The best time to buy whole lobster for exceptional quality versus price is October, November, and December. The worst is January, February, and March. Any other time is okay. Lobsters are sorted by size. "Chickens" are 1 pounders. "Quarters" run about 1¼ pounds, and "halves" are 1½ pounds. "Selects" are 1½ to 2½ pounds. Larger ones are "jumbos." "Culls," which have a claw missing or are very small, are usually good bargains when you're not serving lobsters whole. I tend to buy halves, one per person for a whole-lobster dinner.

Lobster tails are usually from the spiny lobster, a warm-water beast with no claws. Most tails are frozen and I find them pretty good. Like other frozen shellfish buying, watch for ice crystals, which could indicate mishandling.

& CRAYFISH

CAN IT GET ANY BETTER?

Buy whole lobsters alive and kicking. Buy them from a market that does a good business in lobster so that the turnover is greater. The longer the lobster is in the tank, the more meat tissue it loses. I couldn't care less about male or female, but to tell them apart, the last set of swimmers on the underside of the tail, next to the body, is the clue. Soft and feathery is the female. Once you are home with your live lobster, keep it covered with damp newspapers in the coldest part of your refrigerator and cook it within a day or two. Cold slows them down slightly. Please don't stick your hand down in a bag of lobsters. I have and it hurts when they get a hold of you. Allow the lobster to fall out of its bag from the store and onto the counter. Come in from behind and grab the lobster right behind its claws.

There are three general ways of killing the beast. If you are boiling or steaming, you will dispatch the lobster in those ways. When you are going to grill, roast, or stuff lobsters, plunge a knife into the crosshairs on the lobster's head and cut it in half. Some fish markets will do this for you. In this chapter, we will slightly boil the lobster to kill it before moving to the next step.

And what about a south Louisiana party without crayfish?

Crayfish—pronounced like crawfish—cause strong sentiments among their lovers. We only think of the craze they create on the Gulf Coast, but Scandinavia uses crayfish feeds for big parties. Crayfish are most always farmed and sold alive; as whole cooked; or as cooked tail meat, usually frozen, which is the only edible part. When buying live crayfish, make sure they are moving. Plan on about 1 pound a person (there are 15 to 20 per pound), either live or whole cooked. For cooked tail meat, 6 ounces per person usually works. Crayfish are best boiled. The tail meat can be used in recipes with additional elements.

To get to the meat from a whole crayfish, twist off the head, and suck out the head juices, if desired. Then pinch the tail shell and peel the shell from the meat.

Never pass up an invitation to a Gulf Coast crayfish feed.

BOILED LOBSTER

Boiling probably is the simplest method to cook a lobster, but it's also one of the tastiest. Just be sure and use a pot large enough to hold sufficient water to submerge the lobster completely. Get the water to a good rolling boil before the lobster meets its fate. This is also a good technique for partially cooking a lobster when you want to use the meat in a different recipe. Just shorten the cooking time by at least half. I have found that 1½-pound lobsters are the perfect size for most people but also have the sweetest flavor. Big lobsters look impressive but don't have the same intensity of taste that a small one does. Placing the live lobster in the freezer for 10 minutes before cooking makes them a little easier to handle.

SERVES 4

1 Fill a large stockpot about half full of water. Add the salt and bring it to a boil.

2 When the water has come to a rolling boil, plunge the lobsters headfirst into the pot. Clamp the lid on tightly and return the water to a boil over high heat. Reduce the heat to medium and cook the lobsters for 12 to 18 minutes (hard-shell lobsters will take the longer time), until the shells turn bright red and the tail meat is firm and opaque when checked.

3 Lift the lobsters out of the water with tongs and drain them in a colander. Place them underside up on a work surface and, grasping firmly, split the tails lengthwise with a large knife. Drain off the excess liquid. Serve them with melted butter and lemon wedges.

2 to 3 tablespoons kosher salt

4 live lobsters, about 1½ pounds each

8 tablespoons (1 stick) unsalted butter, melted

Lemon wedges for garnish

CRAYFISH BOIL

Crayfish, or mudbugs as they are referred to, were strictly a Louisiana thing for many years. Aquaculture has solved the problem of supply when it comes to live crayfish. Crayfish are farmed throughout the Southern states, and live crayfish are routinely sent throughout the country. If you're in Denver, for instance, you may have to preorder crayfish, but you will be able to get them. So if you've got a Mardi Gras party in mind, let the good times roll.

3 medium onions, halved

3 garlic bulbs, halved crosswise

4 celery ribs, quartered

10 bay leaves

1 cup kosher salt

¾ cup cayenne pepper

¼ cup whole allspice

2 tablespoons mustard seeds

1 tablespoon coriander seeds

1 tablespoon dill seeds

1 tablespoon red pepper flakes

1 tablespoon black peppercorns

1 teaspoon whole cloves

5 pounds whole crayfish

1   Bring 1 ½ gallons of water to a boil in a 20-quart stockpot or canning pot over high heat. Add the onions, garlic, celery, bay leaves, salt, cayenne, allspice, mustard seeds, coriander seeds, dill seeds, pepper flakes, peppercorns, and cloves. Return the pot to a full boil. Reduce the heat to medium, and cook, uncovered, 30 minutes.

2   Add the crayfish. Bring the pot to a full boil over high heat, and cook for 5 minutes.

3   Remove the pot from the heat and let it stand for 30 minutes. Letting the crayfish steep for a while will make them spicier, if you desire.

4   Drain the crayfish. Serve them on large platters or newspaper.

SERVES 8 TO 10, DEPENDING ON IF THEY ARE FROM NEW ORLEANS OR NOT

GRILL-ROASTED LOBSTER

Perfectly cooked lobster on the grill is a sensual experience. I like parboiling the lobsters for a few minutes to start with. Other methods of grilling lobster create problems. I feel a little better about the way the lobster has met his demise. You can actually parboil your lobster an hour or two before you plan to grill. The biggest key to successfully cooking lobster on the grill is not being shy about basting with butter while it's cooking. You do not want the lobster to dry out. Overcooked lobster is a total waste of your time and money.

SERVES 4

1   Light a charcoal fire or preheat your gas grill on high. Oil your grill's cooking grate.

2   Bring a large pot, such as a canning pot, of water to a boil. Add about 1 tablespoon of salt. Plunge the lobsters into the boiling water, cover the pot, and return it to a boil. Cook for 5 to 8 minutes, or until the lobsters are beginning to turn bright red. We are trying to cook them about halfway. Drain. Place each lobster top shell up on a cutting board and, using a large chef's knife, starting at the crosshairs on the back of the head, split it lengthwise through the shell. Remove the intestinal vein. The lobsters can be prepared 1 hour ahead. Cool, cover, and refrigerate.

3   Brush the cut side of the lobsters with melted butter. Place them, cut side down, on the grill, and cook until the tail meat is firm, about 5 minutes.

4   Brush them liberally with melted butter as they grill, and season with salt and pepper. Pass additional melted butter and lemon wedges at the table.

4 live lobsters, about 1$\frac{1}{4}$ to 1$\frac{1}{2}$ pounds each

Kosher or gray sea salt

8 tablespoons (1 stick) unsalted butter, melted, plus additional for serving

Freshly ground black pepper

Lemon wedges for garnish

210

LOBSTER AND CORN FRITTERS

Corn just seems to go with so many varieties of shellfish. Here we pair it with lobster meat in a light batter that's quickly fried. It's like eating tasty puffs of air. How you get to the lobster meat is up to you. You can buy whole lobsters and boil them; lobster meat that has been frozen has become more available and works well in this recipe.

1 cup cooked corn kernels

1$\frac{1}{2}$ cups all-purpose flour

$\frac{1}{2}$ cup cornmeal

1 tablespoon baking powder

$\frac{1}{2}$ teaspoon freshly ground black pepper

$\frac{1}{4}$ teaspoon kosher salt

1$\frac{1}{4}$ cups whole milk

2 tablespoons ($\frac{1}{4}$ stick) unsalted butter, melted

1$\frac{1}{2}$ cups small chunk lobster meat (8 to 10 ounces)

3 large eggs, lightly beaten

Vegetable, peanut, or canola oil for frying

1 Pulse the corn in a food processor until it is partially pureed.

2 In a large bowl, mix the flour, cornmeal, baking powder, pepper, and salt. Add the milk, $\frac{1}{4}$ cup water, and the butter and mix until smooth. Stir in the lobster, eggs, and corn and combine. Allow the batter to rest at room temperature for at least 1 hour before cooking the fritters.

3 In a deep saucepan or pot or electric fry pan, heat 2 to 3 inches of oil until it registers 350 degrees F on a deep-fat thermometer. Dip a tablespoon into the oil to keep the batter from sticking to it. Drop the batter by heaping tablespoons into the hot oil, turning after a minute or 2, until it is golden brown all over. Drain the fritters on paper towels. Serve immediately.

SERVES 4 TO 6

LOBSTER COBB SALAD

Cobb salad is one of those historic dishes. Rather than try and reinvent the wheel, I just thought the addition of lobster meat made for an interesting twist. You could substitute shrimp, scallops, crayfish tails, or Dungeness crabmeat for the lobster.

SERVES 4 TO 6

1 To make the vinaigrette: Whisk together the oil, juice, mustard, salt, and pepper in a small bowl.

2 To make the salad: Cut the avocados in half, remove the seeds, and peel. Cut them into $^3/_4$-inch dice and toss them with the juice.

3 Put the lobster and tomatoes in a bowl. Sprinkle them with the salt and pepper and toss them with enough vinaigrette to moisten. Add the avocados, bacon, cheese, and arugula and toss again. Serve at room temperature.

VINAIGRETTE

5 tablespoons extra-virgin olive oil

$^1/_4$ cup fresh lemon juice (about 2 lemons)

$1^1/_2$ tablespoons Dijon mustard

$^3/_4$ teaspoon kosher salt

$^1/_2$ teaspoon freshly ground black pepper

SALAD

2 ripe avocados

2 tablespoons fresh lemon juice (about 1 lemon)

$1^1/_2$ pounds cooked lobster meat, cut in $^3/_4$-inch chunks

1 pint cherry tomatoes, cut in half or quarters

$1^1/_2$ teaspoons kosher salt

$^1/_2$ teaspoon freshly ground black pepper

8 ounces lean bacon, cooked and crumbled

$^3/_4$ cup crumbled English Stilton or other blue cheese (about 3 ounces)

1 bunch baby arugula or spinach

LOBSTER MARTINIS WITH CITRUS SALSA

All things in a martini glass must be sophisticated, right? This recipe certainly is. The citrus forms a sweet acidic base in which to enjoy lobster. Does it have to be served in a martini glass? Heck, no. But you might feel a little special if it is.

4 whole lobsters, cooked and cleaned (about 12 ounces meat)

3 oranges, peeled and sectioned

1 large grapefruit, peeled and sectioned

¹⁄₂ cup diced red bell pepper (about 1 small)

¹⁄₂ cup thinly sliced red onion

¹⁄₃ cup cider vinegar

¹⁄₃ cup fresh orange juice

¹⁄₄ cup chopped fresh cilantro

¹⁄₄ cup canola oil

1 jalapeño pepper, seeded and minced

¹⁄₄ to ¹⁄₂ teaspoon kosher salt

¹⁄₂ teaspoon freshly ground black pepper

Lettuce leaves for serving

1 Remove the shell from the lobsters, keeping the claw meat intact. Thinly slice the tail meat. Combine the orange and grapefruit sections, bell pepper, onion, vinegar, juice, cilantro, oil, jalapeño, salt, and jalapeño pepper in a large bowl. Add the lobster, tossing until everything is well blended.

2 Spoon the mixture into lettuce-lined martini glasses or small bowls.

SERVES 8

LOBSTER NEWBURG

Legend tells us that Newburg sauce, which is a mixture of cream, butter, eggs, cognac, and black pepper, had its beginning at the old Delmonico's Restaurant in New York City. The tale goes that Ben Wenberg, a fruit importer and a Delmonico's regular, introduced their chef to this lobster dish that he had eaten in his travels. The original name was Lobster Wenberg. Mr. Wenberg at some point got drunk at Delmonico's, started a fight, and was banned from the premises, and lost the honor of having a dish named for him. Thus, Lobster Newburg instead of Lobster Wenberg.

SERVES 4

1 Cut the lobster into small chunks. Melt the butter in a saucepan and, when hot, add the lobster. Cook for 3 to 4 minutes, or until the lobster is firm and tinged with brown.

2 Mix the sherry and brandy together and pour them over the lobster. Remove the pan from the stove. Carefully light the alcohol with a match and flambé the lobster (keep a saucepan lid nearby in case the flame gets out of hand). Using a slotted spoon, transfer the lobster to a plate and set it aside. Add the cream to the pan and stir to heat.

3 In a bowl lightly beat the egg yolks with a fork. Add 2 table-spoons of the warm cream mixture to the yolks and mix to adjust the temperature. Add the tempered eggs to the sauce in the pan, whisking, then put the pan back over low heat and continue to whisk for 3 to 4 minutes to thicken the sauce. The mixture must not boil or the eggs will scramble. Strain the sauce into another pan just in case the eggs have tried to cook. Stir in the lobster and any juices on the plate. Season with a pinch of cayenne. Serve immediately over boiled rice or puff pastry shells.

8 ounces half-cooked lobster meat, from 2 lobsters boiled for 5 minutes (see page 208)

4 tablespoons (½ stick) unsalted butter

1 tablespoon sherry

1 tablespoon brandy

1 cup heavy cream

2 large egg yolks

Pinch of cayenne pepper

4 servings cooked rice or 4 frozen puff pastry shells, baked

LOBSTER POT STICKERS

Pot stickers are just fun things to eat and fun to make. This recipe takes an Asian method and combines it with Caribbean flavors. If you're serving this to company, let them come in the kitchen and enjoy the fun of putting the pot stickers together.

1½ cups tamari or light soy sauce

½ cup cream of coconut (in the bar mix aisle of your market), divided

1 garlic clove, finely chopped

½ teaspoon Asian sesame oil

1 pound cooked lobster meat, coarsely chopped

4 green onions, finely chopped, divided

1 teaspoon grated peeled fresh ginger

1 pound Asian dumpling (*gyoza*) wrappers (about 16)

1 large egg, lightly beaten

1 tablespoon canola oil

2 tablespoons (¼ stick) unsalted butter, divided

1 teaspoon chili-garlic sauce (optional)

SERVES 8

1 Whisk the tamari, ¼ cup of the cream of coconut, the garlic, and sesame oil together in a small bowl. Set aside.

2 Combine the lobster meat, all but 1 tablespoon of the green onions, the remaining ¼ cup of cream of coconut, and the ginger in a medium bowl. Place a dollop of the lobster filling in the center of each dumpling wrapper. Brush the edges with the beaten egg, fold the wrapper into a triangle, and pinch to seal.

3 Heat the oil and butter together in a medium skillet over medium heat. Add the dumplings when the butter stops foaming, and cook for about 2 minutes on each side, until they are golden brown. Remove the dumplings to a platter.

4 Deglaze the pan with the reserved tamari mixture, scraping up any bits on the bottom of the pan. Cook for 3 to 4 minutes, until the liquid is slightly reduced. Add the remaining 1 tablespoon of green onion. Add the chili sauce for additional heat, if desired. Pour the dipping sauce into a sauce bowl.

5 Serve the dumplings with the dipping sauce.

LOBSTER PASTA WITH
HERBED CREAM SAUCE

I like using lobster with pasta. It surprises many people, but it's a delightful surprise. Lobster was just meant for cream sauces. It really enjoys being bathed in this herb-infused cream. You can substitute shrimp or any good lump crabmeat in this recipe. And by the way, this is a good special occasion kind of recipe and is great to impress a crowd because it really stretches the lobster.

SERVES 10

1 Bring a very large pot of salted water to a boil. Add the lobsters. Boil until they are cooked through, about 12 minutes. Cook in batches, if necessary. Transfer the lobsters to a large rimmed baking sheet. Remove the meat from the tails and claws; place the meat in a medium bowl. Remove any roe from the bodies and place it in a small bowl. Cover and chill the meat and roe. Remove the tomalley (the green stuff) from the bodies and discard. Reserve the bodies and shells.

2 Heat the oil in a large heavy-bottomed pot over high heat. Add the reserved lobster bodies and shells. Cook for 3 minutes. Reduce the heat to low. Add the tomato paste and stir; continue cooking for 3 minutes. Stir in the tomatoes, wine, vinegar, garlic, parsley, tarragon, and thyme. Add the cream, and bring it to just under a boil for 2 minutes. Reduce the heat to medium-low, and simmer until the lobster flavor infuses the cream, stirring occasionally, about 20 minutes. Strain the sauce into a large bowl, pressing on the solids to extract as much liquid as possible. Discard the contents of the strainer. The lobster and sauce can be prepared 1 day ahead. Cover separately and refrigerate.

Three 1³/₄-pound live lobsters

3 tablespoons olive oil

¹/₄ cup tomato paste

¹/₂ cup chopped plum tomatoes (about 2 large)

¹/₃ cup dry white wine

2 tablespoons white wine vinegar

2 garlic cloves, sliced

2 teaspoons chopped fresh Italian parsley

1 teaspoon chopped fresh tarragon

1 teaspoon chopped fresh thyme

6 cups heavy cream

1¹/₂ pounds fettuccine

Kosher salt

Freshly ground black pepper

3   Transfer the sauce to a large heavy-bottomed saucepan. Cut the lobster meat into bite-size pieces and coarsely crumble any roe. Add them to the sauce. Gently rewarm over low heat, stirring occasionally.

4   Meanwhile, cook the pasta in a large pot of boiling salted water until it is just tender, stirring occasionally. Drain, and return the pasta to the pot. Add the sauce; toss it over medium-high heat until the sauce coats the pasta, about 4 minutes. Season with salt and pepper to taste. Transfer everything to a large shallow bowl and serve.

LOBSTER THERMIDOR

Lobster Thermidor may be a culinary cliché, but don't tell anybody. This dish is one of my favorite lobster preparations. It may be out of style with the culinary elite, but it's not out of style when it comes to incredible palate pleasure. Give this classic a try with someone close, one of those "just the two of you" moments.

SERVES 2

1 Using a sharp knife, cut the lobster in half lengthwise through the shell. Lift the meat from the tail and body. Remove the cream-colored vein and soft body matter and discard. Cut the meat into ¾-inch pieces, cover, and refrigerate. Wash the meat and shell halves, then drain and pat them dry.

2 Preheat the broiler.

3 Heat 4 tablespoons of the butter in a frying pan over medium heat, add the onions, and stir for 2 minutes. Stir in the flour and mustard and cook for 1 minute, or until it is pale and foaming. Remove the pan from the heat and gradually stir in the milk and wine. Return the pan to the heat and stir constantly until the mixture boils and thickens. Reduce the heat and simmer for 1 minute. Stir in the cream, parsley, and lobster meat, then season to taste with salt and pepper. Stir over low heat until the lobster is heated through.

4 Spoon the mixture into the lobster shells, sprinkle them with the cheese, and dot them with the remaining 2 tablespoons of butter. Place the lobster under the broiler and cook for 2 minutes, or until the cheese is lightly browned. Serve them with some lemon wedges.

1 cooked lobster

6 tablespoons (¾ stick) unsalted butter, divided

4 green onions, finely chopped

1½ tablespoons all-purpose flour

½ teaspoon dry mustard

1 cup milk

2 tablespoons white wine or sherry

¼ cup heavy cream

1 tablespoon chopped fresh parsley

Kosher salt

Freshly ground black pepper

½ cup grated Gruyère cheese (about 2 ounces)

Lemon wedges for garnish

TRADITIONAL LOBSTER ROLL

Thanks to Rebecca Charles, chef-owner of the Pearl Oyster Bar in New York City, lobster rolls have become one of my favorite foods. Up until she opened her doors, lobster salad and lobster rolls were long on the seasonings, short on lobster flavor. Not so with hers. Jasper White, chef-owner of the Summer Shack in Massachusetts and the nation's leading expert on lobster, also makes an exceptional roll. I've borrowed a little from both for this recipe. As with any good lobster roll, one of the keys is taking the time to griddle the bun in butter. Make more of the lobster concoction than you think you'll need because there never seems to be enough of this delicious salad.

1 pound cooked lobster meat, roughly chopped into ¹/₂- and ³/₄-inch pieces

¹/₄ cup very finely chopped celery

¹/₄ cup Hellmann's mayonnaise (the preferred mayonnaise for rolls)

2 tablespoons peeled, seeded, and finely chopped cucumber

Juice of ¹/₂ lemon

¹/₈ teaspoon kosher salt

Freshly ground black pepper

1 tablespoon unsalted butter

2 top-loading hot dog buns (Pepperidge Farm makes them)

Chopped fresh chives for garnish

1 In a large bowl, combine the lobster meat, celery, mayonnaise, cucumber, juice, salt, and pepper to taste. Fold together. Cover the salad and refrigerate it until ready to serve. It will last for up to 2 days, and is better after 1 day.

2 Place a small skillet over low to medium heat, and melt the butter. Place the buns on their sides in the butter. Turn the buns a couple of times so that both sides soak up an equal amount of butter and brown evenly. Remove the buns from the pan and place them on a large plate.

3 Fill the toasted buns with the lobster salad. Sprinkle them with chives and serve.

SERVES 2

OVER-THE-TOP LOBSTER POTPIE

I hated potpies as a kid. You know the kind I'm talking about—frozen in those little aluminum pans. Then I found out how good a potpie can be when you make it from scratch. To gild the lily, why not lobster potpie? Lobster potpies have long been a staple in Maine, where lobsters are always cheap and available. This pie is truly delicious, with a great crust and warm filling, almost like a mother's hug. On a cold winter night, this may be the best thing you can put in your mouth. I like to bake these in individual ramekins, about 4 inches deep and 5 inches wide, but a large round baking dish will work also.

SERVES 4

1   To make the pastry: Combine the flour, butter, and salt in a food processor. Pulse until the mixture has the consistency of coarse sand. Add the water while pulsing until the mixture just comes together.

2   Remove the dough from the food processor and, on a lightly floured work surface, using your hands shape it into a disk about ½ inch thick. Wrap it with plastic wrap and refrigerate for at least 1 hour before rolling it out.

3   To make the pie: In a large sauté pan or pot, melt 2 table-spoons of the butter over medium heat. Add the mushrooms and salt. Cook them slowly until they are lightly browned, about 4 minutes. Place them in a bowl and set aside.

4   Add the remaining 1 tablespoon of butter to the pan and cook the shallots over low heat until they are soft, about 4 minutes. Return the mushrooms to the pan and deglaze the pan with the sherry, scraping up any bits on the bottom of the pan.

PASTRY DOUGH

2 cups soft wheat all-purpose flour, such as White Lily, plus extra for rolling

1 cup (2 sticks) chilled unsalted butter, cut into tiny pieces

½ teaspoon kosher salt

¼ cup ice water

PIE

3 tablespoons unsalted butter, divided

16 shiitake mushrooms, stemmed (julienne any caps that are larger than a quarter)

12 baby portabello mushrooms, quartered

$^1/_8$ teaspoon kosher salt

$^1/_2$ cup chopped shallots (about 4)

1 cup amontillado sherry

$5^1/_2$ cups heavy cream

3 boiling potatoes, cut into $^1/_4$-inch pieces (about 1 cup)

1 cup fresh shelled or frozen green peas, thawed

2 or 3 carrots, cut into $^1/_4$-inch pieces (about $^1/_2$ cup)

Freshly ground black pepper

Meat from four 1-pound lobsters, cooked and removed from the shell, or 12 ounces cooked lobster

1 large egg

1 tablespoon water

5   Raise the heat to medium and reduce the sherry to roughly $^1/_4$ cup, about 5 minutes. Add the cream, potatoes, peas, and carrots. Reduce the sauce by one-third, 5 to 6 minutes. Season to taste with salt and pepper. Remove the pan from the heat and reserve.

6   Preheat the oven to 425 degrees F.

7   On a lightly floured work surface, roll out the pastry dough and, using a ramekin as a guide, cut the pastry around the dish with a paring knife, making it $^1/_4$ inch wider than the dish to allow for the dough to shrink. Repeat for a total of 4 rounds.

8   On a cookie sheet, lay out the pastry rounds and make steam vents in the tops so that the steam can escape when they are on top of the potpies during cooking. Bake the crusts for 8 minutes, or until they are slightly browned.

9   Put a generous amount of lobster meat into each ramekin. Ladle the vegetables and sauce on top, leaving about $^1/_2$ inch from the top. Top each one with a pastry round. Mix the egg and water together in a small dish. Brush the pastry with the egg wash and finish the potpies in the oven for 5 minutes, or until the filling starts to bubble through the steam vents. Serve immediately.

QUICK CRAYFISH ÉTOUFFÉE

Étouffée simply means "smothered," and it is a classic Louisiana Cajun dish. Making an étouffée the traditional way can be time-consuming (see facing page). I've tried to shorten the process a bit here and still maintain the authentic flavor. Forgive my use of canned soup, but sometimes nothing else works.

SERVES 6

1 Prepare the rice according to the package directions.

2 Melt the butter in a large cast-iron skillet or Dutch oven over medium heat. Add the onion, bell pepper, celery, and garlic, and cook, stirring constantly, for 8 minutes, or until the vegetables are tender.

3 In a bowl, stir together the soup and broth. Add them to the vegetable mixture. Stir in the seasoning and cayenne.

4 Cook over medium-low heat 10 minutes, stirring occasionally. Stir in the crayfish, green onions, and parsley; cook 3 minutes, or until everything is hot. Serve the étouffée over the rice.

1 cup long-grain rice

4 tablespoons (½ stick) unsalted butter

1 large onion, chopped

1 green bell pepper, chopped (about 1 cup)

4 celery ribs, chopped (about 1 cup)

4 garlic cloves, minced

One 10¾-ounce can cream of mushroom soup

One 14½-ounce can low-sodium chicken broth

1 tablespoon Cajun seasoning

⅛ to ¼ teaspoon cayenne pepper

1 pound frozen cooked peeled crayfish tails, thawed and well drained

¼ cup chopped green onions

3 tablespoons chopped fresh parsley

TRADITIONAL CRAYFISH ÉTOUFFÉE

OK, for you traditionalists, here's the real deal. What makes this dish worthwhile is taking the time to make a dark roux. This process can't be rushed. You'll have to stay with it constantly because the roux will quickly go from pale brown to burnt in the blink of an eye. You will be rewarded, however, with a dish that has tremendous depth of flavor. Remember, one of the vital questions a suitor would ask a potential wife-to-be in southern Louisiana was quite simply, "Can your mama make a roux?"

1 cup long-grain rice

10 tablespoons (1¼ sticks) unsalted butter, divided

1 pound frozen cooked peeled crayfish tails, thawed and well drained

1 cup chopped onion (about 1 medium)

1 cup chopped green bell pepper (about 1)

½ cup chopped celery ribs (about 3)

4 garlic cloves, minced

6 tablespoons all-purpose flour

2¾ cups low-sodium chicken broth

¼ cup chopped green onions

2 tablespoons chopped fresh parsley

1 tablespoon Cajun seasoning

¼ teaspoon kosher salt

¼ teaspoon cayenne pepper

1 Prepare the rice according to the package directions.

SERVES 6

2 Melt 4 tablespoons of the butter in a large Dutch oven over medium-high heat; add the crayfish and cook 5 minutes, or until it is thoroughly heated. Remove the crayfish from the pot, and keep warm.

3 Add the onion, bell pepper, and celery to the Dutch oven. Cook over medium-high heat 8 minutes, or until tender. Add the garlic, and cook 1 minute. Remove the vegetables, and keep warm.

4 Melt the remaining 6 tablespoons of butter in the Dutch oven over medium heat. Add the flour and cook, stirring constantly, 20 minutes, or until it is caramel colored. Reduce the heat to low, and gradually stir in the broth, green onions, parsley, seasoning, salt, and cayenne. Cook over medium heat 10 minutes, or until slightly thickened. Stir in the vegetables and crayfish and cook 5 minutes to heat through. Serve the étouffée with the hot rice.

WARM LOBSTER TACOS WITH
YELLOW TOMATO SALSA

If Chef Dean Fearing took his lobster taco off the menu at The Mansion on Turtle Creek in Dallas, Texas, he might be drug from the kitchen and shot. By his own admission, it's the most popular appetizer they've ever served. This is a very simplified version to make at home, but it stays true to his sense of creativity.

SERVES 6

1   To make the salsa: In a food processor, pulse the tomatoes 3 or 4 times, or until they are well chopped. Do not puree them, though. In a large bowl, combine the tomatoes and their juices with the shallot, jalapeños, cilantro, vinegar, garlic, lime juice, and salt to taste, and mix well.

2   Cover and refrigerate the salsa for at least 2 hours or until very cold.

3   Preheat the oven to 300 degrees F.

4   To prepare the tacos: Fill a large stockpot with lightly salted water and bring it to a boil over high heat. Add the lobsters and cook for about 8 minutes, or until they are just cooked through. Drain and let the lobsters cool slightly.

5   Wrap the tortillas tightly in foil and place them in the oven for about 15 minutes, or until they are heated through. Keep them warm until ready to use.

6   Remove the meat from the lobster tails, being careful not to tear it apart. Cut the meat into medium-size chunks.

YELLOW TOMATO SALSA

2 pints yellow cherry tomatoes or 1 pound yellow tomatoes, stemmed

3 tablespoons finely minced shallot (about 1 large)

2 jalapeño peppers, seeded and minced

2 tablespoons finely minced fresh cilantro

1 tablespoon white wine vinegar

1 large garlic clove, finely minced

2 teaspoons fresh lime juice (about 1/2 lime)

Kosher salt

TACOS

**Four 1¹/₂-pound lobsters, or
12 ounces cooked lobster meat**

Six 7-inch flour tortillas

3 tablespoons corn oil

**1 cup grated jalapeño Jack cheese
(about 4 ounces)**

1 cup shredded spinach leaves

7   Heat the oil in a medium sauté pan over medium heat and cook the lobster meat until it is just heated through.

8   Spoon equal portions of warm lobster medallions into the center of each warm tortilla. Sprinkle them with equal portions of cheese and spinach. Roll the tortillas into cylinders and place each one on a warm serving plate with the seam facing the bottom. Surround each taco with Yellow Tomato Salsa, and serve.

CRAYFISH CANTONESE

Believe it or not, this recipe originated in the Mississippi Delta, where farming crayfish is a growing industry. Martha Foose, executive chef for Viking Range Corporation, shared this very authentic-flavored recipe with me that she has pulled from the growing Chinese population in the Delta.

SERVES 6 TO 8

1   Rinse the crayfish in cold water and drain.

2   Heat a wok over high heat. Add the salt, and cook until it is lightly browned. Add 1 tablespoon of the oil. When the oil is hot, add half of the garlic. Cook until the garlic is just aromatic. Add the crayfish and stir-fry, adding 1 teaspoon of the sherry. When the crayfish is hot, after 1 to 2 minutes, remove and set it aside.

3   Add the remaining 2 tablespoons of oil to the wok. Heat until it shimmers, then add the remaining garlic and the pork. Stir-fry a few minutes, until the pork cooks through, stirring in the remaining 1 teaspoon of sherry, the soy sauce, black bean paste, and pepper. Add the broth, and bring the mixture to a boil.

4   Stir the cornstarch and water together, then stir them into the sauce to thicken it, using more cornstarch if necessary. Stir in the eggs, letting them cook for 30 seconds, then fold them with a spoon. Repeat, cooking until the eggs are set. Return the crayfish to the wok, stirring the mixture slightly. Sprinkle it with the sesame oil and green onions. Serve over steamed rice.

1 pound shelled crayfish tails

1/2 teaspoon kosher salt

3 tablespoons canola oil, divided

4 garlic cloves, chopped, divided

2 teaspoons dry sherry, divided

8 ounces fresh pork, ground or chopped

2 teaspoons soy sauce

1 teaspoon black bean paste

Dash of freshly ground black pepper

2 cups low-sodium chicken broth

1 tablespoon cornstarch

2 tablespoons water

2 large eggs, lightly beaten

1/2 teaspoon sesame oil

2 to 3 green onions, sliced

Steamed rice for serving

LOBSTER SOUP WITH
MANGO AND AVOCADO

For a south-of-the-border twist on lobster soup, give this dish a try. It is a cold soup, which can be extremely refreshing during the hot summer months. This recipe is a stand-out for a special luncheon or brunch.

6 mangoes (about 5 pounds), peeled, seeded, and cut into $^1\!/_2$-inch cubes, divided

3 cups vegetable broth

1 pickled jalapeño pepper

2 tablespoons sugar

2$^1\!/_2$ teaspoons kosher salt, divided

2 avocados, peeled, seeded, and cut into $^1\!/_2$-inch cubes

1 tablespoon fresh lemon juice

1 pound cooked lobster meat

$^1\!/_2$ cup thinly sliced red onion

$^1\!/_2$ cup chopped fresh cilantro

$^1\!/_2$ cup chopped fresh Italian parsley

1 In a blender or food processor, puree half of the mangoes with the broth, jalapeño, sugar, and 1$^1\!/_2$ teaspoons of the salt. Transfer the mixture to a large bowl and set it aside.

2 Place the avocados in a small bowl with the lemon juice and remaining 1 teaspoon of salt and stir to coat. Stir the avocado mixture into the mango puree. Stir in the remaining chopped mango, the lobster, onion, and cilantro.

3 Refrigerate until ready to serve.

4 To serve, ladle the soup into bowls and top with the parsley.

SERVES 6 TO 8

DECADENT LOBSTER CAKES

Crab cakes, fish cakes, salmon cakes—why not lobster cakes? The folks in Maine might think that we've lost our minds for gussying up lobster this way. But I think you'll find this a fabulous lobster adventure.

SERVES 4 TO 6

1 Preheat the oven to 350 degrees F. Place a rack over a baking sheet.

2 In a large bowl, combine the lobster, mayonnaise, onion, celery, bell pepper, ¼ cup of the breadcrumbs, the egg, capers, parsley, zest, seasoning, Worcestershire sauce, mustard, and hot pepper sauce. Toss the mixture lightly—your hand will work well.

3 Place the remaining ¾ cup of breadcrumbs in a shallow dish. Form the lobster mixture into twelve 2-inch patties using a biscuit cutter as a mold. Carefully dredge the patties in the crumbs. Place the patties in a single layer on a platter, cover with plastic wrap, and refrigerate for at least 30 minutes to 1 hour to chill and set up.

1 pound shredded cooked lobster meat

1 cup good-quality mayonnaise

½ cup finely diced onion (about 1 small)

½ cup finely diced celery (about 3 ribs)

½ cup finely diced red bell pepper (about 1 small)

1 cup plain breadcrumbs, divided

1 large egg, lightly beaten

1 tablespoon drained tiny capers

1 tablespoon chopped fresh Italian parsley

2 teaspoons finely grated orange zest

2 teaspoons Chesapeake Bay–style seasoning

1 teaspoon Worcestershire sauce

½ teaspoon dry mustard

Dash of hot pepper sauce

2 tablespoons canola or peanut oil, plus more if needed

1 tablespoon unsalted butter, plus more if needed

Almost Like Joe's Mustard Sauce (page 325)

Any Region Tartar Sauce (page 322) or your favorite tartar sauce

4 Heat the oil and butter in a nonstick skillet over medium heat. Cook the cakes in batches, until they are golden brown, about 3 minutes per side, adding more butter and oil as necessary. Drain the cakes well on paper towels, place them on the rack, then slide them into the oven while you cook the rest of the cakes. Serve them immediately, and pass Almost Like Joe's Mustard Sauce or Any Region Tartar Sauce at the table.

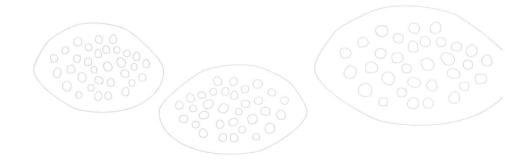

Native Americans thought clams had worth. They used the shells for money. That's where the "how many clams" phrase comes from in our slang today. Of course they also ate the clam meat. When I was growing up in North Carolina, the clams were usually large and went into the soup pot or were fried. They seemed almost secondary to other seafood. When I came to New York, I had a clam awakening.

Their names used to confuse me. Basically there are two types of clams: hard shell and soft shell. Hard shells carry names like littlenecks (the best of the bunch), cherrystones, the large quahogs, and mahogany. Soft shells go by steamers, long necks, and fryers.

Soft shells actually have hard shells; the difference is that the shells are thinner. The giveaway to soft shells is the little neck of meat that sticks out from the shell. There are Pacific clams such as the Manila, the butter clam of the Pacific Northwest, and what about those funny-looking razor clams?

How do you decide what's best? By size. The smaller the clam, the better it is to eat raw or steamed, like a littleneck. The middle-size ones, cherrystones for instance, can do everything a smaller clam can do, plus they are better for stuffing and frying. The larger ones are for chowder and some frying, or chopped for salads. I love cockles, which are not clams but have a similar taste. They are especially good in pasta dishes, and they look great, shell and all.

Buying clams is simple. Hard shells should be tightly shut, except for quahogs, but they should shut quickly when tapped. Soft shells can't fully close when taken from the water. Pull on the little neck that sticks out from the shell. It should have a little give. Soft shells are more perishable than hard shells.

CLAMS &

There is much hoopla about purging clams. Hard shells usually don't contain enough sand to bother. Soft shells do need a purge. It is simple to do. Make a solution with 1 cup of salt, 1 tablespoon of cornmeal, and 3 quarts of water. Dissolve the salt, and let the clams soak in that mixture overnight in the refrigerator.

Opening a clam is much like opening an oyster, but the muscle structure makes it easier. Take a clam, hold it in a towel, then use a clam knife or a table knife (no sharp knives) and wiggle it between the shells. Rock it slightly back and forth while sliding the knife toward the hinge. Slide the knife more along the top shell, to keep the clam whole. Work through the hinge and pop it open. The only time you need to do this is to eat them raw; any other recipe can be started by steaming them open. Some fishmongers will open them for you.

Frozen whole clams can be pretty good, especially on pasta or pizza. Be sure to look for the tag label on a bag of clams, or ask to see it for loose ones. This will tell you where the clams are from and when they were harvested.

COUSINS

BUTTERY GARLICKY
STEAMED CLAMS

Clams and garlic and butter are a trinity to behold. There's something about the earthy, chewy texture of clams that's complemented by the sharp taste of garlic and then smoothed by butter. If you can't find littlenecks, cherrystones or even cockles will work.

SERVES 4

1 Put 1 stick of the butter in a pan large enough to hold all the clams, and place it over medium heat until the butter foams. Add the onions, garlic, and pepper flakes. Cook for 3 minutes, stirring occasionally, being careful not to let the garlic burn.

2 Add the vermouth, raise the heat to high, and cover the pan. Bring the mixture to a rapid boil and add the clams. Cover and continue to cook at a rapid boil, stirring occasionally. When the clams begin to open, which can be in as little time as 1 minute, remove the open ones to a platter as quickly as possible in order not to overcook them, but all the clams should be done in 7 to 8 minutes. Discard any that do not open in that time. Reserve the pan juices, including the garlic, onions, and pepper flakes.

3 Divide the clams equally among 4 bowls or place them on a large platter. Add the parsley and remaining 1 tablespoon of butter to the pan juices. Stir well to combine. Spoon the mixture over the clams. Serve immediately.

9 tablespoons (1 stick plus 1 tablespoon) unsalted butter

2 cups finely sliced green onions, white and green parts

¼ cup very finely minced garlic

2 teaspoons red pepper flakes

1 cup dry vermouth

48 littleneck clams, scrubbed and rinsed

1 cup roughly chopped fresh Italian parsley

DARNED GOOD CLAM CHOWDER

My dream was to come up with a New England–style clam chowder that was creamy, fragrant, and unladened with flour. This is the best attempt that I've come up with so far, and from what I'm told, this is some of the best clam chowder most people have ever eaten. It's not totally true to its New England roots, since I've used bacon instead of salt pork, but I believe the smokiness of the bacon makes a huge difference.

8 pounds cherrystone clams, scrubbed and rinsed, or three 10-ounce cans whole baby clams

4 ounces double-smoked bacon, diced

1 teaspoon peanut oil or canola oil

1 large onion, chopped (about 1 cup)

2 large white potatoes, peeled and cut into ½-inch dice (about 2 cups)

1 cup reserved strained clam cooking liquid or bottled clam juice

3 cups heavy cream

Kosher salt

Freshly ground black pepper

Chopped fresh chives for garnish

SERVES 4

1 To steam the clams, choose a pot large enough to hold them all (a canning pot is good) with a tight-fitting lid, and add 2 cups of water. Place the pot over high heat and bring it to a boil. Add the clams and cover. Steam the clams for about 5 minutes, depending on their size. Remove clams as soon as they open, so keep an eye on them. Reserve the broth for the chowder and discard any clams that don't open.

2 Add the bacon and oil to a 5-quart soup pot over medium heat. Add the onion and cook until it is soft, 5 to 8 minutes. Add the potatoes, and cook for 3 minutes. Reduce the heat to low. Pour in the clam broth, stir, and simmer for 25 minutes. Stir in the cream and continue simmering for another 20 minutes. Check the potatoes. If they are still firm, cook another 5 minutes, or until the potatoes are tender. Add the clams and cook for 5 more minutes. Add salt and pepper to taste.

3 Ladle the chowder into warmed bowls and garnish with the chives.

CLAM FRITTERS

Clam fritters are one of those must-have nibbles from the Carolinas to Maine. Like a light hush puppy filled with luscious clam meat, they are addictive and you'll eat more than you think you have. Stand close to the fryer and get them while they're hot.

SERVES 4 TO 6

1 In a large bowl, mix the flour, cornmeal, baking powder, pepper, and salt together. Whisk in the milk, water, clam juice, and butter. Add the clams and eggs and combine thoroughly. Allow the batter to rest at least 1 hour at room temperature before using it.

2 Preheat the oven to 200 degrees F. Place a rack over a baking sheet.

3 In a deep saucepan or pot or electric fryer, heat 3 inches of oil until it registers 350 degrees F on a deep-fat thermometer. Dip a tablespoon into the oil to keep the batter from sticking to it. Drop a spoonful of batter at a time into the hot oil, but don't add too many at once. Turn the fritters after a minute or two, until they are golden brown all over. Drain them on paper towels. Place the fritters on the rack and put them in the oven to keep warm. Continue with the remaining batter.

4 Serve the fritters immediately with tartar sauce.

1½ cups all-purpose flour

½ cup cornmeal

1 tablespoon baking powder

½ teaspoon freshly ground black pepper

¼ teaspoon kosher salt

1 cup whole milk

¼ cup water

¼ cup bottled clam juice

2 tablespoons (¼ stick) unsalted butter, melted

1½ cups chopped clams, freshly steamed or canned

3 large eggs, lightly beaten

Peanut or canola oil for frying

Any Region Tartar Sauce (page 322) or your favorite tartar sauce

CLAMS CASINO

There are probably as many variations on Clams Casino as there are Italian grand-mothers. What would any Italian festival be without some vendor serving up huge plates of Clams Casino? This version has a bit of heat because of the jalapeño pepper, but it still stays close to the classic.

6 strips bacon

1 small green bell pepper, finely chopped (about ²/₃ cup)

1 small red bell pepper, finely chopped (about ²/₃ cup)

½ cup chopped yellow onion

1 jalapeño pepper, seeded and finely chopped

2 tablespoons (¼ stick) unsalted butter, at room temperature

1 tablespoon Worcestershire sauce

Juice of ½ lemon

24 small cherrystone or large littleneck clams, scrubbed and rinsed, on the half shell

1 Preheat the broiler.

2 Cut each bacon strip into 4 pieces and lightly fry them in a pan over medium heat. You don't want the bacon to become crispy, since it is going to go into the broiler later. Remove and set the half-cooked bacon aside on paper towels.

3 In a medium bowl, add the peppers, onion, and jalapeño to the softened butter, stirring to combine. Add the Worcester-shire sauce and lemon juice.

4 Add a generous pinch of the vegetable-butter mixture to each of the clams on the half shell. Place a piece of the cooked bacon on top of the mixture on each clam.

5 Place the clams on a rimmed baking sheet under the broiler and cook until the vegetables begin to wilt and the bacon is almost crisp, about 3 minutes. Serve them immediately, 6 per person.

SERVES 4

FRIED CLAMS

I don't know anybody who doesn't like fried clams when you start with the real thing, coat them with a perfect breading, and quickly fry them. It will make you forget about all those frozen fried clams that you've eaten in your life. They're great by themselves, but if you take a notion, grill some hot dog buns in butter, add a few tablespoons of tartar sauce, and fill the buns with fried clams, and you'll have a great New England treat.

SERVES 6

1 Combine the egg with the milk in a large bowl. Add the clams, making sure all the clams are covered.

2 Preheat the oven to 200 degrees F. Place a rack over a baking sheet.

3 In a shallow bowl, mix the breadcrumbs, salt, and cayenne together.

4 Pour oil to a depth of 3 inches into a Dutch oven, and place it over medium-high heat. An electric fryer also works. When the oil registers 365 degrees F on a deep-fat thermometer, lift a batch of clams out of the bowl with a slotted spoon, allowing any excess milk to drop off. Place the clams in the crumbs and toss to coat them well, then drop them into the hot oil and fry them until they are golden brown, 2 to 3 minutes. Drain them on paper towels, place them on the rack, and into the oven to keep warm. Continue cooking until all the clams are fried. Serve immediately with tartar sauce, if desired.

1 large egg, lightly beaten

1 cup whole milk

2 pounds freshly shucked frying clams (such as cherrystones or quahogs that have been cut in half)

1 cup fine, dry, unseasoned breadcrumbs

1 teaspoon kosher salt

$1/4$ teaspoon cayenne pepper

Peanut oil for frying

Any Region Tartar Sauce (page 322) or your favorite tartar sauce (optional)

LINGUINE WITH RED CLAM SAUCE

This is a great recipe to convince your kids that they really like clams. You probably want to take the clams out of their shell if you have kids at the table, but once they find out how much they enjoy clams, present this pasta—shells and all.

1 tablespoon olive oil

1 cup chopped onion

6 anchovy fillets, drained and chopped

3 large garlic cloves, chopped

1/2 teaspoon red pepper flakes

Two 14 1/2-ounce cans Italian-style diced tomatoes

3 tablespoons tomato paste

1/2 cup dry red wine

36 cockles or small clams, scrubbed and rinsed

1 pound linguine, freshly cooked

Kosher salt

Freshly ground black pepper

Chopped fresh parsley for garnish

Freshly grated Parmesan cheese for serving (optional)

1 Heat the oil in a large heavy-bottomed pot over medium-high heat. Add the onion and sauté for 3 minutes. Add the anchovies, garlic, and pepper flakes; sauté 2 minutes. In a bowl, mix the tomatoes and tomato paste with the wine. Add them to the pot, and bring the sauce to a boil. Reduce the heat to medium-low and simmer until the sauce is slightly thickened, stirring occasionally, about 5 minutes. Increase the heat and add the cockles. Cover and cook for 2 to 3 minutes, or until they have opened. Discard any that do not.

2 Add the linguine to the sauce and toss to coat. Season with salt and pepper to taste. Transfer everything to a large bowl. Sprinkle it with parsley. Serve the pasta with Parmesan, if desired.

SERVES 4 TO 6

CLAM MISO SOUP

You know that great miso soup that you enjoy so much as part of a Japanese meal? It's pretty simple to make at home, and when you add some clams to it, it gets downright delicious. All the Japanese products here can be found in gourmet and specialty food stores, usually saving you a trip to the Japanese market. Either way, this soup is worth the extra effort. Freeze any leftover dashi to use the next time you make this soup. Or add some small diced bits of tofu, a little green onion, and some sesame oil to the dashi for a wonderful first course soup before any Asian meal.

SERVES 6

1 To make the dashi: Using a small sharp knife, cut several slits all over the kelp. Place the kelp and the water in a large saucepan. Bring them just barely to a simmer over medium-low heat. Remove the kelp and discard.

2 Add the bonito shavings to the saucepan, and barely simmer until the bonito shavings sink, about 3 minutes.

3 Pour the broth through a fine-mesh strainer; discard the bonito shavings. This can be prepared up to 3 days ahead; cover and refrigerate. Makes about 5 cups.

4 To prepare the clams: Finely grate the ginger. Place it in a fine-mesh strainer over a small bowl and press down to extract 1 teaspoon of juice. Set aside.

5 Combine 2 cups of the Dashi and the water in a large pot over medium-high heat. Add the clams. Cover and simmer until the clams open, about 10 minutes, discarding any clams that do not open. Remove the pot from the heat. Remove the clams to a bowl.

DASHI

One 12-inch piece dried kelp (kombu)

6 cups water

³/₄ cup (loosely packed) dried bonito shavings (*katsuo bushi*)

CLAMS

One 3-inch piece fresh ginger

2 cups water

18 littleneck clams, scrubbed and rinsed

3 tablespoons sweet white miso or yellow miso

1 tablespoon red miso

¹/₂ teaspoon tamari or light soy sauce

2 green onions, chopped

6 Remove the meat from the shells, and reserve. In a bowl, strain the broth and any accumulated clam juices through a fine-mesh strainer lined with a coffee filter or a triple thickness of cheesecloth. Return the clam broth to the pot.

7 Mix the 2 misos in a bowl. Bring the broth to a simmer, and add $\frac{1}{4}$ cup broth to the mixed miso, stirring until the miso dissolves. Whisk the miso mixture into the broth. Add the reserved ginger juice and tamari. Keep it warm over medium-low heat (do not boil).

8 Place 3 pieces of clam meat in each of 6 bowls. Ladle the miso broth over, and sprinkle the soup with the onions.

SPICY ASIAN-STYLE NOODLES WITH CLAMS

The Asian countries all seem to have a love affair with foods from the sea. Maybe it's because their basic seasonings blend so well with almost all fish and shellfish. Clams are no exception. This is a straightforward pasta presentation with a few Asian touches. If you want to get really fancy and can find razor clams, use them.

SERVES 4

1 Cook the pasta in a large pot of boiling water until just tender but still firm to the bite, stirring occasionally. Drain well.

2 Return the pasta to the same pot; toss with 1 tablespoon of the oil. Put the pasta in a large bowl and cover to keep it warm.

3 Heat the remaining 1 tablespoon of oil in the same pot over medium-high heat. Add the bell pepper, onion, garlic, ginger, and pepper flakes. Cook until the bell pepper begins to soften, about 2 minutes. Add the water, vinegar, and tamari, and bring them to a boil. Add the clams. Cover the pot and cook until the clams have opened, 8 to 10 minutes, discarding any clams that do not open.

4 Spoon the clams and sauce over the pasta. Sprinkle it with the cilantro and serve.

8 ounces vermicelli pasta

2 tablespoons Asian sesame oil, divided

1 red bell pepper, thinly sliced

1/2 cup chopped onion

6 garlic cloves, chopped

1 tablespoon chopped peeled fresh ginger

1 teaspoon red pepper flakes

1 cup water

3 tablespoons rice vinegar

2 tablespoons tamari or light soy sauce

24 clams, scrubbed and rinsed

1/2 cup chopped fresh cilantro

STEAMED CLAMS WITH SPICY SAUSAGE AND TOMATOES

A taste of Spain or maybe Portugal headlines this recipe. The sausage and tomatoes would be good right by themselves. Adding the clams and the liquid they release puts you on a Mediterranean beach with a glass of cold white wine.

2 tablespoons olive oil

1 pound chorizo sausage, casings removed

$\frac{1}{2}$ cup chopped shallots

4 garlic cloves, chopped

$\frac{1}{4}$ teaspoon red pepper flakes

One 14$\frac{1}{2}$-ounce can diced tomatoes with their juice

1 cup bottled clam juice

2 tablespoons balsamic vinegar

36 littleneck clams, scrubbed and rinsed

$\frac{1}{2}$ cup chopped fresh basil

$\frac{1}{4}$ cup chopped fresh cilantro

Crusty bread for serving

1   Heat the oil in a large heavy-bottomed pot over medium-high heat. Add the sausage, and cook until it is almost cooked through, breaking up any large chunks with a fork, about 10 minutes.

2   Add the shallots, garlic, and pepper flakes. Cook until the sausage is fully cooked, about 5 minutes.

3   Mix in the tomatoes and their juice, clam juice, and vinegar. Bring them to a boil. Add the clams, cover, and cook until the clams open, about 8 minutes, discarding any clams that do not open. Stir in the basil and cilantro. Divide the mixture among 6 bowls and serve with crusty bread.

SERVES 6 AS A FIRST COURSE

WHITE CLAM PIZZA

I'll go out of my way for good pizza. That includes jumping on Metro North and heading
for New Haven and Pepe's Pizza Parlor across from Yale University. I have no idea what
a regular pizza tastes like there. I've never ordered anything but their clam pizza. Garlic,
garlic, and more garlic coupled with freshly chopped clams on a perfect pizza crust create one of those one-of-a-kind food memories. This recipe is sort of a quick variation of
what they do, but if you've got a great homemade pizza dough recipe, please use it
in place of the premade pizza shell. I like to use a variety of cheeses on this pizza and
have found that the store-bought six-cheese blend is perfect. No, it ain't Pepe's, but it's
a whole lot closer to home.

SERVES 4

1 Preheat the oven to 450 degrees F.

2 Dust the bottom of the prepared crust or rolled dough with
cornmeal.

3 Divide the clams evenly over the crust. Top them evenly
with the garlic, bacon, cheese, and oregano. Drizzle the
surface with hot pepper sauce and oil. Bake for 15 minutes,
or until the crust is golden brown and the cheese is bubbly.

One 10-inch premade thin crust
pizza shell, or 1 recipe homemade
pizza dough

2 tablespoons cornmeal

1 cup chopped clams, drained

3 garlic cloves, minced

1 strip bacon, cooked and crumbled

1 cup Italian 6-cheese blend
(about 4 ounces)

1 tablespoon crushed fresh
oregano or 1 teaspoon dried

1/2 teaspoon hot pepper sauce

Olive oil for drizzling

CONEY ISLAND CLAM CHOWDER

I had Manhattan-style clam chowder long before I had New England–style clam chowder. So I'm not opposed to some tomato in my chowder. What surprised me was that the best red clam chowder I've ever tasted was in San Francisco at the Tadich Grill. It was so good I can't even put it in the same class with most Manhattan clam chowders. This recipe is fairly close, and I think it's better than anything you'll ever get in New York.

6 to 7 tablespoons bacon fat

2 cups chopped yellow onions (about 2)

1 green bell pepper, chopped (about 1)

Leaves from 2 or 3 celery stalks, chopped

1 tablespoon minced fresh parsley

1 garlic clove, minced

$\frac{1}{8}$ teaspoon curry powder

One 14$\frac{1}{2}$-ounce can whole tomatoes, juice reserved

5 cups bottled clam juice

$\frac{1}{2}$ cup dry white wine

3 cups water, or as needed

2 potatoes, unpeeled and cut in $\frac{1}{4}$-inch dice

2 cups chopped clams, drained

Kosher salt

Freshly ground black pepper

Pinch of cayenne pepper

1   Place a large soup pot over medium heat. Add the bacon fat. When the fat is shimmering, add the onions, bell pepper, celery leaves, parsley, garlic, and curry powder and sauté for 3 to 5 minutes, until everything is golden. Add the tomatoes and break them up with the back of a spoon. Mix well. Measure out the juice from the tomatoes, clam juice, wine, and enough water to make 8 cups of liquid. Add this to the pot, along with the potatoes.

2   Increase the heat to medium-high, bring the liquid to a gentle boil, then decrease the heat to low and simmer, covered, for 1 $\frac{1}{2}$ hours, until the vegetables are tender and the soup is fragrant and flavorful. Add the clams, salt and pepper to taste, and the cayenne. Simmer for 10 minutes, until warmed through. Ladle the soup into warmed soup bowls, and serve it at once.

SERVES 6

DEVILED CLAMS

I guess deviled clams are eaten everywhere, but I always like to think of them as the Carolinas' version of Clams Casino. "Deviling" anything was the hot food trend along the Mid-Atlantic in the '30s. Think about a time when we thought green bell pepper was exotic! The key to these deviled clams is the lack of filler, allowing the individual ingredients to stand up and be counted. They're just as good when baked in ramekins as they are when baked in the shell.

SERVES 6 TO 8

1 Place the clams and liquid in a medium saucepan and simmer for 5 minutes.

2 Melt the butter in a small saucepan over medium heat. Add the celery, onion, bell pepper, celery leaves, mustard, and pepper, and cook until the vegetables are tender, about 5 minutes. Add them to the clam mixture. Stir in the cracker crumbs and mix well.

3 Preheat the oven to 350 degrees F.

4 Butter the clam shells or individual 4-ounce ramekins and place them on a bed of rock salt in a rimmed baking pan. Fill them evenly with the clam mixture. Bake for 20 minutes, or until the crumbs are nicely browned and the mixture is bubbly. Serve hot.

2 cups finely chopped clams, shells reserved if possible

$\frac{1}{2}$ cup clam liquid or bottled clam juice

4 tablespoons ($\frac{1}{2}$ stick) unsalted butter

$\frac{1}{4}$ cup chopped celery

2 tablespoons minced onion

2 tablespoons minced green bell pepper

2 tablespoons minced celery leaves

$\frac{1}{2}$ teaspoon prepared yellow mustard

$\frac{1}{8}$ teaspoon freshly ground black pepper

$\frac{3}{4}$ cup fresh cracker crumbs

Butter at room temperature for greasing

Rock salt for baking

DOWN EAST CLAM CHOWDER

Down East here refers to the Bogues Bank area of coastal North Carolina, but Rhode Island has a similar version. Both believe in eating their clam chowder unadorned with milk, cream, or tomatoes. So, if you just want the pure taste of clams, pull out your soup pot and fix a batch of this chowder.

4 ounces salt pork, sliced

1 quart coarsely chopped chowder clams

1 quart water

½ cup chopped onion

1 teaspoon kosher salt

¼ teaspoon freshly ground black pepper

4 cups diced potatoes

Oyster crackers for serving

1 In a large soup pot, cook the salt pork over medium heat until it is crisp. Remove the pork and discard it, reserving the renderings. Add the clams, water, onion, salt, and pepper to the pan. Bring them to a boil.

2 Reduce the heat and cook slowly until the clams are tender, about 1 hour. Add the potatoes and cook until they are tender, about 20 minutes more. Ladle the soup into bowls and serve it with oyster crackers.

NOTE: Some folks thicken their chowder with 1 cup of instant mashed potato flakes in addition to the other ingredients. Add them right at the end and cook until the soup is thickened.

SERVES 10 TO 12

LINGUINE WITH WHITE CLAM SAUCE

Every time I make this dish, I think of Art Custer, the late husband of one of the finest food stylists in the business, Delores. In many ways, I owe my food career to Art, who was convinced that everyone should always follow their dreams, at least for three years. This was his dish, and I never passed up an invitation to share it with Delores and Art. You can use canned clams just as easily, but fresh clams make such a difference. Make this meal and think about your dreams.

SERVES 8

1 Bring a large pot of water to a boil. Add the linguine and cook until it is al dente, about 10 minutes. Drain.

2 Meanwhile, heat the oil in a large nonreactive skillet over medium heat. Add the garlic and pepper flakes, and stir until the garlic is soft and slightly golden, 3 to 5 minutes. Add the clams, wine, and juice. Cover and steam until the clams open, about 7 minutes, discarding any that do not open. Shuck the clams, dropping them back into the skillet, or leave them in the shell.

3. Toss the pasta with the clam sauce, and garnish with the parsley. Serve it in bowls, with Italian bread.

1 pound linguine

5 tablespoons extra-virgin olive oil

5 garlic cloves, smashed

About $1/2$ teaspoon red pepper flakes

32 littleneck clams, scrubbed and rinsed

1 cup dry white wine

Juice of $1/4$ lemon

$1/4$ cup chopped fresh Italian parsley

Toasted Italian bread for serving

CLAM DIP

There are probably thousands of variations on shellfish dips, none better than this simple clam dip. You could make this with canned clams, but freshly steamed add another level to this dip. There are also some excellent frozen clam products on the market now that, when thawed, taste pretty darned close to freshly shucked. Use this dip for most any party you can imagine. You'll get raves.

8 ounces cream cheese, at room temperature

2 teaspoons fresh lemon juice

2 teaspoons grated onion

1 teaspoon Worcestershire sauce

1 teaspoon minced fresh parsley

¼ teaspoon kosher salt

⅛ teaspoon hot pepper sauce

1 cup minced cooked clams, liquid reserved (canned minced clams are fine)

Assorted crackers and toasted French bread slices for serving

1 Blend together the cheese, juice, onion, Worcestershire sauce, parsley, salt, and hot pepper sauce in a medium bowl. Add the clams and mix well. Add the reserved liquid until your desired consistency is reached.

2 Chill thoroughly, for at least 2 hours. Serve with assorted crackers and toast.

MAKES ABOUT
2 CUPS

STEAMED MANILA CLAMS WITH DIJON-CAPER SAUCE

Dijon and capers are natural mates. Together with the steaming source and then sauce for clams, they show what a culinary force they can be.

SERVES 4

1 Melt the butter in a large heavy-bottomed nonreactive skillet with a tight-fitting lid over medium heat. Add the garlic and cook, stirring occasionally, until it is soft and just beginning to color, 3 minutes. Increase the heat to medium-high, add the vermouth and herbes de Provence, and bring them to a boil, stirring often, until the liquid has reduced by half, about 5 minutes.

2 Add the clams, cover, and steam until the clams open, 5 to 8 minutes. Discard any shells that do not open. Divide the clams between 4 warm wide soup bowls, leaving the broth in the skillet. Return the skillet to medium-high heat.

3. Add the cream, capers, and mustard to the skillet, stir to combine, and gently boil until the sauce is just thick enough to coat the back of a spoon, 6 to 8 minutes. Season to taste with salt and pepper. Divide the sauce between the bowls of clams.

4 tablespoons (1/2 stick) unsalted butter

10 garlic cloves, thinly sliced

1 cup dry vermouth

2 tablespoons herbes de Provence

48 Manila clams, scrubbed and rinsed

2 cups heavy cream

6 tablespoons drained capers

6 tablespoons Dijon mustard

Kosher salt

Freshly ground black pepper

MUSSELS:

BLACK-LIPPED, GREEN-LIPPED

Almost all mussels are now being farmed, with Prince Edward Island being the key player. However, gathering mussels off the north coast of California is as time honored a tradition as it is on the shores of New England. Mussels may be the biggest joy you find in this book. They are creamy and rich, with great depth to their flavor. Theirs has been a farming success story.

Mussels are always good steamed. They take to many broth-flavoring combinations with ease. Yet, I have found that they can be fried, stuffed, baked, and sauced successfully, leading to much more enjoyment of this bivalve.

Good mussels are simply those with shells that are tightly closed or go that way when tapped. Rarely should cultivated mussels need purging, but wild mussels will benefit from a 30-minute soak in a salt bath ($\frac{1}{2}$ cup salt to 6 cups water). Like all bivalves, they should be scrubbed when you get home, but save the debearding until you are ready to cook. This little tuft of hair sticking out from the mussel is easy to remove by pulling it out with your fingers, but its removal kills the mussel. You may need to have a paper towel in your hand for extra traction if they are slippery. A pair of needle-nose pliers works as well. Mussels store nicely for several days in your refrigerator. Make sure they are getting air. Don't put them in a plastic bag, or they will die.

Ask your fishmonger how many of today's mussels are in a pound. I like to think in terms of a count per person. You also need to judge this by their size. New Zealand green lips are very tasty and large, thus more expensive than black mussels. They can be better for stuffed presentations.

I'm not a raw mussel fan, especially wild mussels. Unless you know the water, they can be dangerous. Farmed mussels are carefully monitored, but I still am cautious about raw ones. Cooked mussels will unlikely make you ill.

Frozen shucked mussels are easier to find these days and are of good quality, especially the green lip variety. Feel free to use them when it's easier than steaming and shucking.

COLD MUSSELS WITH HERB MAYONNAISE

If you've never thought of eating cold mussels, you might be surprised at how good they are. The process is much the same as with other mussel recipes. You steam them to open them and cook the mussels. Then it's just a matter of letting them chill and having a good little sauce to go with them.

SERVES 6 AS A FIRST COURSE

1   Debeard the mussels if necessary. Steam them in the wine in a large covered pot for about 10 minutes, or until they have opened. Discard any unopened mussels and the top shell of each opened mussel. Strain the cooking liquid into a clean saucepan and reduce it until only ¼ cup remains, about 3 minutes. Set aside to cool.

2   Whisk together the mayonnaise, cooled reduced cooking liquid, parsley, and tarragon in a medium bowl and let it sit for 15 minutes to give the flavors time to meld. Add a little bit of the vinegar at a time to taste but don't let the sauce get too thin.

3   Place the mussels in their half shells on a platter coated with rock salt and spoon a little of the sauce over each mussel.

2 pounds mussels (3 dozen), scrubbed and rinsed

1 cup dry white wine

½ cup good-quality mayonnaise

1 tablespoon finely chopped fresh parsley

1 tablespoon finely chopped fresh tarragon

1 tablespoon white wine vinegar (balsamic is a good choice)

Rock salt for serving

CURRIED MUSSELS

Indian seasonings, especially curry, seem to bring out special nuances from mussels. Be sure to serve some type of bread to soak up all the wonderful juices that you will be creating.

2 tablespoons (¹⁄₄ stick) unsalted butter, divided

¹⁄₂ small yellow onion, minced

2 stalks celery, minced

1 Granny Smith apple, peeled, cored, and finely chopped

1 tablespoon Madras curry powder

Pinch of saffron threads

One 14-ounce can coconut milk

¹⁄₃ cup heavy cream

Kosher salt

Freshly ground black pepper

36 black mussels (about 2 pounds), scrubbed and rinsed

2 teaspoons cider vinegar

2 tablespoons minced fresh cilantro

1   Melt 1 tablespoon of the butter in a medium saucepan over medium-low heat. Add the onion and celery and cook until they are very tender, about 15 minutes. Add the apple and the remaining 1 tablespoon of butter, and cook 2 or 3 minutes more, until the apple begins to soften. Add the curry powder and cook 2 minutes more. Add the saffron and stir in the coconut milk and cream. Increase the heat to medium and simmer 3 minutes. Season with salt and pepper to taste.

2   Debeard the mussels if necessary. Add them to the pan and cook, covered, until they open, 4 to 6 minutes. Discard any mussels that do not open.

3   Ladle the mussels into 4 individual bowls and pour the sauce over each portion. Drizzle about ¹⁄₂ teaspoon of vinegar over the mussels, sprinkle them with the cilantro, and serve immediately with the rest of the vinegar alongside.

SERVES 4

EUROPEAN-STYLE STEAMED MUSSELS

Mussels meunière is one of those dishes that you order at a restaurant and love, but think that it must be too difficult to make at home. Nothing could be further from the truth. It is simple, quick, delicious, and elegant enough for company, but it eats too good to just save it for special occasions.

SERVES 8 AS A
FIRST COURSE
OR 4 AS A MAIN
COURSE

1   Debeard the mussels if necessary.

2   Combine the wine, clam juice, shallots, bay leaves, and thyme in an 8-quart pot and bring them to a simmer over medium heat. Let them simmer about 5 minutes.

3   Add the mussels. Cover the pot and turn the heat to high.

4   As the steam builds up, cut your heat back to medium. After about 7 minutes, remove the lid and check to see if the mussels are opening. If not, replace the lid and continue to cook. Then, if it appears that all of the mussels have opened, scoop them out of the pot and divide them equally among serving bowls. Discard any unopened mussels. Return the pot with its steaming liquid to low heat and whisk in the butter, a tablespoon or 2 at a time. Stir in the parsley and then ladle the buttered broth equally over the servings of mussels. Serve immediately.

48 mussels (2 to 3 pounds), scrubbed and rinsed

1 cup dry white wine (such as vermouth)

1 cup bottled clam juice or clam broth

4 shallots, finely chopped

2 bay leaves

½ teaspoon dried thyme or 2 fresh sprigs

6 tablespoons (¾ stick) unsalted butter

4 tablespoons chopped fresh parsley

FRIED MUSSELS

Everything that comes out of the ocean at some point has to be tried fried, and mussels are no exception. My first thought of frying mussels probably generated a frown. But after experimenting, I was pleasantly surprised at how good this bivalve can be when treated to a bath of hot oil.

36 mussels (about 2 pounds), scrubbed and rinsed

1½ cups water, divided

½ cup all-purpose flour

Peanut oil for frying

Kosher salt

1 bunch curly parsley, large stems removed, rinsed and thoroughly dried

Tartar sauce of mayonnaise for serving

1 Debeard the mussels if necessary.

2 Prepare a batter by slowly whisking 1 cup of the water into the flour in a small bowl. Strain this mixture into another bowl, cover, and let it rest.

3 Meanwhile, in a covered pot large enough to hold the opened mussels, steam them in the remaining ½ cup of water for 5 to 10 minutes, until they open. Discard any unopened mussels and save the liquid for another recipe.

4 Heat the oil in a high-sided pan or electric fryer until it registers 350 degrees F on a deep-fat thermometer. Remove the mussels from their shells, dip them in the batter, and gently drop them one by one into the hot oil. Fry the mussels for about 1 minute, take them out with a slotted spoon, and drain them on paper towels. Take care when frying the mussels, as they like to spatter.

5 Arrange the hot mussels on a plate and sprinkle them with salt. For a fun garnish, throw the sprigs of parsley into the hot oil and fry them for about 5 seconds and then spread them over the mussels. Serve with tartar sauce or just plain mayonnaise.

SERVES 6 AS A
FIRST COURSE

ITALIAN-STYLE STEAMED MUSSELS WITH GARLIC AND TOMATOES

Many people like the classic method of steaming mussels as they do in Belgium, with wine and herbs. Here is a fun change of pace, in which you add garlic and tomatoes into the mix. This is a great start to an Italian feast. Not much else other than some pasta is needed.

SERVES 4

1   Debeard the mussels if necessary.

2   Heat the oil and garlic over medium heat in a 4- to 5-quart saucepan for about 3 minutes, but do not brown the garlic. Add the tomatoes and simmer for about 10 minutes, stirring every minute or two, until the mixture starts to thicken.

3   Add the wine and stir. Put the mussels in the saucepan. Cover and steam them for about 10 minutes over medium to high heat, until the mussels open. Discard any unopened mussels. Divide the mussels among 4 bowls. Stir to combine and ladle it over the mussels. Sprinkle the mussels with pepper and the parsley. Serve immediately.

48 mussels (3 to 4 pounds), scrubbed and rinsed

¼ cup olive oil

2 garlic cloves, roughly chopped

3 tomatoes, peeled, seeded, and chopped, or 1½ cups drained chopped canned tomatoes

½ cup dry white wine

Freshly ground black pepper

3 tablespoons finely chopped fresh parsley

JOSEPH'S PORTUGUESE-STYLE STEAMED MUSSELS

Even though my good friend Joseph Therasa has been in the United States for twenty-plus years, he has maintained his coastal Portuguese roots when it comes to food. This is a change of pace with mussels that's well worth trying. The spice from the chorizo sausage perks up the mussels. Try to find Portuguese chorizo if possible.

48 mussels (3 to 4 pounds), scrubbed and rinsed

4 tablespoons extra-virgin olive oil

3 bay leaves

1 medium onion, cut into ¼-inch dice

1 small red bell pepper, cut into ¼-inch dice

1 tablespoon finely chopped garlic

2 medium tomatoes, peeled, seeded, and finely chopped

1 cup dry white wine

4 ounces chorizo sausage, thinly sliced

2 tablespoons chopped fresh Italian parsley

2 tablespoons chopped fresh cilantro

Freshly ground black pepper

1 Debeard the mussels if necessary.

2 In a large 5-quart Dutch oven or soup pot set over medium-high heat, combine the oil and bay leaves. Heat for 1 minute, then add the onion, bell pepper, and garlic. Sauté the vegetables until tender, about 5 minutes. Add the tomatoes, wine, and sausage. Simmer for 5 minutes.

3 Add the mussels. Cover and steam them until the mussels open, 5 to 10 minutes. Check frequently after the first 5 minutes. Discard any that do not open. Remove the mussels to serving bowls. Return the pot to medium heat, and add the parsley, cilantro, and pepper to taste. Cook 1 minute. Spoon the sauce over the mussels, and serve immediately.

SERVES 4

MUSSEL CHOWDER

When you are in the mood for chowder and clams aren't around but the mussels are fresh and glistening, pull this recipe out. Mussel chowder has an elegant and almost mystical taste and feel to it. Mussels themselves are a bit regal, and we get so used to eating them only steamed that to find them in a chowder preparation is a pleasant surprise. This chowder will feed a crowd, but the leftovers reheat nicely for several days. As a matter of fact, it actually improves over a couple of days.

SERVES 6 AS A
FIRST COURSE
OR 8 AS A MAIN
COURSE

1   In a large pot, bring the water to a boil. Debeard the mussels if necessary, then add them to the pot and cover. Reduce the heat to medium, and cook about 8 minutes, or until the mussels open.

2   Remove the mussels to a large bowl and discard any that do not open. Reserve 16 mussels in their shells and shuck the rest. Strain the mussel broth and reserve it.

3   In a large pot, heat the butter and oil. Add the potatoes, 1 teaspoon salt, and ½ teaspoon pepper. Cook over medium heat, stirring occasionally, for about 5 minutes. Add the leeks and shallot and continue cooking, covered, until the vegetables are soft, about 8 minutes more. Add the garlic and reserved mussel broth along with the wine. Simmer for 10 minutes. Add the shucked mussels and the cream, stir, and let the soup simmer for an additional 5 minutes. Add the reserved mussels in their shells and cook an additional 2 minutes, or until they are heated through. Taste and season with salt and pepper.

4   Ladle the chowder into cups or bowls, making sure each serving contains at least 1 of the mussels in the shell.

3 cups water

48 mussels (3 to 4 pounds), scrubbed and rinsed

6 tablespoons (¾ stick) unsalted butter

3 tablespoons olive oil

3 cups finely diced peeled potatoes (about 2 large)

Kosher salt

Freshly ground black pepper

2 small leeks, well cleaned, white and pale green parts thinly sliced

1 large shallot, finely chopped

3 tablespoons minced garlic

¾ cup dry white wine

½ cup heavy cream

MUSSELS AND SAUSAGE WITH SPAGHETTI

I like the rustic feel of this recipe—good spicy Italian sausage against the mellowness of the mushrooms, all bound together with spaghetti. It's plain and simple and oh so filling. Be sure to have a good bottle of red wine to drink with this pasta.

36 mussels (about 3 pounds), scrubbed and rinsed

1 tablespoon olive oil

1 pound hot Italian sausage, casings removed

2 garlic cloves, chopped

3 or 4 plum tomatoes, roughly chopped

10 leaves fresh basil or parsley

½ cup water

1½ pounds spaghetti

1 Debeard the mussels if necessary.

2 Bring a large pot of water to a boil for the pasta.

3 Heat the oil in another large pot over medium heat. Add the sausage, and using a spoon, crumble it into small pieces. Cook the sausage, stirring occasionally, until no pink remains, about 5 minutes. Add the garlic and cook for 1 minute. Stir in the tomatoes and basil and cook 2 to 3 minutes longer. Pour in the water and the mussels, cover, and increase the heat to high. Put the spaghetti in the pot of boiling water.

4 Cook the mussels until they have opened, about 10 minutes. Discard any that do not open. Drain the pasta, place it in a very large serving bowl, and pour the mussels, with their sauce, on top. Let everyone serve themselves at the table.

SERVES 4 TO 6

NEW ZEALAND GREEN-LIP MUSSELS

New Zealand green-lip mussels show up occasionally in your market. Their shells are beautiful and the flavor is just slightly different from the standard black mussel. They tend to like a bit of saffron, which is included in this recipe. Black mussels will work just as well, but give green lips a try.

SERVES 4

1 Debeard the mussels if necessary.

2 Combine the wine, oil, vinegar, salt, pepper flakes, and saffron in a large saucepan over medium heat. Cook, stirring until the saffron releases its yellow color, about 5 minutes.

3 Add the Pernod and clam juice and bring them to a boil. Pour the mussels into the pot, cover, and reduce the heat to medium. Cook for 8 to 10 minutes, or until the mussels have opened. Discard any that do not open.

4 Divide the mussels among 4 bowls and ladle the broth equally over each.

36 green-lip mussels (about 3 pounds), scrubbed and rinsed

$\frac{1}{2}$ cup dry white wine

2 tablespoons olive oil

1 teaspoon white wine vinegar

$\frac{1}{8}$ teaspoon kosher salt

$\frac{1}{8}$ teaspoon red pepper flakes

Pinch of saffron threads, crushed between your fingers

2 tablespoons Pernod

$\frac{1}{2}$ cup bottled clam juice

STEAMED MUSSELS IN THAI
CURRY SAUCE

Some of the most surprising flavors to incorporate into a mussel dish are the sweet, sour, salty standards of Thai cuisine. This is not a spice-ladened dish in terms of heat, but a wonderful combination of flavors. Use this recipe for a first course followed by pad thai or right by itself. Most all the Thai ingredients can now be found in any good supermarket.

36 mussels (about 3 pounds), scrubbed and rinsed

Two 13¹/₂-ounce cans unsweet-ened coconut milk (3 ½ cups)

1 teaspoon Thai red curry paste

1 cup canned low-sodium chicken broth

¹/₂ cup packed fresh basil leaves

2 stalks lemongrass, trimmed, coarsely chopped (about ¹/₃ cup), or 1 tablespoon freshly grated lemon zest

¹/₄ cup fresh lime juice

2 tablespoons fish sauce (*nam pla*)

3 Kaffir lime leaves or 3 table-spoons fresh lime juice plus 1¹/₂ teaspoons grated lime zest

2 tablespoons peanut oil

4 plum tomatoes, diced (about 1 cup)

¹/₂ cup chopped fresh cilantro

1 Debeard the mussels if necessary.

2 Bring the coconut milk to a boil in a large heavy-bottomed saucepan. Reduce the heat to medium, and whisk in the curry paste. Add the broth, basil, lemongrass, juice, fish sauce, and lime leaves. Simmer uncovered 10 minutes. Strain the sauce into a bowl and reserve.

3 Heat the oil in a large, deep skillet over high heat. Add the mussels. Cook for 2 to 3 minutes. Add the strained curry sauce and tomatoes. Cover, and cook until the mussels open, 6 to 8 minutes. Discard any mussels that do not open. Transfer everything to a large serving bowl. Sprinkle it with the cilantro and serve.

SERVES 6 TO 8 AS A FIRST COURSE

COLD GREEN-LIP MUSSELS IN
BEER AND HERBS

More and more supermarkets have frozen precooked New Zealand green-lip mussels in their freezer cases. They're really a great product. They give you a head start on a lot of mussel-based recipes, and I encourage you to seek them out.

SERVES 4

1 Remove the mussels from their package and thaw them on a rack placed over a baking sheet in the refrigerator overnight.

2 Heat the oil in a medium skillet over medium-high heat. Add the tomatoes, onion, beer, garlic, shallot, pepper, and salt and cook for about 2 minutes. The vegetables should still be a little firm. Stir in the chopped herbs. Remove the mixture to a bowl and refrigerate until cool.

3 Arrange the cold thawed mussels on a serving plate. Stir to recombine the sauce and spoon some over each mussel. Serve cool with lots of napkins.

One 2.2-pound bag frozen precooked New Zealand green-lip mussels

1 tablespoon peanut oil

1 cup peeled, seeded, and diced plum tomatoes (about 4)

½ cup finely diced red onion (about 1 small)

¼ cup dark beer

2 garlic cloves, finely diced

1 teaspoon finely diced shallot

1 teaspoon freshly ground black pepper

¼ teaspoon kosher salt

1 teaspoon finely chopped fresh parsley

2 teaspoons finely chopped fresh chervil

1 teaspoon finely chopped fresh chives

1 teaspoon finely chopped fresh basil

TEMPURA-BATTERED MUSSELS

If I convinced you to try fried mussels earlier in this chapter, then getting you to do a little tempura with them should be easy. Tempura is a veil of light batter encasing the mussels. Since you're already set up for tempura, why not throw a few vegetables into the mix, too? Add a salad with a carrot-ginger dressing, a little raw tuna, and you've got a heck of a Japanese meal.

36 large black or New Zealand green-lip mussels, (about 3 pounds), scrubbed and rinsed

½ cup dry white wine

½ cup bottled clam juice

1 teaspoon minced garlic

1 teaspoon chopped shallot

Pinch of red pepper flakes

2 cups all-purpose flour

1 cup cornstarch

12 ounces seltzer water

1 large egg, lightly beaten

½ teaspoon paprika

Kosher salt

Freshly ground black pepper

Peanut oil for frying

Shredded green leaf lettuce for serving

Ponzu sauce for serving (see page 60; optional)

1   Debeard the mussels if necessary.

2   Combine the wine, clam juice, garlic, shallot, and pepper flakes in a pot with a tight-fitting lid. Bring them to a boil and add the mussels. Cover and steam until the mussel shells have just opened, about 8 minutes. Remove them with a slotted spoon and cool. Discard any unopened mussels.

3   Combine the flour and cornstarch in a large bowl. Whisk in the seltzer, egg, paprika, salt, and pepper. Continue whisking until the batter is smooth, adding more seltzer if the batter seems dry. Remove the cooked mussels from their shells. Coat the mussels with tempura batter.

4   Heat the oil in a large, deep sauté pan over medium-high heat until it registers 375 degrees F on a deep-fat thermometer. Fry the mussels several at a time until they are golden, 3 to 5 minutes per batch. Remove and drain them briefly on paper towels. Serve them over the shredded lettuce with ponzu sauce on the side.

SERVES 4

SPICY TOMATO-MUSSEL SOUP

I was served a spicy mussel soup in Rome that intrigued me. Calling it a soup or *zuppa* is a bit of a stretch because the soup is thick—almost like New England chowder—leaning a bit toward a sauce. My Italian is not very good, so trying to get the recipe was difficult. I scoured some of the top Italian cookbooks trying to find a recipe that fit my taste memory. Taking bits and pieces from several recipes, this soup developed.

SERVES 6

1   To prepare the soup base: Heat the oil in a heavy saucepan over medium heat. Add the garlic and pepper flakes and cook 2 to 3 minutes. Add the tomatoes and clam juice, and season with a bit of salt. Simmer, uncovered, until the base begins to thicken, 10 to 12 minutes. Remove it from the heat and keep warm.

2   To prepare the mussels: Debeard the mussels if necessary. Combine the wine, onion, parsley, and oil in a large covered saucepan. Bring them to a boil over high heat. Boil for 1 to 2 minutes. Add the mussels, cover, and cook until the mussels open, 8 to 10 minutes. Discard any mussels that do not open.

3   Divide the mussels among 6 bowls. Strain the mussel broth and add it to the soup base. Quickly reheat the soup, adding additional clam juice if desired. Ladle soup into each bowl, covering the mussels, and garnish with a grinding of pepper. Serve immediately with crusty Italian bread.

SOUP BASE

6 tablespoons extra-virgin olive oil

12 garlic cloves

¾ teaspoon red pepper flakes

One 28-ounce can crushed tomatoes in puree

½ cup bottled clam juice, plus more if necessary

Kosher salt

MUSSELS

1 cup dry white wine

1 small onion, minced

Handful of fresh Italian parsley stems, tied in a bundle with kitchen twine

3 tablespoons olive oil

48 small mussels (about 3 pounds; try to find very small mussels for this dish), scrubbed and rinsed

Crusty Italian bread for serving

Freshly ground black pepper

PACIFIC NORTHWEST-STYLE MUSSELS

You will like the aromatic combination of a fennel bulb and tomatoes in this steamed-mussel presentation. The resulting broth is light and flavorful, and you'll want to have a spoon to get all of it after the mussels are gone.

48 mussels (about 4 pounds), scrubbed and rinsed

4 tablespoons (½ stick) unsalted butter

1 leek, white part only, well cleaned and thinly sliced

1 cup diced fennel bulb (about 1 medium)

¼ cup finely chopped shallots

2 cups diced seeded tomatoes, or one 14½-ounce can diced tomatoes, drained

½ cup chopped fresh Italian parsley

1 tablespoon finely minced garlic

Kosher salt

Freshly ground black pepper

1 cup dry white wine

1 Debeard the mussels if necessary.

2 Melt the butter in a large heavy-bottomed nonreactive pot over medium heat. Add the leek, fennel, and shallots and cook, stirring, until they are softened, 8 to 10 minutes.

3 Add the tomatoes, parsley, and garlic and cook for an additional 2 minutes. Taste and season with salt and pepper.

4 Add the wine and increase the heat to high. Add the mussels, cover, and cook until the mussels have opened, 8 to 10 minutes. Discard any that do not open. Divide the mussels among 4 shallow bowls. Ladle the broth and vegetables over each, and serve immediately

SERVES 4

After years of popularity in the Italian, Greek, and Asian cultures, squid, especially, has reached into mainstream America and octopus is gaining ground. Squid and octopus both are plentiful and relatively cheap compared to other seafood. For the purposes of this book, we will deal with cleaned squid and octopus. Most are sold that way, but, if not, a good fishmonger should be able to clean them for you.

Squid can be stuffed and baked, grilled, cut into rings and fried, or braised in a stew. Most all squid have been frozen, and they take to freezing without any loss of flavor or texture. Buying frozen squid is a better plan than buying squid that has been thawed for who knows how long. Don't lay squid on paper towels unless you want to eat the paper. It adheres and won't come off. Squid must be cooked very quickly or it becomes very tough. However, squid that is braised for an hour or more becomes extremely tender.

TOO GOOD TENTACLES—

Typically, octopuses sold in retail markets have been cleaned. Most have been frozen, which helps tenderize this tough sea creature. Frank Bertoni, a fisherman in Fort Bragg, California, swears by freezing, as do many others. Even a short, weeklong stint in the freezer helps, and six months in the freezer won't hurt them. The Japanese rub the meat with daikon radish, and the Greeks beat it with broom handles. All work, but the best way is to simmer the octopus for an hour or more in water. From that point, you can cut it in chunks and proceed with any recipe. Try octopus grilled for a real taste surprise.

Those who choose to shy away from squid and octopus will be missing some great tastes.

sQUID & OCTOPUS

FRANK AND JACKY'S MENDOCINO COUNTY OCTOPUS SALAD

Frank and Jacky Bertoni have for decades made their living from the Pacific Ocean. Frank fishes for Dungeness crab and other fish, as well as octopus, and this is their favorite way of serving it. One suggestion that they gave me is to always freeze octopus first because it helps to tenderize the meat.

SERVES 4

1   Bring a large pan of water to a boil and add the octopuses. Simmer them for 8 to 10 minutes, or until they are tender, which you can determine by testing them with the point of a knife.

2   To make the dressing: Mix together in a bowl the oil, juice, garlic, mint, parsley, mustard, and cayenne with some salt and pepper to taste.

3   Drain the octopuses well and put them in a bowl. Pour most of the dressing over the top and let them cool for a few minutes before transferring them to the refrigerator. Chill for at least 3 hours before serving the octopuses on a bed of the salad greens. Drizzle the remaining dressing on top and serve with lemon wedges.

1½ pounds cleaned baby octopuses

DRESSING

½ cup olive oil

2 tablespoons fresh lemon juice

1 garlic clove, thinly sliced

1 tablespoon chopped fresh mint

1 tablespoon chopped fresh parsley

1 teaspoon Dijon mustard

Pinch of cayenne pepper

Kosher salt

Freshly ground black pepper

4 cups mixed salad leaves

Lemon wedges for serving

FRIED CALAMARI WITH
RÉMOULADE SAUCE

Please don't get in between my daughter and a plate of fried calamari. The first time she ordered it in my presence, I was floored. Did she really know it was squid? We like calamari with rémoulade sauce, but you could certainly serve it with a bowl of marinara.

SAUCE

1 cup good-quality mayonnaise

4 teaspoons chopped fresh chives

4 teaspoons finely diced cornichons

1 tablespoon chopped fresh Italian parsley

2 teaspoons chopped fresh tarragon

1 teaspoon drained capers

1 teaspoon finely chopped shallot

¼ cup milk

1 teaspoon fresh lemon juice

Fine sea salt

Freshly ground white pepper

CALAMARI

20 small (4- to 5-inch) cleaned squid, bodies only (about 1½ pounds)

Canola or corn oil for deep-frying

1 cup milk

1 cup all-purpose flour

Fine sea salt

2 lemons, halved

1 To make the sauce: Whisk together the mayonnaise, chives, cornichons, parsley, tarragon, capers, and shallot in a large bowl. Whisk in the milk, juice, and salt and pepper to taste. You can make this sauce a day ahead and refrigerate it, covered.

2 To prepare the calamari: Cut the squid across the bodies into ½-inch rings.

3 Heat the oil in a deep pot or deep fryer until it registers 375 degrees F on a deep-fat thermometer. Dip the calamari in the milk and then toss them in the flour. Shake off the excess flour and carefully drop the calamari into the fryer, in batches if necessary to prevent overcrowding. Fry until they are golden brown, about 1 minute. Do not overcook. Drain the calamari on paper towels.

4 Season them with salt. Pile them on 4 plates and place half a lemon on each plate. Place the sauce in individual serving bowls and serve immediately.

SERVES 4

GREEK-STYLE CALAMARI

The Greeks seem to have a special way with tentacled sea creatures. I've had more memorable squid and octopus dishes prepared by Greek hands than those of any other culture. This recipe certainly captures their love of squid.

SERVES 4 TO 6

1   Preheat the oven to 325 degrees F.

2   To make the stuffing: Mix the rice, pine nuts, currants, onions, parsley, oil, and zest in a bowl. Season well with salt and pepper. Add enough egg to moisten all the ingredients. Fill each calamari tube three-fourths full with the stuffing. Secure the ends with toothpicks. Place the calamari in a single layer in a casserole dish.

3   To make the sauce: Heat the oil in a medium sauté pan, and add the onion and garlic and cook over low heat for 2 minutes, or until the onion is soft. Add the tomatoes, wine, and oregano and bring them to a boil. Reduce the heat, cover, and cook over low heat for 10 minutes, or until the sauce has thickened slightly.

4   Pour the sauce over the calamari, cover, and bake for 20 minutes, or until the calamari is tender. Remove the toothpicks before cutting the calamari into thick slices for serving. Spoon the sauce over the calamari just before serving.

STUFFING

1½ cups cooked rice, chilled

½ cup pine nuts

½ cup dried currants

2 green onions, chopped

2 tablespoons chopped fresh parsley

1 tablespoon olive oil

2 teaspoons grated lemon zest

Kosher salt

Freshly ground black pepper

1 large egg, lightly beaten

2 pounds plus 4 ounces cleaned squid, bodies only, washed and patted dry

SAUCE

1 tablespoon olive oil

1 onion, finely chopped

1 garlic clove, crushed

4 large ripe tomatoes, coarsely chopped

¼ cup good-quality red wine

1 tablespoon chopped fresh oregano

GRILLED OCTOPUS

Grilled octopus is a wonderful treat that many of us don't indulge in. You might want to try grilled octopus in a restaurant first to make sure you like it, but I'm pretty convinced you will. Note that you precook the octopus.

One 2- to 3-pound cleaned octopus

1 bay leaf

½ cup extra-virgin olive oil

¼ cup fresh lemon juice (about 1 lemon)

4 garlic cloves, pressed

1 teaspoon dried oregano

1   Precook the octopus by placing it and the bay leaf in a medium saucepan, covered with water. Over medium heat, bring it to a boil, then lower the heat to simmer, and cook for at least 1 hour, possibly more, until a knife slides to the center of the octopus fairly easily. Drain the octopus in a colander and reserve.

2   Light a charcoal fire or preheat your gas grill on high. Oil your grill's cooking grate.

3   Cut the octopus into large chunks. Whisk the oil, juice, garlic, and oregano together in a small bowl. Toss the octopus pieces in this mixture.

4   When the fire is ready, use tongs to drain the octopus pieces well and place them on the grill. Brush them often with the vinaigrette. Grill until the octopus pieces are slightly crisp on all sides, just a few minutes. Serve immediately.

SERVES 4

MARINATED SQUID AND
OCTOPUS SALAD

No respectable Italian antipasti bar would be without a marinated squid and octopus salad. They really are delicious when combined into one event. You could certainly do this salad with all squid or all octopus, if you desire.

SERVES 6

1 To prepare the seafood: Mix the oil and vinegar together in a bowl. Cut the squid into ¼-inch rounds. Cut the octopus bodies in half lengthwise. Place the squid and octopus in the oil and vinegar mixture, cover, and refrigerate overnight.

2 To make the vinaigrette: In a medium nonreactive bowl, combine the vinegar with the shallot. Add the oil in a steady stream, whisking slowly to emulsify, or use a blender or food processor. Season with salt and pepper to taste. Set the dressing aside.

3 To make the salad: Cook the onion slices in the oil in a large skillet over high heat, until they just begin to color, about 5 minutes. You can also brush them with oil and grill them. They should not become soft. Set them aside.

4 Remove the marinated octopus and squid from the refrigerator. Heat a large cast-iron pan over high heat, and cook the octopus and squid until they are golden brown. Remove them from the heat and season with salt and pepper.

5 To serve, toss the salad greens with enough Sherry Vinaigrette to lightly coat them. Add the mango and onion slices and toss. Distribute the salad equally among 6 salad plates and top with equal portions of the squid and octopus.

SEAFOOD

½ cup extra-virgin olive oil

¼ cup sherry vinegar

12 ounces cleaned squid

1 pound cleaned octopus

SHERRY VINAIGRETTE

⅓ cup good sherry vinegar

2 tablespoons finely chopped shallot

1 cup olive oil

Kosher salt

Freshly ground black pepper

SALAD

½ cup thinly sliced (⅛ inch thick) red onion

2 tablespoons olive oil

6 cups mixed salad greens

1 mango, peeled, pitted, and julienned

VIETNAMESE-STYLE STUFFED SQUID

I particularly like this Vietnamese take on stuffed squid. The Asian flavors are a refreshing change of pace that I think you'll enjoy. Many grocery stores now carry lemongrass in the produce section, or you can find it at an Asian market.

½ ounce cellophane noodles, soaked in cold water for 30 minutes, drained, and squeezed dry

1 pound medium (40-count) shrimp, peeled and deveined

12 large cleaned squid (about 2 ½ pounds)

½ cup finely chopped shallots (about 3)

3 tablespoons Thai fish sauce

3 tablespoons finely chopped fresh cilantro, plus sprigs for garnish

3 tablespoons finely chopped fresh basil

One 3-inch piece of lemongrass, thinly sliced, then finely chopped (optional)

1 large egg, lightly beaten

3 garlic cloves, finely chopped

2 teaspoons sugar

½ teaspoon kosher salt

Freshly ground black pepper

3 tablespoons peanut oil

Fresh mint sprigs for garnish

1 Cut the noodles into approximately ½-inch lengths.

2 Chop the shrimp into coarse dice by hand or in a food processor. Chop the squid tentacles similarly to the shrimp. Combine the shrimp and squid in a large bowl with the noodles and add the shallots, fish sauce, cilantro, basil, lemongrass, egg, garlic, sugar, salt, and pepper to taste. Stir the mixture well.

3 Fill each squid body about three-fourths full of stuffing, and close each body with a piece of wooden skewer or a toothpick.

4 Preheat the oven to 375 degrees F.

5 Heat an ovenproof skillet over medium heat. Add the oil, and brown the squid on all sides, then transfer the skillet to the oven for about 12 minutes, or until the squid is heated through.

6 Remove the skewers or toothpicks and slice each squid into about 4 slices. Arrange them on individual warmed plates. Garnish each plate with a sprig of mint or cilantro and serve.

SERVES 6 AS A
FIRST COURSE
OR 12 AS AN
HORS D'OEUVRE

WARM BEAN AND OCTOPUS SALAD

My first experience with octopus was at a Greek restaurant in Manhattan. I was in an awkward situation, because I was with clients and felt like I had to try this dish that they had ordered for the table. Fortunately, it was love at first bite. This is one of my favorite octopus preparations. The interesting chewiness of the octopus against the soft texture of the beans makes for a wonderful mouthfeel and a pleasing eating event.

SERVES 6 AS A FIRST COURSE

1 Bring a pot of water large enough to hold the octopus to a boil. Add the octopus and cook for 5 minutes. Drain the octopus and let it cool. Cut the tentacles into 2-inch chunks, and the center section into 1-inch-square chunks.

2 In a heavy pot large enough to hold the beans and octopus, heat 2 tablespoons of the oil and, when it shimmers, add the onion and garlic and cook until the onion is soft. Pour in the beans with their soaking liquid, the sage, and the octopus. Bring them slowly to a simmer, partially cover the pot and simmer very slowly for 2 hours. Make sure the beans stay covered with liquid, adding more water as needed. Stir the beans every 30 minutes or so, scraping against the bottom of the pot, so the beans don't stick. But don't stir the beans to a mush. After the beans have cooked for 1 hour, add the salt. If there seems to be a lot of water left in the pot after 1 ½ hours of cooking, remove the lid so any excess water evaporates; the finished beans should be fairly dry.

3 Pour the hot beans and octopus into a large bowl. Stir in the juice, parsley, and the remaining oil to taste. Season to taste with pepper and salt, if necessary. Serve the salad warm or at room temperature.

One 2-pound cleaned octopus

½ to ¾ cup extra-virgin olive oil, divided

1 cup finely chopped red onion (about 1)

1 garlic clove, finely chopped

1 cup dried cannellini or navy beans, rinsed and soaked in 3 cups water for 3 hours or overnight

2 fresh sage leaves

2 teaspoons kosher salt

½ cup fresh lemon juice (about 2 lemons)

3 tablespoons chopped fresh parsley

Freshly ground black pepper

MEDITERRANEAN SQUID STEW

Squid takes on a host of Mediterranean flavors in this stew. Slightly Portuguese in its concept and method, it has Spanish overtones as well. But this dish would be just as happy in Italy or Greece.

3 tablespoons olive oil

2 cups chopped green bell peppers

1 cup chopped onion

2 large garlic cloves, minced

³/₄ cup chopped seeded tomato (about 1 large)

1 bay leaf

¹/₂ cup dry white wine

1 pound russet potatoes, peeled and cut into 1-inch cubes

1¹/₂ cups bottled clam juice

Generous pinch of saffron threads, crushed

12 ounces cleaned squid, bodies only, cut into 1-inch rings

Kosher salt

1 Heat the oil in a large heavy skillet over medium heat. Add the peppers, onion, and garlic and cook for 10 minutes, or until the vegetables are soft. Add the tomato and bay leaf and cook for 3 minutes more.

2 Add the wine and boil until it is reduced by half, 3 to 4 minutes. Reduce heat to a simmer and add the potatoes, clam juice, and saffron. Cook until the potatoes are tender, stirring occasionally, about 20 minutes. Add the squid, and simmer just until it is cooked through, about 2 minutes.

3 Season to taste with salt, and serve immediately.

SERVES 4 TO 6

FRIED SQUID, PAPAYA, AND
FRISÉE SALAD

Rice flour provides an extremely light coating in this fried squid recipe. While there are Asian notes featured in this dish, they're not overpowering. The flavors here are clean, light, and enjoyable. If you can't find frisée, use baby spinach, endive, or any other bitter salad green.

SERVES 6 AS A
FIRST COURSE
OR FINGER
FOOD

1   To make the dressing: Heat the canola oil in a medium heavy skillet over medium-high heat. Add the garlic and cook until it is golden, about 2 minutes.

2   Add the carrot and pepper and cook for 2 minutes. Add the vinegar, juice, and sugar. Bring them to a boil, stirring until the sugar dissolves.

3   Remove the skillet from the heat and cool. Stir in the chili oil. Season to taste with salt. Pour the dressing into a bowl, cover, and refrigerate for up to 1 day.

4   To prepare the squid: Cut the squid bodies into ½-inch-thick rounds. Place them in a large colander set over a bowl. Refrigerate them for at least 1 hour to drain.

5   Place 1 cup of the all-purpose flour, 1 cup of the rice flour, the soy sauce, vinegar, oil, and sugar in a large bowl. Gradually add the water, whisking until the batter is smooth. If necessary, whisk in more water, little by little, until the batter reaches a heavy-cream consistency. Let the batter stand at least 1 hour at room temperature.

SPICY-SOUR DRESSING
1 tablespoon canola oil

3 garlic cloves, thinly sliced

¼ cup finely diced carrot

¼ cup finely diced red bell pepper

7 tablespoons rice vinegar

5 tablespoons fresh lime juice

¼ cup packed brown sugar

1 tablespoon chili oil

Kosher salt

SQUID

1½ pounds cleaned small squid

1½ cups all-purpose flour, divided

1½ cups rice flour, divided

2 tablespoons soy sauce

1 tablespoon rice vinegar

1 teaspoon peanut oil

1 teaspoon sugar

1¼ cups water, plus more if needed

Kosher salt

Peanut oil for frying

Freshly ground black pepper

SALAD

4 cups frisée lettuce (about 2 heads)

2 cups peeled and seeded ½-inch dice fresh papaya (about 2 papaya)

One 6-ounce can sliced water chestnuts, drained and dried

½ cup whole roasted salted cashews

⅓ cup thin strips peeled fresh ginger

Toasted sesame seeds for serving

6 Mix the remaining ½ cup of all-purpose flour and ½ cup of rice flour in a large bowl. Add the drained squid. Toss until all the squid is coated. Dump the squid into a strainer and shake off any excess flour. Sprinkle the squid generously with salt. Add the squid to the batter.

7 Pour the oil into a large heavy-bottomed saucepan to a depth of 1½ inches. Heat the oil over medium heat until it registers 360 degrees F on a deep-fat thermometer. Working in batches, pull the squid pieces from the batter and allow the excess to run off. Drop the squid by handfuls into the oil and stir often with tongs to keep the pieces separated. Fry until the squid is crisp and brown, no more than 4 minutes per batch. Using a slotted spoon or spider, remove the squid to paper towels to drain. Sprinkle it with salt and pepper.

8 To make the salad: Combine the frisée, papaya, water chestnuts, cashews, and ginger in a large bowl. Add enough dressing to coat them lightly. Divide the salad equally among 6 plates. Pile hot squid on top of the salads. Sprinkle them with sesame seeds. Serve, passing the remaining dressing.

SPICY SQUID SALAD

Laced with red pepper flakes and complemented with the full richness of olives, this spicy squid salad will satisfy your hankering for something piquant without burning your taste buds with too much heat. Don't be bashful about increasing the amount of red pepper for your particular heat level. The squid can hold up to increased heat without losing its integrity.

SERVES 6 AS A
FIRST COURSE

1 In a medium bowl, stir together the oil, juice, garlic, and pepper flakes. Stir in the celery and olives. Reserve.

2 Slice the squid bodies crosswise into ¼-inch rings. Cut the tentacles in half lengthwise. Rinse the squid and drain it thoroughly.

3 In a large saucepan, bring 3 quarts of water to a rolling boil. Add 2 tablespoons of salt. Add the squid pieces and cook just until they turn opaque, not more than 1 minute. Drain but do not rinse. Add the hot squid to the olive dressing and toss to coat. Check the seasoning and add salt if needed. Cover and refrigerate the salad for at least 3 hours, or overnight.

4 Serve the salad as part of an antipasto platter, or on small salad plates as a first course, with crusty bread.

²/₃ cup extra-virgin olive oil

¹/₃ cup fresh lemon juice
(about 2 lemons)

4 garlic cloves, minced

³/₄ teaspoon red pepper flakes

¹/₂ cup minced celery
(about 4 ribs)

20 drained pimiento-stuffed green olives, quartered crosswise

2 pounds cleaned squid

Sea salt

Crusty bread for serving
(optional)

CARIBBEAN SQUID

This is a fun dish. It will take you straight to the Caribbean Islands. The jalapeño, sweet bell peppers, and cilantro all combine for a very regional taste. Add some hot white rice and a lightly dressed green salad, and you've got a dinner that will transport you miles from where you are.

2 tablespoons olive oil

¹/₂ cup minced onion
(about 1 small)

1 garlic clove, minced

¹/₄ jalapeño pepper, seeded and minced

1 cup minced red bell pepper
(about 1)

2 pounds cleaned squid

1 cup dry white wine

2 tablespoons tomato paste

¹/₄ cup minced fresh cilantro

Kosher salt

Freshly ground black pepper

1 In a large nonreactive skillet, warm the oil over medium heat. Add the onion, garlic, and jalapeño and cook until the onion is soft, about 5 minutes. Add the bell pepper and cook for 3 minutes.

2 Cut the bodies of the squid into ¹/₂-inch rings. Stir the wine and tomato paste into the onion and pepper mixture, and cook for 5 minutes. Add the rings and tentacles to the mixture, and cook for 3 to 4 minutes, until the squid is just tender. Add the cilantro, and salt and pepper to taste. Serve warm.

SERVES 4 TO 6

SEAFOOD, ALL MIXED

THE BIG BOOK OF FISH & SHELLFISH

How could I not mix up some seafood? If the flavors and textures of the individual fish or shellfish are worth having, it just makes sense to me to double or triple the pleasure. Heck, some of these recipes go crazy with many types in one dish.

Classics, some very modern and a few with new twists, can be found in these pages. All of these recipes can be adapted for entertaining. Some, like Charleston Seafood Country Captain and Fred's Slightly Twisted Bouillabaisse, are such great one-pot meals that the cook can enjoy the time with friends and family instead of being buried in the kitchen, tied to a stove.

I think you will enjoy this chapter, and as your confidence builds in preparing fish and shellfish, you will discover other combinations that you enjoy.

CHARLESTON SEAFOOD COUNTRY CAPTAIN

Country Captain has its roots in the Low Country of South Carolina, and was especially popular in Charleston. Spices that we take for granted today were exotic and expensive a century or so ago, making this a special-occasion dish for even the well-to-do. It remains a great choice for entertaining today, with its one-pot qualities. Typically made with chicken, this seafood version is equally successful. Many of my Southern friends in New York City and other cities outside the South routinely serve this recipe to guests and earn rave reviews.

SERVES 6 TO 8

Melt the butter with the oil in a large heavy-bottomed saucepan over medium heat. Add the onions, bell pepper, garlic, and curry powder. Stir and cook until the onions and peppers are soft, about 5 minutes. Add the apples, stir, and cook an additional 5 minutes. Add the wine, bring it to a boil, and cook until the liquid is almost evaporated, about 10 minutes. Stir in the crushed tomatoes, diced tomatoes, sage, sugar, and salt and pepper to taste. Reduce the heat to low and simmer, uncovered, stirring occasionally, until the sauce is thick, 30 to 40 minutes. Add the cream and continue cooking for an additional 5 minutes.

2 tablespoons (¼ stick) unsalted butter

2 tablespoons olive oil

2 cups thinly sliced yellow onions (about 2)

¾ cup thinly sliced green bell pepper (about 1)

2 garlic cloves, pressed

2 tablespoons curry powder

2 cups diced peeled Granny Smith apples (about 2)

½ cup dry white wine

One 28-ounce can crushed
tomatoes

One 14½-ounce can diced
tomatoes

1 tablespoon chopped fresh sage

1 teaspoon sugar

Kosher salt

Freshly ground black pepper

½ cup heavy cream (optional)

1 pound medium (40-count)
shrimp, peeled and deveined

1 pound grouper fillets, cut into
1-inch chunks

8 ounces dry-pack sea scallops,
sliced in half if large, or bay
scallops, side muscles removed

8 ounces lump crabmeat, picked
over for shell

6 cups hot cooked rice

Toasted almonds for garnish

Golden raisins for garnish

Orange zest for garnish

Chopped green onions for garnish

Mango chutney for serving

2 Remove the sauce from the heat. Stir in the shrimp, grouper, scallops, and crabmeat. Cover and allow the seafood
to cook in the hot sauce until the shrimp are pink and the
scallops and fish are cooked through, 5 to 10 minutes.

3 Spoon the cooked rice onto individual plates and ladle the
seafood sauce liberally over the rice. Garnish with almonds,
raisins, zest, and green onions. Serve at once. Pass mango
chutney at the table.

FISH AND SHRIMP CHOWDER

My first experience with this chowder was at Pam Hoening's home, overlooking the Hudson River near Wappingers Falls, New York. We were working on a cookbook cover together with others, and she wanted to serve lunch for us all. Pam is quite a foodie and cook. The results of her efforts may be the best mixed chowder you'll ever eat.

SERVE 6

1 Melt the butter in a large soup kettle over medium heat. Add the onions and cook until they're soft, about 5 minutes. Add the potatoes, clam juice, broth, bay leaf, salt, and pepper. Bring them to a boil, then reduce the heat to a simmer, and cook over low heat for 20 minutes, or until the potatoes are tender.

2 Add the fish, cream, and milk. Bring to a boil again and add the shrimp. Stir and simmer for 3 minutes, until the shrimp are pink and are just beginning to form a C shape. Add the parsley and ladle the chowder into warm soup bowls.

3 tablespoons unsalted butter

2 cups finely chopped onions (about 2 medium)

4 cups diced peeled potatoes ($^1/_2$-inch pieces)

2 cups bottled clam juice

2 cups low-sodium chicken broth

1 bay leaf

$^3/_4$ teaspoon kosher salt

$^1/_2$ teaspoon freshly ground black pepper

12 ounces tilefish, anglerfish, grouper, or monkfish, or any other firm-fleshed fish, cut into chunks

1 cup heavy cream

$^3/_4$ cup milk

1 pound medium (40-count) shrimp, peeled, deveined, and cut in half

$^1/_2$ cup minced fresh parsley

FRED'S SLIGHTLY TWISTED
BOUILLABAISSE

This is classic bouillabaisse, and at the same time not, but everyone who has eaten it raves about how good it is.

¼ cup olive oil

2 cups thinly sliced onions

1 thinly sliced fennel bulb

4 garlic cloves, minced

Three 28-ounce cans diced tomatoes

2 quarts chicken stock or broth

2 cups bottled clam juice

1 tablespoon grated orange zest

Pinch of saffron

8 ounces dry-pack sea scallops, side muscles removed

8 ounces monkfish, membrane removed (see page 65)

8 ounces grouper, tuna, or sea bass

1 pound mussels, scrubbed and rinsed

1 pound large (24-count) shrimp, peeled and deveined

¼ cup chopped fresh cilantro (optional, but good) or Italian parsley

Kosher salt

Freshly ground black pepper

¼ cup freshly grated Parmesan cheese (about 1 ounce)

1 Heat the oil in a soup pot or Dutch oven over medium heat until hot. Add the onions and fennel and cook until they are tender, 5 to 6 minutes. Add the garlic and cook until you can smell the garlic.

2 Add the tomatoes, stock, clam juice, zest, and saffron. Bring them to a boil, reduce the heat, and simmer for 45 minutes. The broth can be made ahead to this point. Cover and refrigerate. (It improves if made ahead.)

3 Slice the scallops in half, horizontally. Cut the fish into 1-inch chunks. Debeard the mussels.

4 Bring the broth mixture to a boil. Add the mussels, cover, and cook about 5 minutes. Add the shrimp, cover, and cook 2 minutes. Add the fish, cover, and cook 3 minutes. Finally add the scallops, cooking only 1 minute more, until firm. Stir in the cilantro or parsley and salt and pepper to taste. Serve the bouillabaisse with the cheese on the side.

SERVES 8 TO 10

GREEN CURRY WITH MUSSELS, SHRIMP, AND CALAMARI

Thai green curries are a bit milder than the red, but no less flavorful. If the thought of seven or eight jalapeños scares you, cut down on the amount. All the different flavors of the seafood enhance the broth.

SERVES 4 TO 6

1 Combine the onions, bell peppers, cilantro, jalapeños, garlic, galangal, ginger, and lemongrass in a food processor and pulse until they are evenly minced and almost a puree.

2 Heat the oil in a large heavy-bottomed saucepan over medium heat. Add the onion mixture and cook, stirring constantly, 5 to 6 minutes, or until a strong garlic aroma is noted.

3 Stir in the coconut milk and water, bring them to a boil, then decrease the heat, and simmer for 10 minutes. Season with salt and sugar to taste.

4 Add the seafood, cover, and simmer until the mussels open, 4 to 6 minutes. Discard any mussels that do not open. Divide the curry among individual soup bowls and serve it immediately.

2 medium onions, diced

2 cups chopped green bell peppers (about 2)

1/2 bunch fresh cilantro, stemmed

7 or 8 jalapeño peppers, seeded and chopped

4 garlic cloves

Four or five 1/8-inch slices galangal or peeled fresh ginger

One 2-inch piece fresh ginger, peeled and sliced

1 tablespoon thinly sliced lemongrass

1/4 cup vegetable oil

One 14 1/2-ounce can coconut milk

1 1/2 cups water

Kosher salt

Sugar

20 to 25 black mussels (about 1 pound), scrubbed and rinsed

8 ounces medium (40-count) shrimp, peeled and deveined

8 ounces cleaned squid, bodies cut into rings

MUSSELS, CLAMS, AND SHRIMP WITH SAFFRON RISOTTO

Milanese-style risotto, with its saffron base, makes an amazing bed for seafood, especially mussels, clams, and shrimp. Risotto is one of those foods many don't think they can make at home. Actually it is easy and therapeutic.

2 cups canned low-sodium chicken broth

¹/₄ teaspoon saffron threads

2 tablespoons extra-virgin olive oil

¹/₄ cup chopped shallots

1 cup Arborio rice or medium-grain white rice

4 garlic cloves, minced

¹/₂ cup dry white wine

1 cup bottled clam juice

20 mussels (about 1¹/₂ pounds), scrubbed and rinsed

12 littleneck clams, scrubbed and rinsed

12 large (24-count) shrimp, peeled and deveined, tails left intact

¹/₄ cup sliced green onions

Lemon wedges for garnish

SERVES 4

1 Put the broth and saffron in a saucepan over medium heat.

2 In a separate, 3-quart saucepan, heat the oil over medium heat until it shimmers. Add the shallots and cook for 2 minutes. Stir in the rice, making sure to coat every grain with oil. Add the garlic and cook, stirring, for another 2 to 3 minutes. Add the wine, and cook until it is absorbed by the rice, 2 to 3 minutes.

3 At this point, start adding the warm broth, ¹/₂ cup at a time. Stir each addition until it is almost absorbed. The process should take about 20 minutes.

4 After about 10 minutes, pour the clam juice into another 3-quart saucepan. Bring it to a boil and add the mussels and clams. Cover and cook for 5 to 8 minutes, or until they open. Remove and keep them warm, discarding any that do not open. Add the shrimp to the same pan, cover, and remove from the heat. Let the shrimp steep about 4 minutes, or just until they are cooked through and have a gentle C shape.

5 When the risotto is tender but still has a bit of bite to it, divide it among 4 bowls and divide the seafood equally between the bowls. Garnish each serving with the green onions and with lemon wedges.

NORTH COAST CIOPPINO

Cioppino certainly has it roots in northern Italian fishing villages, where a tomato and seafood stew called *ciuppin* was commonplace. Cioppino soon became the first "signature" dish among San Francisco's earliest restaurants on Fisherman's Wharf, and is now widespread over the coastal areas of Northern California. Like so many recipes, this one has a million interpretations, but you will find this one a good place to start.

SERVES 8

1   If using whole crab, remove the legs and claws and break the bodies in half. Clean the bodies and discard the innards (you can have your fishmonger do this for you). Set the crab pieces aside.

2   Place the clams in a saucepan, and add 1 cup of the wine. Steam, covered, over medium heat for 4 to 6 minutes, or until the clams open. Remove the clams, discarding any that do not open. Reserve the cooking liquid.

3   In an 8-quart soup pot, heat the oil over medium heat. Add the onion, bell pepper, and garlic and sauté, stirring occasionally. Cook for approximately 5 minutes, or until the vegetables start to soften.

2 fresh or frozen cooked whole Dungeness crabs (approximately 1½ to 2 pounds each), 4 cooked blue crabs, or 1 pound fresh lump crabmeat, picked over for shell

24 littleneck or cherrystone clams, scrubbed and rinsed

3 cups dry white wine, divided

⅓ cup olive oil

1 cup finely chopped yellow onion (about 1 medium)

½ cup coarsely chopped green bell pepper (about 1)

3 large garlic cloves, finely minced

One 28-ounce can peeled tomatoes

One 14½-ounce can diced tomatoes

2 tablespoons tomato paste

1 teaspoon Worcestershire sauce

1 teaspoon freshly ground black pepper

½ teaspoon dried oregano

**½ teaspoon dried basil or
1 tablespoon finely chopped fresh**

**2 pounds firm white fish such as
sea bass, cod, or halibut, cut into
1-inch pieces**

**12 ounces dry-pack sea scallops,
side muscles removed, cut in half
if large**

**12 ounces large (24-count)
shrimp, peeled and deveined**

Chopped fresh parsley for garnish

4   Add the tomatoes (slightly crushing them through your hands), remaining 2 cups of wine, the tomato paste, Worcestershire sauce, pepper, oregano, basil, and the clam cooking liquid. Partially cover and simmer for 20 to 30 minutes. Add the fish chunks, scallops, shrimp, and crab pieces or crabmeat. Simmer for approximately 5 minutes, or until all the seafood is cooked through. Do not stir. Add the clams and simmer long enough to just reheat them, about 5 minutes. Sprinkle with the parsley and serve immediately in big bowls with lots of napkins.

SEAFOOD PAELLA

Don't try this recipe on a busy weeknight after work. Spain's national dish takes some time. Cook paella when you have time to savor the experience. This one is strictly seafood, no chicken or pork. It is a great party dish to get your friends involved in the making.

SERVES 6

1 To make the aioli: Mash the garlic and salt with the back of your knife to form a paste. Transfer it to a medium bowl.

2 Whisk in the mayonnaise, oil, and juice. Cover and refrigerate until cold. This can be prepared 1 week ahead and kept refrigerated.

3 To make the fish stock: Bring the clam juice and water to a boil in a large pot. Add the shrimp shells, parsley, and bay leaf and bring them to a simmer. Reduce the heat and simmer 20 minutes.

4 Strain the stock into a large measuring cup, pressing on the solids with the back of a spoon. If the stock measures more than 5½ cups, return it to the pot and simmer until it is reduced to 5½ cups. Mix in the wine and saffron. This can be prepared 1 day ahead. Cover and refrigerate.

5 Preheat the oven to 375 degrees F.

6 To make the paella: Cut the tomatoes in half crosswise. Coarsely grate them onto a large plate, discarding the skins. Transfer the tomato pulp to a sieve and drain. Set aside.

7 Bring the fish stock to a simmer. Cover and keep it warm over very low heat. Place a 14-inch paella pan or heavy skillet over two stove-top burners or one very large burner. Add the oil and heat it over medium-high.

AIOLI
8 garlic cloves, minced
¾ teaspoon kosher salt
2 cups mayonnaise
2 tablespoons extra-virgin olive oil
1 teaspoon fresh lemon juice

FISH STOCK
5 cups bottled clam juice
2 cups water
8 ounces medium (40-count) shrimp, peeled and deveined, shells reserved
2 sprigs fresh parsley
1 bay leaf
½ cup dry white wine
1 teaspoon saffron threads

PAELLA

3 medium tomatoes

¹/₂ cup olive oil

1 pound monkfish or other firm-fleshed white fish, cut into 1-inch pieces

Kosher salt

1 pound cleaned squid, bodies cut into ¹/₄-inch rings

1¹/₂ cups finely chopped green bell pepper

12 garlic cloves, minced

2 teaspoons paprika

1 tablespoon minced fresh parsley, plus extra for garnish

1 bay leaf, crumbled

3 cups paella, Arborio, or other short-grain rice

¹/₂ cup shelled fresh or frozen peas

18 small mussels (1¹/₄ to 1¹/₂ pounds), scrubbed and rinsed

One 4-ounce jar pimientos, drained and sliced

8 Add the shrimp and monkfish to the pan. Season with salt and cook for 2 minutes, rotating the pan occasionally for even heat. Remove the shrimp and fish to a bowl.

9 Add the squid to the pan and cook 2 minutes. Add the pepper and sauté 3 minutes. Mix in the garlic and cook 1 minute. Add 3 tablespoons of the aioli and the paprika and stir to combine. Stir in the tomato pulp, 1 tablespoon of parsley, and bay leaf and cook 2 minutes.

10 Add the rice and stir to coat it with the tomato mixture. Add the fish stock and peas and cook until the rice is partially cooked and the liquid is thick, stirring frequently, about 15 minutes. Season to taste with salt. Remove the pan from the heat.

11 Add the shrimp, monkfish, and any accumulated juices in the bowl to the paella. Arrange the mussels (on their sides) and pimientos decoratively atop the paella. Transfer the paella to the oven and bake until the rice is almost tender, about 10 minutes.

12 Remove the paella from the oven. Cover the pan with aluminum foil and let it stand 20 minutes at room temperature. Remove the foil and sprinkle the paella with parsley and serve, passing the aioli separately.

SHELLFISH NORFOLK STYLE

This is an old-fashioned method of doing shellfish that should never be overlooked. You can make it with a mixture of seafood or just one kind, and around Bogues Bank, North Carolina, you'll see this listed on restaurant menus as "panned in butter."

SERVES 6

1 Melt the butter in a 12-inch sauté pan over medium heat. Add the shrimp and cook until they begin to turn pink, turning once, 3 to 5 minutes. Add the scallops and continue cooking for another 3 minutes.

2 Carefully stir in the crabmeat, vinegar, and hot pepper sauce and continue cooking for about another 4 minutes, until everything is heated through. Add salt and pepper to taste and serve the seafood immediately over rice. Have extra vinegar and hot pepper sauce at the table.

8 tablespoons (1 stick) unsalted butter

8 ounces medium (40-count) shrimp, peeled and deveined

8 ounces bay scallops, side muscles removed

8 ounces lump crabmeat, picked over for shell

¼ cup sherry vinegar

3 dashes hot pepper sauce

Kosher salt

Freshly ground black pepper

3 cups hot cooked rice

STUFFED FLOUNDER

Here we cook a whole flounder stuffed with a crabmeat mixture. It's sort of like eating fish stuffed with a crab cake. The moisture of the flounder bastes the crabmeat as they cook together for an incredible sensation of the ocean. If you like, throw a little diced country ham into the stuffing, and you will have a taste of the coastal South.

Four 12-ounce to 1-pound whole flounders

8 tablespoons (1 stick) unsalted butter, 4 tablespoons melted

¾ cup chopped onion (about 1 medium)

⅓ cup chopped celery (about 1 rib)

⅓ cup chopped red or green bell pepper

1 pound crabmeat, picked over for shell

2 cups small pieces white bread

2 large eggs, lightly beaten

1 tablespoon chopped fresh parsley

1 tablespoon amontillado sherry

Kosher salt

Freshly ground black pepper

Juice of 1 lemon

1 Preheat the oven to 350 degrees F.

2 Lay the white side of the fish up on a cutting board and make an incision in each fish along the center of the fish down to the backbone, stopping just shy of the head and tail. Slip your knife in between the flesh and the backbone and run the knife down the ribs on both sides of the backbone.

3 Heat 4 tablespoons of the butter in a large sauté pan. When it foams, add the onion, celery, and bell pepper and cook until the onion gets soft, about 5 minutes. Set aside and let cool.

4 Toss the vegetables with the crabmeat, bread, eggs, parsley, and sherry in a large bowl, seasoning with a little salt and pepper.

5 Stuff the fish with the mixture. Brush a glass baking pan large enough to hold the fish with some of the melted butter, and add the fish to the pan. Mix the remaining melted butter with the lemon juice and pour it over the fish. Bake for 30 to 45 minutes, or until the fish flakes easily with a fork. Serve immediately with some of the pan juices.

SERVES 4

SMOKED SALMON AND
CRAB CAKES WITH ONION
AND MUSHROOM CHUTNEY

If corned beef and cabbage is getting tiresome to your family for Saint Patrick's Day, try this Irish-American twist. The smoked salmon amazingly complements the crabmeat and the onion and mushroom chutney. Mashed potatoes are usually a good side on Saint Patty's Day, and are the binder for the seafood cakes, so make a little extra. While not necessary, the chutney gives this dish another Irish tone and sets off these two seafoods.

SERVES 4 TO 6

1 To make the chutney: Add the leek, onion, water, and ¼ teaspoon of salt to a small saucepan and bring the water to a boil over high heat. Cover, reduce the heat, and cook for 5 minutes, then uncover and cook for an additional 2 minutes, until thickened.

2 Meanwhile, in a medium sauté pan, heat the oil over medium heat. Add the shallot, and cook for 2 minutes. Add the mushrooms and thyme and sauté for 5 minutes, or until the mushrooms have picked up some color.

3 Remove the thyme sprig, and add the mushroom mixture to the leek and onion mixture.

4 Put the combined mixture into a blender, add the butter, milk, and juice and pepper to taste and run the machine until a nice puree has developed. (This can be made a day ahead, and kept, covered, in the refrigerator. Warm it before serving. Thin with warm water if necessary.)

ONION AND MUSHROOM CHUTNEY

1 large leek, pale green and white parts only, well cleaned and chopped

1 sweet onion, such as Vidalia, chopped

¾ cup water

Kosher salt

1 tablespoon olive oil

2 tablespoons chopped shallot

1 cup chopped cleaned shiitake mushrooms or baby portabellos

1 sprig fresh thyme

2 tablespoons (¼ stick) unsalted butter

2 tablespoons milk

Fresh lemon juice

Freshly ground black pepper

SEAFOOD CAKES

³/₄ **cup mashed potatoes**

¹/₄ **cup breadcrumbs**

¹/₄ **cup chopped green onions**

2 large eggs, lightly beaten

2 tablespoons chopped fresh thyme

2 tablespoons fresh lemon juice

4 ounces smoked salmon, chopped

8 ounces lump crabmeat, picked over for shell

Lemon wedges for garnish (optional)

5 To make the seafood cakes: Combine the potatoes, bread-crumbs, onions, eggs, thyme, and juice in a medium bowl. Fold in the salmon and crab.

6 Shape the mixture into 8 cakes, using your hands, an ice cream scoop, or a ring mold, and place them on a baking sheet coated with cooking spray. Cover and refrigerate for at least 1 hour or up to overnight.

7 Preheat the broiler. Remove the cakes from the refrigerator and uncover. Broil them about 6 inches from the heat, for about 4 minutes, or until they are light brown. Turn them over and cook an additional 3 to 4 minutes, until browned on the other side.

8 Serve the cakes immediately, with the Onion and Mushroom Chutney and lemon wedges, if desired.

MOUNTAIN TROUT EN PAPILLOTE WITH CRAB ROMESCO SAUCE

Ann Cashion, James Beard Award–winning chef-owner of Cashion's Eat Place in Washington, D.C., served a dish very much like this at a special dinner for the Southern Foodways Alliance at Blackberry Farm Inn near Knoxville, Tennessee. I needed one more course for a dinner that I had auctioned off to benefit the Tammy Lynn Center for mentally handicapped children, so I borrowed from Ann; this is the result, and it got rave reviews at the dinner. Chef Cashion used smoked trout, which you can certainly substitute for the fresh trout here.

SERVES 8 AS A FIRST COURSE OR 4 AS A MAIN COURSE

1 To make the sauce: Place the tomatoes, bread, almonds, hazelnuts, and garlic in a food processor and pulse to break them up roughly.

2 Add the pimientos, rosemary, oregano, pepper flakes, sugar, salt, paprika, and pepper. Pulse until the nuts are finely ground.

3 With the machine running, gradually pour in the vinegar and then drizzle in the oil. The sauce should be the consistency of thick salad dressing. Taste to make sure the sauce has plenty of piquancy and enough salt.

4 Preheat the oven to 475 degrees F.

ROMESCO SAUCE

4 Roma tomatoes, chopped

1 slice thick country-style white bread

½ cup toasted almonds

½ cup toasted hazelnuts

6 garlic cloves, peeled

4 large roasted pimientos or 2 large roasted red bell peppers (about 1 cup)

1 tablespoon chopped fresh rosemary

1 tablespoon chopped fresh oregano

1 ½ teaspoons red pepper flakes

1 teaspoon sugar

1 teaspoon kosher salt

1 teaspoon smoked Spanish paprika

¼ teaspoon freshly ground black pepper

¼ cup sherry vinegar

½ cup extra-virgin olive oil

TROUT

4 tablespoons (½ stick) unsalted butter, at room temperature

Eight 6-ounce fillets mountain trout

⅓ cup finely minced shallots (about 2)

¼ cup chopped fresh chives

¼ cup chopped fresh parsley

Kosher salt

Freshly ground black pepper

8 ounces lump crabmeat, picked over for shell

5   To prepare the trout: Cut eight 16-by-20-inch sheets of parchment paper. Fold each one in half and trace a half-heart shape. Cut the traced shape and unfold the paper into a heart. Take the butter and rub a little on half of each heart. Top each with 1 fillet of fish. Equally sprinkle on the shallots. Divide the chives and parsley equally over each fillet. Season with salt and pepper. Spoon 2 tablespoons of the Romesco Sauce over each fillet. Then equally divide the crabmeat over each fillet on top of the sauce.

6   Fold the parchment over so that the edges align. Beginning at the top or bottom, seal the packets by making small overlapping folds each about ½ inch wide. At this point, the packets can be refrigerated for up to 4 hours.

7   Place the packets on a baking sheet and bake for 10 min-utes. Transfer each packet to its own serving plate and take them immediately to the table. Let everyone carefully cut into their packets at the same time and enjoy the wonderful fragrance as the steam lets loose.

STUFFED PETRALE SOLE

My friend Gene Mattiuzzo shared this recipe with me. Gene has been my West Coast teacher and guide on the Pacific's bounty. He basically grew up on Noyo Harbor in Northern California, and runs the sales division of Caito Fisheries on the harbor. Gene makes his own wine with grapes from the nearby Alexander Valley, and only eats great food. This recipe uses petrale sole, as well as Dungeness crabmeat, making it a Northern California double treat. The stuffing makes superb crab cakes as well.

SERVES 4

1   Melt the butter over low heat in a large skillet. When the butter starts to foam, add the celery, onion, and bell pepper and cook for 5 minutes, or until the vegetables are soft. Add the crabmeat and cook for 2 minutes. Stir in the bread-crumbs, parsley, juice, mustard, and salt and pepper to taste. Remove the pan from the heat and reserve.

2   Preheat the oven to 400 degrees F.

3   Place 4 equal amounts of stuffing on a rimmed baking sheet that has been sprayed with cooking spray. Wrap 2 fillets around each mound of stuffing. Bake for 20 minutes, or until the fish slightly flakes.

4   Transfer each serving carefully to one of 4 plates, and serve with the lemon wedges.

2 tablespoons (¼ stick) unsalted butter

½ cup chopped celery

½ cup chopped onion

¼ cup chopped green bell pepper

1 cup Dungeness crabmeat (about 8 ounces), picked over for shell

1 cup Japanese panko bread-crumbs, cracker crumbs, or breading mix

2 tablespoons chopped fresh parsley

1 teaspoon fresh lemon juice

¼ teaspoon dry mustard

Kosher salt

Freshly ground black pepper

Eight 4- to 6-ounce petrale sole fillets

Lemon wedges for garnish

CRAB-STUFFED LOBSTER TAILS

For many of us, frozen lobster tails are our only lobster choice. If they have been handled well, they will be great, especially when stuffed with crabmeat. Be sure to drain them after thawing.

1 tablespoon kosher salt

4 lobster tails, thawed and drained if frozen

8 ounces fresh lump crabmeat, picked over for shell

2 tablespoons freshly grated Parmesan cheese

2 tablespoons fine dry bread-crumbs

2 tablespoons (¼ stick) unsalted butter, melted, plus extra for dipping

1 tablespoon chopped fresh parsley

1 garlic clove, minced

1 teaspoon fresh lemon juice, plus extra for dipping

¼ teaspoon Chesapeake Bay–style seasoning

¼ teaspoon freshly ground black pepper

Lemon halves for garnish

1 Combine 2 quarts of water and the salt in a large Dutch oven, and bring it to a boil. Add the lobster tails, and return it to a boil. Cover, reduce the heat, and simmer 5 minutes. Drain, cool, and reserve.

2 Cut the top side of each tail shell lengthwise, using kitchen shears. Cut through the center of the meat, and remove the vein. Loosen and lift the meat out of the shell. This step will make it easier to serve. Rinse the shells and return the meat to the shell intact.

3 Preheat the oven to 400 degrees F.

4 Drain the crabmeat. Combine the crabmeat, cheese, bread-crumbs, 2 tablespoons of butter, parsley, garlic, 1 tablespoon of juice, seasoning, and pepper; toss gently. Spoon the mixture into the lobster tails. Place them on a baking sheet.

5 Bake for 12 minutes, or until the stuffing is thoroughly heated. Serve with the extra melted butter mixed with the extra lemon juice to taste, and lemon halves.

SERVES 4

"SMOTHERED"
SHRIMP AND LOBSTER

This is from Lafayette, Louisiana, food writer Sandra Day. Proud of her crayfish, she admits to liking shrimp and lobster as well. Here is a key tip to a smooth sauce: "Hot roux and cold liquid equal no lumps."

SERVES 6 TO 8

1   Heat the oil in a cast-iron Dutch oven over medium heat. When the oil is very hot, slowly whisk in the flour. Continue to whisk constantly until the roux turns a rich red-brown color, about 30 minutes.

2   Add the chopped onion, celery, bell pepper, green onions, and garlic, and cook, stirring, until the vegetables have softened, about 5 minutes.

3   Stirring constantly, slowly pour in the clam juice. Continue stirring until the sauce is smooth. Raise the heat and bring the mixture to a boil, still stirring constantly. Reduce the heat to a simmer and cook until it is thickened, 5 to 10 minutes.

6 tablespoons vegetable oil

1/2 cup plus 2 tablespoons all-purpose flour

1 cup finely chopped onion (about 1)

1/2 cup finely chopped celery (about 2 ribs)

1/2 cup finely chopped green bell pepper (about 1)

1/4 cup thinly sliced green onions (about 2)

1 1/2 tablespoons finely minced garlic

1 1/2 cups bottled clam juice

4 ripe plum tomatoes, peeled and cut into ¼-inch dice

2 teaspoons Worcestershire sauce

1 teaspoon dried thyme

¾ teaspoon dried oregano

½ teaspoon hot pepper sauce

½ teaspoon kosher salt

¼ teaspoon freshly ground black pepper

2 pounds medium (40-count) shrimp, peeled and deveined

8 ounces cooked lobster meat, cut into 1-inch pieces

2 tablespoons chopped fresh Italian parsley

6 to 8 cups hot cooked white rice

4   Add the tomatoes, Worcestershire sauce, thyme, oregano, hot pepper sauce, salt, and pepper. Cover partially and simmer to blend the flavors, 30 minutes.

5   Stir in the shrimp and lobster and cook 2 to 3 minutes, or until they are heated through. Stir in the parsley, and serve immediately over the hot rice.

Canned, salted, and smoked seafood are perfect choices for a quick, healthy, yet delicious dish. For a fish and seafood book to leave these out would be a mistake.

Canned tuna, for years, has been one of the top five seafoods consumed in this country. A tuna salad sandwich is a lunchtime standard, and I know you will like the one included here. More recently, high-end, olive oil–packed tuna imported from Italy and Spain is sold as either solid chunks or tuna belly, which reminds us that tuna has reached great culinary heights in many guises.

CANNED, SALTED

Have you tried canned salmon lately? You should. It's not just the leftovers from salmon processing anymore; high-quality types of salmon are getting canned.

Salt cod is a mainstay in many cultures. When soaked overnight, it makes a wonderful transformation, especially cod salted on the bone. Nowhere near as salty as you might think, salt cod stands up to bold preparations with eggs, sausage, and fried potatoes.

Smoked fish, another type of preserved seafood, uniquely incorporates flavor from the richness of the land and sea. Keeping preserved seafood in the home can be a delicious change of pace.

A & FEW SMOKED

CORN AND HOMINY CLAM CHOWDER

The two varieties of corn products, the creamed corn and the hominy, coupled with the fire-roasted tomatoes make for an interesting blending of flavors for the canned clams. The longer you cook this, the more stew like it becomes, so you're in charge. A bowl of this the first cool fall night will be mighty good.

SERVES 10 TO 12

1 Heat the oil in a 3-quart saucepan over medium-high heat. Add the onion and cook until it is soft, about 2 minutes. Stir in the rice and cook an additional minute. Add the clam juice, increase the heat, and bring it to a boil. Reduce the heat to a simmer and cover. Cook for 10 to 12 minutes, or until the rice is almost done but still a little crunchy.

2 Add the creamed corn to the saucepan. Pour in the tomatoes, clams, and Italian seasoning. Continue cooking for another 10 minutes. Drain the hominy and add it to the saucepan. Cook until the hominy is just heated, about 3 minutes. Add salt and pepper to taste. Ladle the chowder into warm bowls and serve.

STEWS TO SAUCES
Chefs love using stews as sauces nowadays. if you have some of this leftover. try using it under a piece of grilled fish or a crisp-crust sauteed dish.

1 tablespoon olive oil

1 cup chopped onion (about 1 medium)

1/4 cup long-grain or basmati rice

3 cups bottled clam juice

One 10-ounce package frozen creamed corn

One 14 1/2-ounce can fire-roasted diced tomatoes

One 10-ounce can whole baby clams

1/2 teaspoon Italian seasoning

One 15 1/2-ounce can white hominy

Kosher salt

Freshly ground black pepper

CREAMY CRAB AND SPINACH CASSEROLE

What the traditional casserole should be—mushroom soup, a frozen vegetable, and cheese. They were great when your mom made them, and this one would make her smile. You could also use fresh crabmeat.

Two 10-ounce packages frozen spinach

One 10 ¾-ounce can cream of mushroom soup

2 cups shredded sharp Cheddar cheese (about 8 ounces), divided

¼ cup dry sherry

¼ cup half-and-half

3 to 4 teaspoons Worcestershire sauce

Freshly ground black pepper

Two 6 ½-ounce cans crabmeat, drained and flaked

½ cup fresh breadcrumbs

2 teaspoons unsalted butter, melted

Paprika for sprinkling

1 Preheat the oven to 350 degrees F.

2 Cook the spinach according to the package directions, without seasoning. Drain well, squeezing out as much moisture as you can.

3 Combine the soup, 1 cup of the cheese, the sherry, half-and-half, Worcestershire sauce, and pepper in a medium saucepan. Cook over medium heat, stirring constantly, until the cheese melts.

4 In a bowl, combine the spinach and ⅓ cup of the soup mixture, mixing well. Spread half of this in a buttered 10-by-6-by-2-inch baking dish. On top of this spread half of the crabmeat. Repeat the layers, ending by pouring the remaining two-thirds of the soup mixture over the top.

5 Combine the breadcrumbs and butter, mixing well; sprinkle it over the soup mixture. Top with the remaining 1 cup of cheese, and sprinkle the top with paprika. Bake for 30 minutes, or until golden brown. Serve hot or at room temperature.

SERVES 6

FRED'S FABULOUS TUNA SALAD

When I had my catering business, I could never make enough of this salad. My neighbors still pester me to make it. I love to take this salad and put it on pumpernickel bread with sprouts, crisp bacon, and a garden-fresh tomato slice. That's good eating.

SERVES 6 TO 8

1   Drain the tuna well in a colander for at least 30 minutes. Transfer it to a large bowl and add the relish, garlic, and thyme. Stir to combine.

2   Fold in the mayonnaise. Add the lemon juice if desired. Taste and season with salt and pepper to taste. Cover and refrigerate until chilled. This keeps covered in the refrigerator for 3 to 4 days.

Six 6-ounce cans chunk light tuna packed in water

¹/₂ cup sweet pickle relish

1 teaspoon garlic powder

1 teaspoon dried thyme

²/₃ cup good-quality mayonnaise

1 tablespoon fresh lemon juice (optional)

Kosher salt

Freshly ground black pepper

KIDS' FAVORITE TUNA CASSEROLE

Every baby boomer has a tale about tuna casserole night. Do you remember? They were pretty good, if you're honest. This one has those chow mein noodles for crunch, but the peanuts make it special.

One 10³/₄-ounce can cream of mushroom soup

1 cup chopped celery

One 6-ounce can chunk light tuna packed in water, drained

¹/₂ cup salted peanuts

¹/₄ cup chopped onion

2 tablespoons chopped green bell pepper

¹/₈ teaspoon freshly ground black pepper

¹/₂ (5¹/₂-ounce) can chow mein noodles

1 Preheat the oven to 350 degrees F.

2 In a bowl, combine the soup, celery, tuna, peanuts, onion, bell pepper, and pepper. Pour them into a 1 ¹/₂-quart casserole dish. Sprinkle the casserole with the noodles.

3 Bake, uncovered, for 30 minutes, until the casserole is slightly golden but still moist.

SERVES 4 TO 6

LEMON-SCENTED TUNA ANTIPASTO

I ran this recipe in my newspaper column and got an avalanche of e-mails. People raved about how different imported olive oil–packed tuna tasted. The Italian and Spanish are the best; be sure and check the label. Also be prepared to pay $4 to $8 for this tuna, but it is worth every penny.

SERVES 4 AS A
FIRST COURSE
OR 2 AS A LIGHT
LUNCH

1 Gently toss the tuna, celery, olives, capers, parsley, oregano, zest, and garlic together in a large bowl. Try to keep the tuna as chunky as possible. Grind some black pepper over the mixture.

2 In a small bowl, whisk the juice and oil together. Pour this over the tuna mixture and lightly toss.

3 Divide the pepper strips into mounds in the center of each of 4 salad plates. Divide the tuna mixture over each mound of peppers, and drizzle with additional oil, if desired. Sprinkle each plate with a pinch of sea salt. Serve immediately.

1 cup imported tuna packed in oil, drained

1 cup chopped celery hearts and leaves

12 oil-cured black olives, pitted and sliced in half

1 tablespoon capers, drained

1 tablespoon chopped fresh parsley

½ tablespoon chopped fresh oregano

1 teaspoon finely minced lemon zest

½ teaspoon finely minced garlic

Freshly ground black pepper

2 tablespoons fresh lemon juice

2 tablespoons high-quality extra-virgin olive oil, plus extra for garnish

2 roasted red bell peppers, cut into strips

Coarse sea salt

SALMON CARBONARA

I used to make this in college when I was low on money. My suite mates liked it so much that they started asking me to make big batches. It is not as heavy as the bacon version, and it is wonderful for a late-night supper.

One 7³/₄-ounce can red salmon

8 ounces spaghetti

1 cup freshly grated Parmesan cheese (about 4 ounces), plus extra for garnish

¹/₂ cup chopped fresh parsley

¹/₄ cup (¹/₂ stick) unsalted butter, melted

2 large eggs, lightly beaten

¹/₈ teaspoon coarsely ground black pepper

1 Drain the salmon, and flake it into small chunks. Set aside.

2 Cook the spaghetti according to the package directions. Drain well. In the pot you used for the pasta, combine the spaghetti, cheese, parsley, butter, eggs, and pepper, tossing to coat. Add the salmon, and toss gently. Place the pot over medium heat and cook for 4 to 5 minutes, stirring until the eggs are cooked.

3 Spoon the spaghetti into a serving dish, and sprinkle it with extra cheese. Serve immediately.

SERVES 4

SALMON CROQUETTES WITH
LEMON-HERB CREAM

If it was Friday, it was salmon croquette day in the school cafeteria. These are not those salmon croquettes. First we start with canned smoked salmon. If you can't find the canned, use the same weight of smoked salmon. The fresh herbs in the lemon sauce never saw the light of day at my school.

SERVES 4 TO 6

1   To make the croquettes: Put the salmon, breadcrumbs, eggs, shallots, garlic, juice, and salt and pepper to taste in a food processor. Pulse the ingredients several times. Scrape down the bowl and then process until the ingredients are finely chopped. Stir in the chives.

2   In a large skillet, heat the butter and oil over medium heat. Moisten your hands, and shape the salmon mixture into 2-inch semiround balls. This will make about 15 croquettes. Add them to the skillet in batches and cook them until golden brown on all sides, about 5 minutes per batch. Set them aside to drain on paper towels.

3   To make the sauce: Pour off the fat from the skillet. Melt the butter over medium heat. Add the shallots and cook until they are soft, 2 to 3 minutes. Add the cream and juice; bring them to just below a boil, and cook until the sauce has thickened, 10 to 15 minutes, stirring often.

SALMON CROQUETTES

Three 6¼-ounce cans alder-smoked skinless salmon, pin bones removed

1½ cups fresh white breadcrumbs

3 large eggs, lightly beaten

3 medium shallots, coarsely chopped

3 medium garlic cloves

1½ teaspoons fresh lemon juice

Kosher salt

Freshly ground white pepper

3 tablespoons chopped fresh chives

6 tablespoons (¾ stick) unsalted butter

3 tablespoons olive oil

LEMON-HERB CREAM SAUCE

3 tablespoons unsalted butter

3 medium shallots, finely chopped

3 cups heavy cream

6 tablespoons fresh lemon juice

3 tablespoons chopped fresh chives

3 tablespoons chopped fresh dill

3 tablespoons chopped fresh parsley

8 ounces spaghetti, linguine, or fettuccine, cooked (optional)

4 Stir the chives, dill, and parsley into the sauce. Then serve in one of two ways: Add the salmon croquettes to the sauce, and simmer for 3 to 5 minutes more, until they are heated through, then serve immediately over pasta. Or, serve the browned salmon croquettes on plates and pass the sauce separately.

SIMPLE CLAM SAUCE

Here is a garlic lover's pasta sauce. Garlic-infused olive oil is the basic coating for the pasta, with clams, parsley, and oregano being the center-stage stars. OK, it is canned clams with garlic and herbs, but still one of the best pastas you can prepare. Keep this recipe handy and you will always be a gourmet.

SERVES 6

1   In a large skillet, heat the oil over medium heat. Add the garlic and cook until it just begins to turn golden, 3 to 4 minutes. Be careful not to burn the garlic. If you do, start over.

2   Add the clams and parsley and cook for 1 minute more. Add the clam juice, oregano, basil, pepper flakes, and salt and pepper to taste, and gently boil for about 3 minutes, until everything is heated through. Pour the sauce over the pasta and serve immediately with Italian bread to sop up the sauce.

9 tablespoons olive oil

6 garlic cloves, chopped

Three 10-ounce cans whole baby clams, drained

6 tablespoons chopped fresh parsley

1¼ cups bottled clam juice

2 tablespoons chopped fresh oregano or 2 teaspoons dried

2 tablespoons dried basil

1½ teaspoons red pepper flakes (optional)

Kosher salt

Freshly ground black pepper

12 ounces spaghetti or linguine, cooked

Italian bread for serving

SMOKED OYSTER SPREAD

My father loved smoked oysters. It was understood that no one opened a tin of smoked oysters without asking him. He would have loved this spread. So rich and deep in flavor, it is lapped up even by folks not so crazy about oysters.

Two 3-ounce cans whole smoked oysters, drained

5 ounces cream cheese

1½ teaspoons fresh lemon juice

1 teaspoon light cream or half-and-half

½ teaspoon minced onion

½ teaspoon minced garlic

Dash of Worcestershire sauce

16 French bread rounds, toasted

1 Preheat the oven to 375 degrees F.

2 Put the oysters, cream cheese, juice, cream, onion, garlic, and Worcestershire sauce in a food processor and pulse a few times until they are well combined but not mushy.

3 Using a teaspoon, place 1-inch mounds of the mixture on the bread rounds and bake for 10 minutes, until the topping is bubbly. Serve immediately.

SERVES 16 AS AN HORS D'OEUVRE

TONNATO SAUCE

This cold tuna sauce is traditionally served with cold veal breast. Try it over a poached chicken or turkey breast for a new taste sensation. This sauce has a raw egg in the ingredients. If you need or want to avoid raw eggs, use a product like Egg Beaters. The result will be a little less rich, but it will still be satisfying.

SERVES 6

1   Blend the anchovies, egg, ½ teaspoon of the lemon juice, and the salt and pepper to taste in the bowl of a food processor. Add the oil in a slow stream while the food processor is running.

2   Add the tuna and the remaining 1 teaspoon of lemon juice and puree until smooth. Transfer the sauce to an airtight container and refrigerate until chilled.

3   When you serve it, garnish with capers.

5 oil-packed anchovy fillets, drained

1 large egg, lightly beaten

1½ teaspoons fresh lemon juice, divided

Pinch of kosher salt

Pinch of freshly ground black pepper

½ cup olive oil

One 6-ounce can white tuna packed in olive oil, not drained

Capers for garnish

WEST AFRICAN TUNA CASSEROLE

One of the positive things that came from the West African influx into this country was the black-eyed pea. First a staple of the South, and now a legume that's enjoyed all over the country, the black-eyed pea adds an interesting dimension to this tuna casserole. The peas remove this casserole from the typical soup-based ones. Try this and you may really like it.

2 cups drained cooked black-eyed peas

1 tablespoon olive oil

$\frac{1}{2}$ cup finely chopped onion

One 14$\frac{1}{2}$-ounce can diced tomatoes

One 8-ounce can tomato sauce

2 teaspoons crushed red pepper flakes

Two 6$\frac{1}{2}$-ounce cans flaked tuna packed in water, drained

$\frac{1}{2}$ teaspoon kosher salt

1 cup cornflake crumbs

4 tablespoons ($\frac{1}{2}$ stick) unsalted butter, melted

1   Preheat the oven to 350 degrees F.

2   Place the peas in an 11-by-7-inch ovenproof baking dish.

3   In a small sauté pan, heat the oil over medium-high heat and add the onion. Cook until it is soft. Spread the onion evenly over the peas.

4   Stir in the tomatoes, tomato sauce, and pepper flakes. Cover and bake for 15 minutes. Remove the pan from the oven, and uncover. Stir in the tuna and salt. Cover the dish and bake an additional 10 minutes.

5   Mix the crumbs and butter together. Remove the casserole and the cover and evenly sprinkle the top of the casserole with the crumbs. Return the casserole to the oven, uncovered, for an additional 5 to 10 minutes, or until the topping is a nice golden brown. Let it sit for 15 minutes before serving.

SERVES 6

SCRAMBLED EGGS WITH SALT COD, ONIONS, AND POTATOES

My first assistant in New York City was Joseph Therasa, a great cook who moved from Portugal while in his teens. He introduced me to the "Ironbound" section in Newark, New Jersey, where a huge population of folks with Portuguese ties have settled. The restaurants and food markets are a delight, especially when you are with someone who knows the territory. If Portugal had a top-five national dish list, this one would certainly be on it. This is Joseph's version. Remember, the Portuguese seem to care nothing about cholesterol.

SERVES 4

1   Rinse the salt cod and then soak it in water in the refrigerator for 24 hours. Change the water occasionally. Drain the cod. Now remove any bones and skin. With your fingers, shred the cod. Set it aside.

2   Sauté the onions and garlic in the olive oil in a large heavy skillet over medium-low heat, stirring often, 5 to 6 minutes—just until the onions are slightly brown. Turn the heat down low, cover the skillet, and allow the vegetables to steam for 10 minutes. Add the cod, mix well, re-cover the pan, and cook over low heat 25 minutes, stirring.

3   Meanwhile, pour the peanut oil into a medium heavy sauté pan set over medium-high heat, and heat until it registers 375 degrees F on a deep-fat thermometer. Pat the strips of potato as dry as possible with a towel. Fry them in several batches, separating the strips as they fry with a long-handled fork, until they are golden, 3 to 4 minutes. With a skimmer or slotted spoon, lift the potatoes out onto paper towels to drain.

8 ounces salt cod

3 cups thinly sliced onions (about 3 to 4)

2 large garlic cloves, minced

¼ cup olive oil

2 cups peanut oil

2 medium Idaho potatoes, peeled and cut lengthwise into matchstick strips

10 large eggs, lightly beaten

2 tablespoons coarsely chopped fresh Italian parsley, divided

¼ teaspoon coarsely ground black pepper

12 large oil-cured black olives

4   When the cod has steamed for 25 minutes, add half the fried potatoes to it and cook, stirring constantly, about 2 minutes. Add the eggs, half the parsley, and the pepper and cook over medium-low heat, stirring the eggs occasionally, 2 to 3 minutes, until they are just set.

5   Mound the egg mixture on a heated platter, sprinkle it with the remaining parsley, add the remaining fried potatoes, and garnish with the olives. Serve at once.

SMOKED SALMON RILLETTES

If you are a fan of the classic pork rillettes, or even if you've never heard of them, this turn with salmon will delight you. Rillettes are usually meats cooked in highly seasoned fat, then pounded into a paste, placed in pots, and covered with fat to preserve them. It is much the same as a smooth confit. The use of both fresh and smoked salmon results in a lighter-tasting nibble, yet it still has that rich, wonderful mouthfeel of a rillette. For a cocktail party, these are perfect with just about any wine or spirit. Smoked salmon rillettes are also a surprising first course when served over greens.

SERVES 16 TO 20 AS AN HORS D'OEUVRE OR 8 AS A FIRST COURSE

1 Place the fresh salmon and thyme in a heavy-bottomed saucepan and cover it with the broth. Gently heat the broth to a simmer and cook the fillet, turning it once, for 8 to 10 minutes, or until it is almost cooked through. It will still be somewhat translucent in the center. It is very important not to overcook the salmon.

2 Let the salmon cool in the broth to room temperature. Cover and refrigerate.

3 Melt 2 tablespoons of the butter in a heavy-bottomed sauté pan over medium heat. Add the smoked salmon, shallot, and nutmeg and sauté, stirring occasionally, for about 2 minutes, or until the salmon turns mostly opaque. Remove the salmon from the pan to a plate, cover tightly, and refrigerate until it is thoroughly cooled.

1½ pounds skinless salmon fillet

1 small sprig fresh thyme or ¼ teaspoon dried

1 cup fish broth, clam broth, or chicken broth

1 cup (2 sticks) plus 2 tablespoons (¼ stick) unsalted butter, at room temperature, divided

8 ounces skinless smoked salmon, cut into small pieces

1 tablespoon minced shallot

¼ teaspoon ground nutmeg

4   Remove the cold poached salmon from the broth and pat it dry. Cut it into slices about ¼ inch thick. Place the slices, the cold smoked salmon plus any of its juices, and the remaining 1 cup of softened butter on a baking sheet with sides. Using 2 forks or even your fingers (clean, of course), gradually mix all of the ingredients together. You are looking for small, thin shards of salmon that are held together with creamy butter.

5   Place the salmon rillettes in a container, cover tightly with plastic wrap, and refrigerate for at least 4 hours or overnight. The rillettes will keep, covered, for 3 days in the refrigerator. Remove them from the refrigerator at least 1 hour before serving.

6   To serve as an hors d'oeuvre, spread the rillettes on toast points or crackers. To serve as a first course, divide the salmon equally on top of 8 salad plates with a salad of baby greens dressed with a simple vinaigrette.

SMOKED BLUEFISH
PASTA SALAD

Smoked bluefish is so different from other smoked fish. The flavor is bolder, and the smoking creates a rich and creamy texture. It blends perfectly with the pasta in this dish.

SERVES 6

1 Pull the smoked fish into shreds. In a large bowl, mix it with the pasta, oil, bell peppers, onion, soy sauce, parsley, cilantro, vinegar, and salt and pepper to taste.

2 Garnish the salad with endive and lemon wedges.

12 ounces smoked bluefish or tuna

1 pound penne pasta, cooked

6 tablespoons olive oil

½ cup diced yellow bell pepper

½ cup diced red bell pepper

½ cup chopped red onion

1 ½ tablespoons soy sauce

1 tablespoon chopped fresh parsley

1 tablespoon chopped fresh cilantro

2 teaspoons balsamic vinegar

Kosher salt

Freshly ground black pepper

Endive spears for garnish

Lemon wedges for garnish

HOME-CURED SALMON

Home curing salmon in a Swedish gravlax kind of way is fun. A great party dish, or a simple lunch, it makes a stunning first course when served like carpaccio. This version is my favorite and has a Southwestern twist.

1 pound center-cut salmon fillet, pin bones removed

1½ tablespoons kosher salt

1 tablespoon light brown sugar

2 teaspoons freshly grated lime zest

1½ tablespoons gold tequila

1 teaspoon coarsely ground black pepper

1 cup chopped fresh cilantro

SERVES 8

1 Place the salmon skin side down on a large piece of plastic wrap. Combine the salt and sugar in a small bowl, and evenly rub the mixture over both sides of the fish.

2 Spread the zest over the skinless side of the salmon, then drizzle the tequila over the salmon and rub the pepper over both sides. Press the cilantro leaves into both sides of the salmon.

3 Double-wrap the salmon tightly in plastic wrap. Sandwich it between 2 small rimmed baking sheets. Place several cans, a brick or two, or a couple of heavy books on the top sheet. Refrigerate the assembly for 36 hours, turning the package once.

4 To serve, slice the fillet ⅛ inch thick using a long, thin-bladed knife, like a ham knife. Slice at almost a parallel angle to the board to get a wide surface area.

5 Tightly wrapped, the salmon will keep for about 1 week in the refrigerator and up to 2 months in the freezer. Remove it from the freezer about 6 hours before serving, and place it in the refrigerator to defrost.

SAUCES, SIDES & SWEETS THAT COMPLETE THE MEAL

Every seafood meal needs a little something to go alongside, as a lure to dip in, or to capture your sweet tooth. This chapter has those things.

Sauces have always been part of the seafood experience. Making your own just tastes better, and here you will find some simple guides to the classics. Don't stop with just the ones here in this chapter. The book is full of sauce recipes. Don't be afraid to swipe a sauce from one type of seafood to use with another.

Cabbage mixtures and potatoes have long been at the table when seafood was present. Have you ever made really good French fries at home? In these pages, you will find the perfect method. And my mom's coleslaw has just the right tang for fried and even grilled seafood.

Of course, we need something sweet, and there are some first-rate pies that are blissful endings to a seafood feed or any other dinner.

Enjoy.

ANY REGION TARTAR SAUCE: THE STANDARD OF SEAFOOD SAUCES

This is an "either/or" tartar sauce. By adjusting the type of pickle used, a regional recipe will develop. Using all dill pickles results in a more northern and Midwest style of tartar sauce that many companies mimic on your grocery store shelves. All sweet pickles brings this sauce to the South, that place where sweetness will always reign supreme. My favorite is a little of both, dill and sweet.

MAKES ABOUT
1 ½ CUPS

Mix all the ingredients together in a medium bowl. Chill for at least 1 hour before serving.

1 cup mayonnaise

½ cup finely chopped dill pickles or sweet pickles

¼ cup minced onion

2 tablespoons chopped fresh parsley

1 tablespoon dill or sweet pickle juice

CAJUN TARTAR SAUCE

Cajun tartar sauce is a spicy cross between the traditional and a rémoulade. Note the use of fresh horseradish, which adds a slightly different pungency. Try this sauce with most anything fried.

1 cup mayonnaise

2 tablespoons Creole mustard

2 tablespoons thinly sliced green onions, green parts only

2 teaspoons chopped drained capers

2 teaspoons Worcestershire sauce

1 teaspoon hot pepper sauce

1 teaspoon fresh lemon juice

1 teaspoon finely grated fresh horseradish

1 garlic clove, finely chopped

Kosher salt

Freshly ground black pepper

In a medium bowl, combine the mayonnaise, mustard, onions, capers, Worcestershire sauce, hot pepper sauce, juice, horseradish, garlic, and salt and pepper to taste. Mix well, cover, and refrigerate for 1 hour for the flavors to blend.

MAKES ABOUT 1 1/2 CUPS

FRED'S CRAB LOUIS SAUCE

Based on Swan Oyster Depot's Louis sauce, I have found that there's more for this sauce to do besides dress crabmeat. It is super with fried or cold boiled shrimp, scallops, fried oysters, and most any breaded fish. I use Bennett's chili sauce because it has a chunkier body than others. Add some additional pickles if you can't find Bennett's.

**MAKES ABOUT
1 ½ CUPS**

1 In a medium bowl, whisk together the mayonnaise, chili sauce, olives, chives, juice, Worcestershire sauce, and horseradish. Season with salt and pepper to taste.

2 Chill for a few hours or overnight for the flavors to commingle.

1 cup mayonnaise (without sugar), such as Duke's or JFG

¼ cup Bennett's chili sauce

2 tablespoons minced pitted black olives

1 tablespoon chopped fresh chives

2 teaspoons fresh lemon juice

1 teaspoon Worcestershire sauce

1 teaspoon prepared horseradish sauce

Kosher salt

Freshly ground black pepper

ALMOST LIKE JOE'S MUSTARD SAUCE

Joe's Crab Shack in Florida probably is better known for their sauce than anything else. Developed for stone crab claws, the sauce is also excellent with all types of crab cakes and any type of fritter. It also plays well with cold seafood.

1 cup mayonnaise

3½ teaspoons Coleman's dry English mustard

2 tablespoons half-and-half

2 teaspoons Worcestershire sauce

1 teaspoon A.1. Steak Sauce

⅛ teaspoon kosher salt

Put the mayonnaise and mustard in a small bowl and whisk them together to blend. Add the half-and-half, Worcestershire sauce, steak sauce, and salt, whisking until the mixture is creamy. Refrigerate, covered, until ready to use.

MAKES ABOUT 1⅓ CUPS

UPSCALE TARTAR SAUCE

A tartar sauce with a little uptown attitude. The capers and cornichons also give the sauce a European flair. This is good with poached items and pan-roasted fish. It also works well with fried calamari.

MAKES ABOUT
1 3/4 CUPS

In a large bowl, mix the mayonnaise, onion, capers, cornichons, juice, salt, and pepper thoroughly. Refrigerate, covered, until ready to use.

1¹/₂ cups Hellmann's mayonnaise

2 tablespoons chopped red onion

2 tablespoons roughly chopped capers

2 tablespoons chopped cornichons

2 tablespoons cornichon juice

¹/₄ teaspoon kosher salt

¹/₄ teaspoon freshly ground black pepper

PACIFIC NORTHWEST-STYLE MARINADE

This style of marinade is used very frequently in the Oregon and Washington coastal areas, with salmon especially. It is also good for large shrimp. You'll only need to let the fish marinate for 30 to 40 minutes to pick up the flavors. Grill, bake, or broil the fish or shellfish.

²/₃ cup packed brown sugar

²/₃ cup granulated sugar

²/₃ cup soy sauce

1 teaspoon grated peeled fresh ginger

In a medium bowl, whisk together the sugars, soy sauce, and ginger, to taste. This makes enough marinade to do 4 to 6 pieces of salmon or a couple of pounds of shrimp. It will keep for 4 to 5 days in a covered container in the refrigerator.

MAKES ABOUT 2 CUPS

RÉMOULADE SAUCE

This is the gold standard of New Orleans seafood, an across-the-board seafood-friendly sauce. A little brighter and sweeter than other rémoulades in the book, this sauce will work with almost all shellfish, but is extremely good with fried seafood, especially panfried fish.

MAKES ABOUT 2 ½ CUPS

In a large bowl, mix together the mayonnaise, celery, onions, parsley, ketchup, horseradish, mustard, Worcestershire sauce, capers, garlic, hot pepper sauce, paprika, anchovy, and salt. Cover and chill for several hours before serving. This keeps for several days refrigerated.

1 cup mayonnaise

6 tablespoons finely minced celery

6 tablespoons finely minced green onions

3 tablespoons finely chopped fresh parsley

3 tablespoons ketchup

3 tablespoons prepared horseradish

2 tablespoons coarse-grain mustard

2 tablespoons Worcestershire sauce

1 tablespoon chopped capers

1 teaspoon minced garlic

1 teaspoon hot pepper sauce

1 teaspoon paprika

1 teaspoon finely minced anchovy

$^1/_2$ teaspoon kosher salt

CHARRED CORN SALAD WITH
MUSTARD VINAIGRETTE

Inspired by a dish from the late Pierre Franey, whom I truly miss, this is my favorite side dish for crab cakes. When fresh corn is not available, frozen corn, thawed, works almost as well; just brown the corn in a sauté pan. This salad has a nice bite, making it a wonderful contrast to crab. Also try it with soft-shell crabs, grilled fish, or even a steak.

4 ears fresh corn, shucked

3 tablespoons Dijon mustard

3 tablespoons cider vinegar

Juice of ¹/₂ lemon

1 teaspoon chopped garlic

1 teaspoon chopped shallot

¹/₂ teaspoon sugar

¹/₄ teaspoon cracked mustard seeds

¹/₂ cup olive oil

I Light a charcoal fire or preheat your gas grill on high. Oil your grill's cooking grate.

2 Grill the corn until it starts to char, turning the ears so that they cook evenly. Be sure the corn doesn't burn. Conversely, pan roast the corn until it begins to color, about 5 minutes. Allow it to cool. Remove the kernels from the cobs and reserve the kernels in a bowl.

3 Make the vinaigrette by combining the mustard, vinegar, juice, garlic, shallot, sugar, and mustard seeds in a blender or food processor and blending well. Add the oil slowly, with the motor running, emulsifying the dressing.

4 When ready to serve, pour the vinaigrette over the corn and combine.

SERVES 6

BUTTERMILK HUSH PUPPIES

There are many tales about the how and where of hush puppies. They are such a standard all through the South, I have been so amused that restaurants from New York City to San Francisco have them listed on menus as appetizers and charge an arm and a leg for them. Now just make your own.

MAKES 5 DOZEN

1 Combine the flour, cornmeal, sugar, salt, and pepper in a large bowl; stir in the onion and, if desired, the jalapeño.

2 In a separate large bowl, whisk together the buttermilk and egg, and stir in the flour mixture.

3 Pour the oil to a depth of 3 inches in a Dutch oven or an electric fryer. Heat until it registers 375 degrees F on a deep-fat thermometer.

4 Drop the batter by level tablespoonfuls into the oil and fry it in batches 5 to 7 minutes, or until golden. Drain the hush puppies on paper towels. Serve hot.

2 cups self-rising flour

2 cups self-rising white cornmeal mix

1 teaspoon sugar

½ teaspoon kosher salt

½ teaspoon freshly ground black pepper

1 large onion, grated (about ½ cup)

1 jalapeño pepper, seeded and minced (optional)

2 cups buttermilk

1 large egg, lightly beaten

Peanut oil for frying

FRENCH FRIES

Even in our carb-crazed days, French fries are hard to give up. They round out many a seafood dinner. Here's the way to perfect fries using a double-fry method.

4 large, long russet potatoes

Peanut oil for frying

Kosher salt or coarse sea salt

1 Slice the potatoes lengthwise into sticks ¼ inch thick. Place them in a bowl, cover with water, and refrigerate 8 hours.

2 Drain the potato sticks, and lay them out on dish towels to dry. Be sure they are completely dry before frying.

3 In a deep fryer or Dutch oven, heat 2 inches of oil until it registers 300 degrees F on a deep-fat thermometer. Add the potatoes a handful at a time. Cook until they are slightly limp, 1½ to 2 minutes. Do not brown them. Remove them with a spider, basket, or slotted spoon. Transfer the potatoes to a rack set over a baking sheet, and separate the sticks. Repeat with the remaining potatoes.

4 Increase the heat to 375 degrees F. Again add the potatoes in batches to the oil. Fry them until they are brown on the edges and crisp. Drain, and transfer them to a bowl lined with paper towels. Immediately season them with salt, tossing to coat. Serve hot.

SERVES 4

GREEN TOMATO SALSA

Green tomatoes are as versatile as their ripe red relatives. A soft, sour flavor makes green tomatoes an ideal foil for dramatic crabmeat. This salsa is especially good with soft-shell crabs that have been grilled. Also try it with grilled tuna steaks.

MAKES 3 CUPS

Combine the tomatoes, vinegar, oil, seasoning, juice, garlic, and salt in a medium bowl. Stir to blend. Let the flavors marry in the refrigerator for at least 30 minutes; longer is better.

3 cups chopped seeded green tomatoes (about 6)

¹⁄₃ cup balsamic vinegar

¹⁄₄ cup olive oil

1¹⁄₂ teaspoons Chesapeake Bay–style seasoning

Juice of 1 lime

¹⁄₂ teaspoon finely chopped garlic

Pinch of kosher salt

MASHED POTATO AND
GOAT CHEESE GRATIN

Sounds upscale, but it's not. Mashed potatoes, laced with the tart tanginess of goat cheese, are superb beside any piece of baked or grilled seafood (without any Asian tones). Even if you don't know goat cheese, this recipe will make you appreciate it. Make it a day ahead and bake right before serving.

4 pounds russet potatoes, peeled, cut into 1-inch pieces

4 large garlic cloves

14 tablespoons (1³/₄ sticks) unsalted butter, divided

Two 3¹/₂-ounce packages, fresh goat cheese, such as Montrachet, crumbled

¹/₂ cup heavy cream

³/₄ cup thinly sliced green onions

Kosher salt

Freshly ground black pepper

1   Butter a 13-by-9-by-2-inch oval glass baking dish. Place the potatoes and garlic in a large pot of cold salted water. Boil until the potatoes are tender, about 20 minutes. Drain the potatoes and garlic, and then return them to the pot.

2   Meanwhile, heat 12 tablespoons of the butter, the cheese, and cream in a small heavy-bottomed saucepan over low heat, stirring until smooth, about 4 minutes. Remove the pan from the heat.

3   Mash the potatoes and garlic until almost smooth. Stir in the goat cheese mixture and onions. Season to taste with salt and pepper. Transfer the mixture to the prepared baking dish. You can make this 1 day ahead; cover and refrigerate.

4   Preheat the oven to 400 degrees F.

5   Melt the remaining 2 tablespoons of butter. Drizzle it over the gratin, and place the dish in the oven. Bake until it is golden on top and bubbling around the edges, about 40 minutes. Let it stand 10 minutes, and serve.

SERVES 8 TO 10

CHEESE-GARLIC BISCUITS

I know people who go to Red Lobster just for the biscuits. These are close, and really make a meal special. You can also use them with a steamed clam and mussel recipe to soak up all those good steaming liquids or with any of the good soups and chowders in this book.

MAKES 12
BISCUITS

1   Preheat the oven to 450 degrees F.

2   In a large bowl, stir together the baking mix, milk, and cheese until a soft dough forms. Beat it vigorously for 30 seconds.

3   On an ungreased baking sheet, drop the dough by spoonfuls. Bake until the biscuits are golden brown, 8 to 10 minutes.

4   In a small bowl, mix together the margarine and garlic powder, and brush it over the biscuits before removing them from the baking sheet. Serve warm.

2 cups buttermilk baking mix

$^2/_3$ cup milk

$^1/_2$ cup shredded Cheddar cheese (about 2 ounces)

4 tablespoons margarine, melted

$^1/_4$ teaspoon garlic powder

SEARED GREEN BEAN SALAD

I love this side dish for what it's not. A cross between a European-style potato salad and a Southern green bean salad, it is perfect for a seafood feast or any sort of outdoor entertaining. The lack of mayonnaise lightens the dish and also makes it safer for parties and picnics. Of course, this salad is so good it will be gone before you know it, so make plenty.

1 pound small Yukon Gold potatoes

½ cup extra-virgin olive oil

2 pounds green beans, trimmed

2 tablespoons sesame seeds

1 large shallot, sliced paper thin

Juice of 1 large lemon (about 2 tablespoons)

2 teaspoons sesame oil

1 teaspoon freshly ground black pepper

Kosher salt

1 Cut the potatoes into quarters, place them in a pot, cover with cold water, and bring them to a boil over high heat. Cook 4 minutes, to slightly precook them. Drain and place them, cut sides up, on a towel to dry.

2 Coat a large frying pan with a thin layer of the olive oil and place it over high heat. When the oil becomes fragrant, arrange enough of the beans to cover the bottom of the pan. Sear them on one side for 3 minutes. Do not turn. Transfer the beans to a bowl and cover. Repeat this in batches with the remaining beans, adding them to the bowl and covering it.

3 Place the potatoes, cut sides down, in the pan with a thick layer of the olive oil. Fry them over medium-low heat for 20 minutes, until the bottoms are crisp and browned. Fry only one side; do not turn. Reserve to a plate and set aside.

4 In a dry pan, roast the sesame seeds. Add the roasted seeds, shallot, juice, sesame oil, pepper, salt, and about 1 tablespoon of the olive oil, or more to taste, to the green beans. Add the potatoes and toss. Chill before serving.

SERVES 10

MOTHER'S COLESLAW FOR FISH

There is slaw for barbeque and fried chicken. Then there is the proper slaw for a fish fry, and this is the one. Creamy, with a vinegar bite that complements that fried-food flavor, it can be served with any fried or coated seafood.

SERVES 6

1   Fill a large bowl or one side of a clean sink with ice water. Remove the outer leaves and soak the cabbage in ice water for 15 minutes to crisp. Drain the crisped cabbage on paper towels.

2   Meanwhile, make the dressing by whisking together the mayonnaise, vinegar, sugar, salt, and pepper. The dressing should be fairly thick. Set it aside.

3   Grate the cabbage quarters on the coarsest side of a box grater or in a food processor. In a large bowl, mix the cabbage and dressing and refrigerate the coleslaw for at least 2 hours or overnight before serving.

1 head green cabbage (about 2 pounds), cut into quarters

³/₄ cup good-quality mayonnaise

2 tablespoons cider vinegar

1 teaspoon sugar

1 teaspoon kosher salt

¹/₄ teaspoon freshly ground white pepper

JICAMA-GINGER SLAW

Jicama, the Mexican "potato," is a crisp addition to a standard slaw. It is also low in sugars, making it a good choice for people who need to watch such things. Jicama is very accommodating to other flavors, and plays the role of side dish with dignity. This recipe is from Chef Brett Jennings, of Elaine's on Franklin in Chapel Hill, North Carolina.

2 cups matchstick-size strips peeled jicama (about 1)

2 cups matchstick-size strips peeled carrots (4 to 6)

2 cups matchstick-size strips red bell peppers (about 2)

¼ cup matchstick-size strips peeled fresh ginger (one 2-ounce piece)

½ cup rice vinegar

1 tablespoon sugar

2 teaspoons packed grated lemon zest

Kosher salt

Freshly ground black pepper

1 Toss the jicama, carrots, bell peppers, and ginger in a large bowl to combine. Whisk the vinegar, sugar, and zest together in a small bowl to blend.

2 Pour the dressing over the vegetables and toss to combine. Season the slaw to taste with salt and pepper. Let it stand at least 20 minutes and up to 2 hours, refrigerated, tossing occasionally. Drain well before serving.

SERVES 6

APPLE COLESLAW

This is a fancier take on the classic side for seafood—coleslaw. The apple brings a sweet-tart note that is very refreshing against any seafood. This slaw is especially good with grilled and marinated items. It's also great for a crowd.

SERVES 12

1 In the bowl of a food processor, combine the apple, bell pepper, and celery and pulse until they are very finely chopped.

2 Transfer them to a nonreactive bowl and add the vinegar, sugar, salt, celery seed, caraway, garlic powder, onion powder, and pepper. Stir to combine, and let the mixture stand 10 minutes.

3 Stir in the mayonnaise and buttermilk and refrigerate 1 hour.

4 Add the green cabbage, red cabbage, and carrot and toss. The slaw is best if made and refrigerated at least 1 hour before serving.

½ green apple, peeled and cored

½ green bell pepper

1 stalk celery, coarsely chopped

¼ cup cider vinegar

1½ tablespoons sugar

1½ teaspoons kosher salt

1 teaspoon celery seed

1 teaspoon caraway seed

½ teaspoon garlic powder

½ teaspoon onion powder

½ teaspoon freshly ground black pepper

1¾ cups good-quality mayonnaise

½ cup buttermilk

1 medium green cabbage (about 2½ pounds), quartered, cored, and very thinly sliced

1½ cups shredded red cabbage

1 carrot, shredded

ROASTED POTATO SALAD WITH ROSEMARY AND PARMESAN CHEESE

Another make-ahead side dish that is full of flavor. These potatoes are better at room temperature, allowing you to make them early in the day, or even the day before, and letting you concentrate on your family or friends.

3 pounds red-skinned new potatoes, well scrubbed and patted dry

3 tablespoons olive oil

Kosher salt

Freshly ground black pepper

1 tablespoon finely chopped fresh rosemary

¹⁄₃ cup grated Parmesan cheese

1   Preheat the oven to 400 degrees F.

2   Quarter the larger potatoes; halve the smaller ones.

3   In a large bowl, toss the potatoes with the oil. Add salt to taste and a generous grinding of pepper and toss again. Transfer them to a large rimmed baking sheet that will hold them in a single layer. Roast the potatoes, stirring them occasionally, until they are crisply browned and tender inside, about 1 hour.

4   Remove the potatoes from the oven and cool slightly. Transfer them to a large bowl, add the rosemary, and toss. Cool the potatoes completely, then add the Parmesan, and toss again. Serve them at room temperature.

SERVES 6 TO 8

GERMAN CHOCOLATE PIE

A killer pie! Simple to make, with flavors that everybody loves. I developed this pie to prove to my mother that I really could cook, and it worked so well that she's more than happy to let me cook for her instead of me getting her home cooking. German chocolate pie finishes any seafood meal with a winning flourish. It's also a fabulous potluck or family-reunion dessert.

SERVES 6 TO 8

1 Preheat the oven to 375 degrees F.

2 Melt the chocolate and butter in a pan over low heat. Remove them from the heat. Blend in the milk. Set aside.

3 Mix the sugar, cornstarch, and salt together in a medium bowl.

4 Beat in the eggs and vanilla. Blend in the chocolate mixture. Pour the filling into the pie shell.

5 In a bowl, combine the coconut and nuts and sprinkle them on top of the chocolate mixture. Bake the pie for 45 minutes, or until the coconut is toasted.

4 ounces Baker's German sweet chocolate

4 tablespoons (½ stick) unsalted butter

One 12-ounce can evaporated milk

1½ cups sugar

3 tablespoons cornstarch

⅛ teaspoon kosher salt

2 large eggs, lightly beaten

1 teaspoon pure vanilla extract

One 9-inch unbaked deep-dish pie shell

1½ cups flaked sweetened coconut

1 cup chopped pecans

REAL KEY LIME PIE

If you think Key lime pie is green, then you have never had the real thing. Key limes are sweeter and more mellow than the standard Persian lime. Until a few years ago, your only choice for Key lime juice was the bottled, which is good, but Key limes are now beginning to show up in larger supermarkets, sometimes labeled as Mexican limes. Give them a try. By the way, a Key lime pie is pale yellow.

CRUST

7 tablespoons unsalted butter, melted

1½ cups graham cracker crumbs (about 10 crackers)

3 tablespoons sugar

FILLING

4 pasteurized egg yolks

One 14-ounce can sweetened condensed milk

½ cup fresh Key lime juice (8 to 10 Key limes), or bottled Key lime juice

1½ cups heavy cream

2 tablespoons sugar

1 Preheat the oven to 375 degrees F.

2 To make the crust: Butter a 9-inch glass pie plate with some of the melted butter, and set it aside. Combine the graham cracker crumbs, sugar, and remaining butter in a medium bowl, then pour them into the pie plate. Spread the crumbs evenly on the bottom and up the sides of the pie plate. Using your fingertips, firmly press down on the crumbs to form a crust. Bake the crust until it is lightly browned, about 8 minutes. Remove it from the oven, and set it on a wire rack to cool to room temperature.

3 To make the filling: Whisk the egg yolks in a large bowl, then gradually add the milk, whisking until smooth. Add the juice, and mix until just combined.

4 Pour the filling into the prepared crust. Cover the pie with plastic wrap, being careful not to let it touch the surface of the filling, and refrigerate it until well chilled, at least 6 hours or overnight is best.

5 Just before serving, put the cream and sugar into a large, well-chilled bowl. Beat the cream with a whisk or an electric beater on high speed until the cream just forms soft peaks. Place a dollop on each slice of pie, or spread it over the pie before slicing.

SERVES 8

KAREN BARKER'S VINEGAR PIE

Karen Barker, pastry chef and co-owner of the award-winning Magnolia Grill in Durham, North Carolina, is a pie phenom, and I am so pleased to be able to include this recipe for you. Now don't go making judgments before you've made this pie. Vinegar? Have I lost my mind? Try it, then check on my mental state. Karen makes the following comments: "A close cousin of Southern-style chess pie, this dessert is a perfect end to a rich crab dinner. To dress it up just a bit, serve it with a dollop of sweetened whipped cream and some lightly sugared sliced strawberries." One taste of this pie and you will know why she was both *Bon Appétit*'s and the James Beard Foundation's Pastry Chef of the Year.

SERVES 8

1   Preheat the oven to 425 degrees F.

2   Cover the pie shell with parchment paper and fill it with dry beans or other pie weights. Bake it for 10 minutes, remove it from the oven, uncover, and lightly brush it with a bit of egg white to seal the bottom crust. Return it to the oven to bake for an additional 10 minutes. While the shell is baking, put together your filling.

3   Combine the sugar, eggs, flour, cornmeal, and salt in a medium bowl and whisk them to combine. Add the butter, milk, and vanilla and whisk them in. Add the vinegar and mix to blend thoroughly. Reserve.

4   When the pie shell is opaque and just starting to brown, turn the oven to 325 degrees F. Pour the filling into the shell and place it on the bottom rack in your oven. Bake it approximately 45 minutes, until the filling is slightly puffed, set around the edges, and still a bit jiggly in the center. Cool it completely before serving.

One 9-inch unbaked pie shell

1 large egg white

1½ cups sugar

3 large eggs, at room temperature

1 tablespoon all-purpose flour

1 tablespoon yellow cornmeal

¼ teaspoon kosher salt

8 tablespoons (1 stick) unsalted butter, melted

2 tablespoons milk, at room temperature

2 teaspoons pure vanilla extract

¼ cup cider vinegar

inDex

TABLE OF EQUIVALENTS

The exact equivalents in the following table have been rounded for convenience.

LIQUID/DRY MEASURES

U.S.	METRIC
¼ teaspoon	1.25 milliliters
½ teaspoon	2.5 milliliters
1 teaspoon	5 milliliters
1 tablespoon (3 teaspoons)	15 milliliters
1 fluid ounce (2 tablespoons)	30 milliliters
¼ cup	60 milliliters
⅓ cup	80 milliliters
½ cup	120 milliliters
1 cup	240 milliliters
1 pint (2 cups)	480 milliliters
1 quart (4 cups; 32 ounces)	960 milliliters
1 gallon (4 quarts)	3.84 liters
1 ounce (by weight)	28 grams
1 pound	454 grams
2.2 pounds	1 kilogram

LENGTH

U.S.	METRIC
⅛ inch	3 millimeters
¼ inch	6 millimeters
½ inch	12 millimeters
1 inch	2.5 centimeters

OVEN TEMPERATURES

FAHRENHEIT	CELSIUS	GAS
250	120	½
275	140	1
300	150	2
325	160	3
350	180	4
375	190	5
400	200	6
425	220	7
450	230	8
475	240	9
500	260	10